WORKERS,
PARTICIPATION,
AND
DEMOCRACY

Recent Titles in
Contributions in Political Science
Series Editor: Bernard K. Johnpoll

Power and Policy in Transition: Essays Presented on the Tenth Anniversary of the National Committee on American Foreign Policy in Honor of Its Founder, Hans J. Morgenthau
Vojtech Mastny, editor

Ideology and Soviet Industrialization
Timothy W. Luke

Administrative Rulemaking: Politics and Processes
William F. West

Recovering from Catastrophes: Federal Disaster Relief Policy and Politics
Peter J. May

Judges, Bureaucrats, and the Question of Independence: A Study of the Social Security Administration Hearing Process
Donna Price Cofer

Party Identification, Political Behavior, and the American Electorate
Sheldon Kamieniecki

Without Justice for All: The Constitutional Rights of Aliens
Elizabeth Hull

Neighborhood Organizations: Seeds of a New Urban Life
Michael R. Williams

The State Politics of Judicial and Congressional Reform: Legitimizing Criminal Justice Policies
Thomas Carlyle Dalton

With Dignity: The Search for Medicare and Medicaid
Sheri I. David

American Prince, American Pauper: The Contemporary Vice-Presidency in Perspective
Marie D. Natoli

Shadow Justice: The Ideology and Institutionalization of Alternatives to Court
Christine B. Harrington

Daniel Bell and the Agony of Modern Liberalism
Nathan Liebowitz

The Flacks of Washington: Government Information and the Public Agenda
David R. Morgan

WORKERS, PARTICIPATION, AND DEMOCRACY

Internal Politics in the British Union Movement

JOEL D. WOLFE

Contributions in Political Science, Number 136

GREENWOOD PRESS
WESTPORT, CONNECTICUT • LONDON, ENGLAND

Library of Congress Cataloging in Publication Data

Wolfe, Joel D.
  Workers, participation, and democracy.

  (Contributions in political science, ISSN 0147–
1066 ; no. 136)
  Bibliography: p.
  Includes index.
  1. Labour Party (Great Britain)—Decision making.
2. Trades Union Congress—Decision making. 3. Great
Britain—Politics and government—1910–1936.
4. Democracy. I. Title. II. Series.
JN1129.L32W58 1985   322'.2'0941   85–5413
ISBN 0–313–24692–0 (lib. bdg.)

Library of Congress Catalog Card Number: 85–5413
ISBN: 0–313–24692–0
ISSN: 0147–1066

First published in 1985

Greenwood Press
A division of Congressional Information Service, Inc.
88 Post Road West, Westport, Connecticut 06881

Printed in the United States of America

10 9 8 7 6 5 4 3 2 1

Dedicated to my parents
Florence A. Wolfe
and the late
Harold M. Wolfe

Contents

Tables

Acknowledgements

I should like to express my gratitude to the social scientists and historians, both in Britain and the United States, whose help and criticism in the writing of this book have been invaluable. My very warm thanks are extended, in particular, to my following friends and colleagues for their detailed and ungrudging assistance: Gerard Braunthal, George Kateb, James S. Coleman, Joel Krieger and Dennis F. Thompson. At various stages I also benefitted from the help of David Easton, Kenneth Prewitt, Alfred Havighurst, Adrian Hayes, Rodney Barker and Joe Finney among others. Special thanks to my wife, Maureen, for her encouragement and help. Any shortcomings must be attributed to me.

The English Speaking Union (Chicago Chapter) is to be thanked for a year's financial support for research at the London School of Economics during the project's inception. I am grateful also to the British Library of Political and Economic Science for access to B. Webb's Diary, the Beveridge Papers, and specialized trades union documents as well as its general collection; to the Public Record Office for MacDonald's Diary; to the Trades Union Congress Library for permission to quote from the 1916 and 1917 Congress Reports; to the Labour Party Library for permission to quote from unpublished War Emergency: Workers National Committee documents as well as to examine the Middleton Papers and the Labour Party Letter Files; to the National Union of Railwaymen for use of the *Railway Review*; to the Amalgamated Union of Engineering Workers for permission to cite the Amalgamated Society of Engineers' *Monthly Journal*; and to the National Union of Mineworkers for permission to quote from the Miners' Federation of Great Britain Special Conference Report, February 8–9, 1916. Finally, I wish to acknowledge the kindness of Betty Steele for use of Amherst College's word processing facilities.

WORKERS, PARTICIPATION, AND DEMOCRACY

Introduction

Is participatory democracy possible in modern large-scale union and party organisations? The current debates about democratic socialism, union and party democracy, and workplace democracy focus attention on the importance of participation by the working people in the crucial decisions that affect their lives. Tony Benn, a leading left-wing proponent of democratic socialism in the British Labour movement, argues that, while monetarism threatens the very fabric of social stability, corporatism constitutes arbitrary rule from above.[1] Consequently, the extension of full participatory democracy into all spheres of the political economy is now more necessary than ever. If industrial societies are going to solve the problems of rising unemployment and stagflation, the full participation, responsibilities, and energies of the working population will be required.[2] Arguments for greater participation were at the center of recent Labour Party internal power struggles that eventuated in both an electoral college for selecting the Party Leader and the mandatory re-selection of all incumbent Members of Parliament. The ideal of greater participation in internal decision-making is also a fundamental principle of the Green Party in West Germany. Similarly, the current enthusiasm for workplace democracy in Europe and America reflects a rising concern for improved productivity and greater satisfaction with work and constitutes the leading objective in the larger movement for economic democracy.[3] As proponents of greater participation make clear, its purpose is to provide better decisions in the sense of providing the guidance and legitimacy authorities need to solve the current political and economic crises and a fuller realization of individual citizenship rights and human potentials.[4]

Yet, these arguments advancing the ideal of participatory democracy fail to analyse important, if often neglected, questions concerning its viability and reality in industrial society. For example, the recent British Labour Party campaign for greater internal democracy has in some cases simply represented a subterfuge by which a militant minority has taken control of local constituency parties. Often impervious to the undesirable, advocates of participatory democracy have argued that participation fosters the very conditions essential to its success. According to one proponent, "Participation develops and fosters the very qualities necessary for it; the more individuals participate the better able they become to do so."[5] Moreover, a democratic political system necessitates the existence of a participatory society, particularly in industry.[6] Following the leading themes of Rousseau and J. S. Mill, other recent defenders of participatory democracy continue to emphasize the importance of active participation in political affairs as a means to self-development and fulfillment, although they fail to explain how it is possible to have genuine and not illusory control.[7]

Unfortunately, those who analysed the internal political processes of mass organisation have provided powerful arguments rejecting the optimistic view that participation is self-sustaining and self-fulfilling. Moise Ostrogorski, Max Weber, and Robert Michels all argued that the internal political dynamics of mass organisations precluded their governance by direct or participatory democracy.[8] Among these, Michels' "iron law of oligarchy" represents the most powerful attack on the possibility of participatory democracy in modern industrial and political organisations committed to formal democratic procedures. By invoking the "bureaucratic principle," Michels' work marks the high point of the elite theorists' attack on Marxism at the turn of the century. Michels' concern was not to challenge Marx simply on the grounds that those who controlled the means of production constituted another instance of a long succession of ruling elites. Rather, his concern was to show that possession of the means of administration was an alternative basis of power, one that was more universal and effective than the control of the means of production alone. Insofar as Michels was concerned, socialism fails to provide a democratic solution to the administrative problems it faces in both the technical and psychological spheres. Those who occupy leadership positions in a party or trade union develop interests which coincide with the interests of the bureaucratic stratum that runs the organisation. Consequently, the elimination of the capitalist class system would not bring the much desired reduction in the "domination of man by man" but, on the contrary, would give rise to an expansion of bureaucratic control over the lives of men. As Michels concluded, "The socialist might conquer, but not socialism, which would perish in the moment of its adherents' triumph."[9] The effect of these arguments is to dismiss the idea that participatory democracy involves strictly structural changes in modern organisations. Formal procedures, while necessary, do not and cannot assure popular control.

To advocate participatory democracy in complex organisations, then, requires moving beyond simplistic demands for greater involvement of citizens in a greater number of decisions affecting their lives. It requires a theory of power relations that explains how the majority of members can actually initiate and shape organisational policy in formally representative institutions. The focus on the educative effects of participation ignores the organisational, sociological, and psychological constraints that can limit the influence of membership participation in formally representative institutions. The traditional theory of participatory democracy also ignores how the organisational environment contributes to or inhibits increased rank-and-file participation and influence. It does this because it fails to systematically link the environment of work to class formation and to examine how the environment affects the internal dynamics and levels of participation in working-class organisations. In short, if the theory of participatory democracy is to support the cause of democratic socialism, it must confront the reality of industrial society and provide defensible explanations and proposals concerning the conditions under and extent to which a fully participatory political and social order is feasible.

The aim of this book is to present a theory of participatory democracy in industrial and political organisations already committed to representative democracy. The achievement of participatory democracy in unions and socialist parties is particularly important, both because they are central to political decision-making and because participatory democracy in unions prefigures its extension to other economic and political spheres.[10] This constructive task involves presenting a theory of power and participatory democracy that resolves the fundamental challenge which Michels' "iron law of oligarchy" presents to both direct and representative democracy. Michels argued that technical, sociological, and psychological factors in large-member organisations made membership influence impossible. Consequently, an alternative theory must comprise an analysis of how members determine and use their own interests and support to control the organisational agenda and policy.

Participatory democracy, according to this view, involves office-holders in both informal and formal representative organisations bending to capture the support they need to function effectively by adopting the demands of their membership. Leaders subject to participatory democracy either directly as a result of the informal bonds of group membership or indirectly as delegates to higher-level councils have "power for" but not "power over" their members. Leaders' tasks would be to creatively and effectively serve their members' expressed interests in a more egalitarian future. This might involve simply following members' mandates or, more likely, coordinating members' interests through plans and campaigns that follow and enlarge upon the imperatives of those interests.

Because participatory democracy in modern industrial societies must involve, as Macpherson argues, "direct democracy at the base and delegate democracy at every level above that,"[11] the theory being advanced expands upon Macpherson's by explaining the power relations that give members active control of their officials' policy decisions at successive levels of complexity. In so doing, this theory gives realism to the ideals of theorists of participatory democracy by responding to Michels' indictment of democracy and by advancing the concept of democracy beyond the idea of elite competition. Democratic elitism, represented by the theories of Schumpeter and Lipset, conceptualizes democracy as a competitive process, thereby reducing citizens' power to the unintentional and indirect by-product of electoral contests. A theory of participatory democracy, on the other hand, must argue for more substantive influence by membership than formally democratic arrangements can provide. In delegate councils and executive bodies, participatory democracy occurs when leaders respond to the active assertion of the interests and support of non-elite participants.

Support for the utility of this theory of participatory democracy comes from an analysis of the policy processes by which the British labour movement adopted its first socialist program, laying the groundwork for the commitment to socialism in Clause IV of the Labour Party's 1918 constitution, and committed itself to a peace-by-negotiation foreign policy during the 1914–18 war. While the policy processes of participatory democracy were not fully matured or recognized, the historical cases are significant because they are representative of a period in which considerable experimentation with participatory democracy occurred in several European countries and in which theorists like G. D. H. Cole and Antonio Gramsci first seriously attempted to apply the ideals of participation to modern industrial circumstances.[12] In Britain, the influence of syndicalism, guild socialism, and shop stewards' movements both reflected aspirations for participatory control of unions and industry and encouraged the processes of mass-based workers' control of trade unions and socialist parties.[13] The upsurge and growth of workplace organisation during the war made it a permanent feature of twentieth century British trade unionism. Pressures for popular control also produced changes in the internal structure of some unions and resulted in the reorganisation of the Labour Party. While these structural innovations are important, they can serve to contain as well as express rank-and-file interests. Participatory democracy, then, depends on how members make use of structure to shape issues and determine leaders' decisions. Thus, by investigating the policy-making processes in formally representative institutions with direct democracy at the base and delegate democracy at higher levels, these cases underscore the complex and fluid relationship between structure and power relations, a relationship central to a realistic and modern conception of participatory democracy.

The historical cases are also significant because the exceptional wartime conditions that underpin the cases of participatory democracy reinforce the generalizability of the study's conclusions. The war strengthened leaders by making organisational survival, in the face of a more powerful and assertive state, more important than doctrinal principles, a situation that compelled internationalist commitments to give way to an outpouring of patriotism. As Michels concluded about the effect of the war, "The party gives way, hastily sells its internationalist soul, and, impelled by the instinct of self-preservation, undergoes transformation into a patriotic party."[14] Only as hardship and oppression gradually mounted did loyalty and sacrifice to the national cause come into question. Even then, the advantages to leaders from the external threat never disappeared. While elite theory is correct in suggesting that the war would strengthen leadership, it must be recognized that rank-and-file participation in a wide variety of representative institutions occurred in spite of the strengthening of these oligarchical tendencies. In other times and organisations, the advantages favouring leaders may be less, encouraging episodes of participatory democracy even more. Thus, in liberal democratic political systems, with less extreme conditions, the conditions underlying participatory democracy may be more favourable than during World War I.

The plan of this study, thus, is both theoretical and empirical. Chapters 1 and 2 present a theory of power and participatory democracy in complex representative organisations. This theory examines the power relationship between officeholders and rank-and-file members as the informal bases of collective action among workers increasingly is subjected to the influence and constraints of formal, bureaucratic structures in branch, district, and national organisations committed to policy-making through the procedures of representative democracy. Because this theory of participatory democracy is a response to the fundamental challenge to democratic theory presented by Michels' theory of oligarchy, it is first developed through a presentation and critique of Michels' theory and the revised theories of democracy,[15] which attempt to reply to elite analysis by emphasizing competition between interest groups, parties, and leaders. Chapter 3 summarizes the wartime conditions that fostered participatory democracy. Chapters 4 through 7 test this theory by examining internal policy processes at successive levels of formality and complexity in the pyramidal structure of both the British Trades Union Congress and the Labour Party during the First World War. This involves examining the sources and internal decision-making processes of rank-and-file organisation; the influence of rank-and-file movements on policy-making on critical wartime issues in the major unions, and, finally, the rank-and-file influences upon the policy-making activities of national unions, political activists, and executives of the two national federations, the Trades Union Congress and the British Labour Party. Finally, Chapter 8 concludes by summarizing our explanation of participatory democracy, discussing the relative merits of democratic elitism and participatory democracy, and briefly assessing the current prospects for participatory democracy in the advanced industrial societies.

CHAPTER 1

Elitism and Democracy

For elite theorists, the history of all past and future societies is the history of their ruling minorities. Their original and primary villain is Marxist socialism, which identified a perpetual ruling minority in the property-owning class and projected the eventual transcendence of the "master–subject" relationship between employer and wage-laborer with the advent of a classless society. The elite theorists sought to deny both the dream and the reality of Marxist analysis. By their theory of circulating elites, they countered the socialist effort to identify the people's oppressor as the owners and managers of capital; they contended that elites were diverse in their origin, even though universal and timeless in their existence. The voice of the "people" could never be heard. If the circulation of elites reduced the Marxist empirical claim that society was throughout history ruled by owners of property, the recognition of the functional importance of elites for the day-by-day operation of every society diminished the plausibility of the belief in the utopian "classless" society. The inherent and immutable incompetence of the mass, expressed either as out-and-out lack of self-sufficiency or as an unruly and directionless aggressiveness threatening all forms of "civilization," necessitated the rise of a ruling minority for the very maintenance of society itself. Elite theory, then, assumes that domination and execution of function are identical; those who run a social system also control it. As Max Weber put it, "Every domination both expresses itself and functions through administration. Every administration, on the other hand, needs domination, because it is always necessary that some power of command be in the hands of somebody."[1]

Of all elite theories, Michels' "iron law of oligarchy" more than any other comprises the main argument against the possibility of participatory democracy in modern industrial organisations. In *Political Parties*,[2] Michels proposed a theory of large-membership organisation in which he argued that in organisations committed to the realization of democratic values, oligarchical tendencies inevitably prevail, constituting a major obstacle to the realization of those values. Finding electoral accountability as a criterion of democracy unsatisfactory, Michels thought that it was more accurate to consider the degree of responsiveness of leadership to the expectations and desires of the constituency. In his discussion of the responsiveness of the leadership to its followers, Michels' concern is with the way in which organisational processes determine how party ideology is translated into party policy. Out of this concern, Michels examined the effects of political processes on organisations with formally democratic constitutions.

Michels explained how and why the internal processes of mass-membership organisations nominally committed to substantive democracy invariably produce leadership domination. To give explanatory power to Mosca's earlier assertion that it was inevitable that the social order should be divided between the ruling few and the ruled majority, Michels made use of Marx's notion that the expropriation of the means for production from the many and its concentration in the hands of a minority of property-owners produced the inequality of power between bourgeoisie and proletariat. Just as the expropriation of the means of production gave power because it concentrated resources among the few, the expropriation of control and status by elected officeholders would render the majority impotent.

This rationalization of internal power relations in trade unions and political parties underlies and reinforces the unequal resources of power possessed by leaders and members. Any process of popular control invariably yields to a division of labour as a result of the need for organisational efficiency and effectiveness. Problem-solving requires a "rationalization" of administrative and executive tasks. The need to act orients the party increasingly toward formal or procedural specialization and division of labour. In terms of effective action, according to Weber, "bureaucratic administration is, other things being equal, always from a formal technical point of view, the most rational type."[3]

At the same time, the consequence of such formal rationalization is that the masses come to depend upon the leadership by default. As Michels notes:

The technical specialization that inevitably results from all extensive organisation renders necessary what is called expert leadership. Consequently, the power of determination comes to be considered one of the specific attributes of leadership, and is gradually withdrawn from the masses to be concentrated in the hands of the leaders alone.[4]

The technical and mechanical impossibility of carrying on practical work by a system of direct discussion among large numbers of people makes leadership necessary and requires, as the duties become more complicated, that the leadership exhibit a particular aptitude for the task. The inherent incompetence of the mass interacts with the need for efficient policy-making to give rise to a "political class" that is both in control of and indispensable to the organisation.

Michels further contends that the officeholder's control of the initiation and administration of policy serves not only as the basis of his domination but as the source of interests that diverge from the original aims of the organisation as well as the interests of the membership. The expropriation process itself causes the interests of the leaders and the led to deviate through a self-reinforcing pattern. The leadership position confers power, develops skills, and produces a middle-class life style, consequences that make it easier for the leader to maintain his power and to increase his status. Through this process the leaders' actions come to focus increasingly on the effect of the policy on the power relations inside the organisation rather than on the achievement of professed external goals. Michels writes:

The interests of the body of employees are always conservative, and in a given political situation these interests may dictate a defensive and even reactionary policy when the interests of the working class demand a bold and aggressive policy; in other cases, although these are very rare, the roles may be reversed. By a universally applicable law, every organ of the collectivity, brought into existence through the need for the division of labour, creates for itself, as soon as it becomes consolidated, interests peculiar to itself. The existence of these special interests involves a necessary conflict with the interests of the collectivity.[5]

The forsaking of initial organisational goals in favour of promoting the persistence of the organisation itself modifies party ideology in addition to party policy. Threats to leaders' authority or office motivate them to preserve their position even if it requires using repressive methods. Any such threatening action is characterized as giving aid to the evil and powerful opponents with which the organisation is struggling. As the leaders work to buttress the benefits conferred on them by their superordinate position, they seek to rationalize the use of policy to maintain their position within the organisation itself rather than to achieve initial ideological goals. Thus, ideology becomes an important instrument to be manipulated by officials in their own interests.

Because officeholders adopt instrumental doctrines, a competitive struggle among opposing contenders produces ideologies which, while mobilizing the mass opinion, serve only the interests of the antagonists. While leaders must appear to be responsive to the preferences of their members, they are in fact only seriously threatened when a new leader or a new group of leaders is on the point of becoming dominant by introducing views that cannot be assimilated by the old. In such instances, it seems

as if the old leaders, unless they are willing to yield to the opinion of the rank and file and to withdraw, must consent to share their power with the new arrival. If, however, we look more closely into the matter, it is not difficult to see that their submission is in most cases no more than an act of foresight intended to obviate the influence of their younger rivals.[6]

While these elite struggles originate from a wide variety of differences among elites, they result in the manipulation of ideology in order to appeal for mass support. Ultimately, these contests for supremacy are only resolved as a consequence of tests of membership opinion, contrived and manipulated though that may be. Because the mass membership lacks the competence, energy, organisation, and goals necessary for independent action as a result of their expropriation by the officials, the members cannot push forward their interests in an effort to influence the leadership. Any benefits which befall the masses are merely unintended by-products of the elite battles initiated by counter-elites who formulate mass interests and mobilize mass support for their challenge to those already in positions of power. Bystanders in the struggle for effective power, the masses play no direct role and democracy makes no headway. Regardless of the outcome of skirmishes among elites, the dominance of the ruling minority remains unchallenged and unchallengeable.

The most important efforts to defend democratic ideals against the challenge contained in the theory of oligarchy so far have come from those who espouse a model of democracy emphasizing elite competition The elitist theory of democracy broadens Michels' contention that leaders shape both policy and ideology to allow for those outside the authority-structure to be taken into account by decision-makers. At the same time, the elitist theory of democracy tacitly adheres to the assumption that control over administrative duties confers domination. Max Weber, the first to set out this line of thought, developed a notion of "passive" democracy which can be contrasted with what he terms "immediately democratic Administration" wherein the ruler may be regarded as the servant of the ruled because the executives only carry out resolutions carried by fully participatory assemblies.[7] For Weber, the mass can influence policy-making by affecting the selection of leaders or by bringing "public opinion" to bear upon leaders through representatives from among their midst. He writes:

The *demos* itself, in the sense of a shapeless mass, never "governs" larger associations, but rather is governed. What changes is only the way in which the executive leaders are selected and the measure of influence which the *demos*, or better, which social circles from its midst are able to exert upon the content and the direction of administrative activities by means of "public opinion."[8]

Further, as social and economic differences within the masses are diminished, public opinion can exert a monolithic force which the elites must take into account. The decisive aspect for the expansion of the domain of influence commanded by public opinion is "the *leveling of the governed* in the face of the governing and bureaucratically articulated groups, which in its turn may occupy a quite autocratic position, both in fact and in form."[9]

Joseph Schumpeter used the notion of market competition to refashion Weber's insight into a theory of democratic elitism that has gained widespread currency today. Rejecting the classical notion of democracy as impractical, Schumpeter argued that it is more accurate to characterize democracy as a system in which the electorate chooses among competing leaders, who decide political issues. In *Capitalism, Socialism, and Democracy*,[10] he contends that the will of the masses does not flow from its own initiative. Rather the will itself is being shaped by competing teams of leaders.

Voters do not decide issues. But neither do they pick their members of parliament from the eligible population with a perfectly open mind. In all normal cases the initiative lies with the candidate who makes a bid for the office of member of parliament and such local leadership as that may imply. Voters confine themselves to accepting this bid in preference to others or refusing to accept it.[11]

Moreover, parties further restrict electoral initiative, without being dependent on the particular needs of the voters.

A party is a group whose members propose to act in concert in the competitive struggle for political power. If that were not so it would be impossible for different parties to adopt exactly or almost exactly the same program. . . . Party and machine politicians are simply the response to the fact that the electoral mass is incapable of action other than a stampede, and they constitute an attempt to regulate political competition exactly similar to the corresponding practices of a trade association.[12]

While Schumpeter was careful to conceive of democracy in the sense of a competitive leadership as an historical upshot of the bourgeois state, he saw it as a method equally applicable to an emerging socialist era.

Following Schumpeter, investigations of intra-organisational democracy have centred on the role of competition among opposition in different guises. In an important test of Michels' theory, Lipset, Trow, and Coleman located democracy in the institutionalization of a two-party system in the International Typographical Union.[13] These authors suggest that "without a sophisticated organised opposition, the members have no way of discovering for themselves what is possible."[14] Such opposition groups function through the development of organisational subgroups which claim the loyalties of members in addition to the larger organisation. Similarly, J. David Edelstein, recognizing that the institutionalization of a two-party system is too narrow a criterion for democracy, suggests closeness of electoral contests as a wider criterion. Close elections result from competition among contenders of equal status, power, and reputation, selected by voters of equal electoral strength.[15] Consequently, the indices of union democracy are the frequency of the incumbents being defeated and the closeness of such contests. In making his argument, Edelstein stresses the role of formal procedures in assuring the equality of electoral competition. Broadening the concept of elite competition still further, Roderick Martin adopts the notion of the "status of the opposition" as the distinguishing characteristic of democracy. Arguing that formal organisation is a dependent rather than an independent variable, Martin formulates the conditions that promote the rise and survival of factions, based upon the assumption that union "leaders will not tolerate faction unless constrained to do so."[16] In a later work, Martin further elaborates the internal and external factors that determine the outcome of the struggle between union bureaucrats and the rank-and-file workplace organisation.[17] Finally, John Hemingway argues that the presence of conflict signifies an absence of effective control by leaders over their members. "When issues arise over which leaders and members disagree, the parties must strategically deploy resources to secure the compliance of the opposition, and the outcome to their conflict will demonstrate the balance of control."[18] Bargaining among factions is the normal pattern of internal union government, according to Hemingway.

The democratic elitist challenge to Michels stands largely on its redefinition of democracy. Electoral competition among leaders permits those outside the authority-structure to have access to political power,[19] instead of merely determining which elite faction would prevail as Michels contends.[20] These elitist theories of democracy dismiss the spirit of earlier versions of liberal democracy by restricting the role of citizens or members. As Michael Margolis argues about recent democratic theories,

They abandon the traditional liberal concern for individual self-improvement, particularly that achieved through political participation. Instead these theorists presume that given the proper social arrangements the virtues of political leaders can be substituted for the virtues of the people.[21]

Democratic elitism, then, salvages democracy by making order and stability the prerequisite for the satisfaction of citizen choices.

Further, democratic elitism, while correctly criticizing Michels for ignoring the "sources and consequences of controversy," fails to confront the argument that values and biases operating through the political process can limit the scope of issues. As Bachrach and Baratz point out in identifying a second face of power, the values built into a political system tend to permit only "safe" issues onto the public agenda and prevent those issues threatening the *status quo* from receiving consideration.[22] The further suggestion that there is conflict over covert interests in addition to overt issues raises concern for the identification of "non-decisions" and their role in policy-making. One result has been to re-conceptualize the hallmark of power as the control over values, the transition of a covert interest into an overt issue.[23]

Other attempts to clarify the problem of how issues emerge as matters of political controversy in systems of effective power lead up the blind alley of "objective" interest analysis. These efforts distinguish theoretically defined "objective" or "real" interests from subjective (covert or overt) interests. In one instance, Ralf Dahrendorf argues that authority relationships involve inherent conflict between superordinates and subordinates, between those in possession of role-defined interests and those excluded from them.[24] In a second instance, Steven Lukes posits that there is "latent" conflict over wants and preferences between those exercising power and those subject to it, especially if the subordinates were to be aware of their "real" interests. Lukes maintains "that men's wants may themselves be a product of a system which works against their interest, and, in such cases, relates the latter to what they would want and prefer, were they able to make the choice."[25] In order to analyse an exercise of power when there is objective rather than subjective conflict, Lukes argues that one must posit a relevant counterfactual, showing that B would have otherwise done b had it not been for A. This involves (1) justifying the belief that agent B should have recognized and acted upon certain "real" interests and (2) identifying the means by which agent A prevented B from carrying out his "real" interests. By positing "real" interests to agents, objective interest analysis links interests with ideals.[26] Because the concept of interest bridges explanation and normative judgment, the notion of interests used determines which types of issues become the focus of moral evaluation.[27] While positing objective interests is therefore unavoidable, the analyses of Dahrendorf and Lukes are, nonetheless, limited because they fail to explain the transformation of objective interests into subjective motivations of quiescence or, alternatively, protest. As a result, all power relationships involve contradictory interests. The logical result is a conceptualisation of the divergence of interests between decision-makers and non-elites that is too simple, one that unnecessarily posits the masses' permanent exclusion from the material resources that constitute their only means to redress inevitable inequities.[28]

While these analyses have yielded valuable conceptual results, they fail to provide an adequate rebuttal to the challenge contained in the theory of oligarchy. Democratic elitism and its critique both retain a one-sided, top-down analysis that implies a natural division of power and interest between leaders and followers. Like elite theory, their assumption that power is aggregated through the accumulation and manipulation of resources relies on the proposition that the division of labour generates specialized interests which may not only conflict with but invariably predominate over those of the membership. Consequently, leaders' interests increasingly focus on the power relations inside the organisation. The result is to narrow debate and to limit participation.[29]

While democratic elitism does represent one effort to revive democratic theory in the face of elitist challenges, it fails to go far enough. Since intra-organisational democracy involves contests between groups of leaders or between particular leaders and an undifferentiated mass, the analysis of conflict among opposing leaders neglects the actual relations of control between leaders and followers. What needs explanation is why, under certain circumstances, leaders are compelled to act on behalf of their membership rather than to exercise power over them or why attempts are made, by the organised membership, to alter the structure of authority itself. To pose these questions as a critique of Michels' theory of oligarchy and democratic elitism is not to condemn these theories as invalid. Rather, this critical analysis provides the basis from which to construct a more defensible theory of participatory democracy in hierarchical representative organisations.

CHAPTER 2

A Theory of Participatory Democracy

A defensible theory of participatory democracy must be able to answer the challenge that the theory of oligarchy raises for democratic theory. An adequate response must establish both that the members are the originators of issues and party controversy and that the organised rank and file also shape policy decisions and administration. In making this claim, it is necessary to go beyond Michels' theory of power in order to escape its self-validating character. While democratic elitists strive to give the masses access to decision-making through elite competition, they fail to give the members any active role in shaping organisational agendas. And, even when they admit that the elites are forced to adopt the policy-initiatives of their members, the democratic elitists argue that the officials still control effective decision-making and day-to-day administration of policy. In other words, Michels and his democratic elitist challengers take too narrow a view of the sources of values and of the ways in which control over policy is distributed.

This chapter explicates the dynamics of power relations that enable members to exercise control over leaders at various levels in complex representative organisations. In large-scale, hierarchical representative systems, participatory democracy will involve "direct democracy at the base and delegate democracy at every level above that."[1] Given this structure of representation, participatory democracy involves power relations that give members active control of their officials' policy decisions. As a result, leaders have "power for" but not "power over"

their members. To originate issues and to shape policy decisions, organisational members must develop autonomous control of interests and
support. The creation of community—common interests, responsibilities, and obligations that constitute a moral imperative toward solidarity—among workers provides this autonomy. The environment of
effective power fosters community when it facilitates members becoming aware of and expressing ultimate interests in greater justice or
reciprocity in social relations. In turn, workers' community enables
them to control their interests and support and to enforce a predominance
of members' interests over those of the leadership. This theory of participatory democracy, thus, broadens the elite theorists' conception of
power to include the possibility of rank-and-file initiation and determination of organisational policy by conceptually enlarging the possible
sources of values and types of interests and the various ways in which
control over policy is distributed.

THE ENVIRONMENT OF EFFECTIVE POWER

Conflict over values—goals of action and standards of decision—is
not confined to systems of effective policy-making. Any system of
effective power is set within a larger environment made up of subsystems
which generate conflict about the proper ends of action. According to
Giddens, "we can say that power has two aspects: a 'collective' aspect,
in the sense that the 'parameters' of any concrete set of power relationships are contingent upon the overall system of organisation of a
society, and a 'distributive' aspect, in the sense that certain groups are
able to exert their will at the expense of others."[2] In other words, power
has a "collective" or "environmental" aspect which shapes the elements of any system of effective power—values and modes of control.
In contrast to Michels and the democratic elitists, the distinction between
an "environmental" and an "effective" aspect of power makes it possible to appreciate that the sources of values and interests within the
political system can lie in its external conditions where conflict over
scarce values originates. Instead of being shaped wholly by internal
norms of technical necessity, systems of effective power are also shaped
by a wide range of external factors covered by the concept of environment. The result is a wider variation in effective power relations than
is entailed in elite analysis.

An adequate notion of environment must be systemic, dynamic, and multifaceted. The exchange between organisations and their environments involves not only structural constraints and possibilities but the creation of moral energies that motivate aspirations and actions. For this reason, Habermas' conceptualization of the interaction between social systems and their environments as the appropriation of outer nature through production and the appropriation of inner nature through socialization by means of the medium of utterances that require justification is useful.[3] The truth-based mediation of the interrelation between social systems and environments limits the potential for domination contained in the extension of rationality to production or social administration and provides a moral basis for individual autonomy. Marcuse's conception of a one-dimensional society focuses on this key issue of individual autonomy in industrial society, even if it exaggerates the capacity of the productive apparatus to constitute a total social system.[4] Culturally defined meaning is not susceptible to reproduction through rationalization, and efforts to compensate for the loss of meaning with material rewards run up against the problem of expectations outstripping available goods.[5] In short, the environment involves structural factors from the realm of physical nature and the cognitive and emotional capacities of the human mind. Either may or may not be compatible with imperatives of the particular social system, creating a potential conflict between the needs of administrative rationality and the needs of social integration.

A complex notion of the environment provides the basis for analysing how the source of political goals and modes of control result in fluid and diverse relations of effective power. This proposition constitutes the critical pre-condition for a discussion of participatory democracy in modern organisations. The environment's determinative effect provides the basis for explaining how power differentials contained in environmental subsystems are converted into systems of effective power. Instead of directing attention toward individual elites or institutional structures, the analysis presented here explains internal power relations as a system property, a system which is structured by those conflicts over values in its internal and external environments which affect the power relations between various subsystems and the larger system. Recognizing that subsystems also involve exchanges between environment and system, this analysis attempts to examine how the environment shapes power in subsystems and how these subsystems, in turn, shape the overall pattern of power. The effect on any given system or subsystem is to enlarge the categories involved in the analysis of power to include values shaped by both leaders and members and to allow for the control over policy by either leaders or the rank and file.

The distinction between these two aspects of power then makes it possible to appreciate variation in power relations within particular organisational structures. Despite Michels' argument that representative structures inevitably yield to oligarchy, it needs to be recognized that the consequence of structure on power relations is always Janus-faced. Because democracy in modern organisations will necessarily involve leadership, formal procedures, and social pluralism, representative structures can either lead to oligarchy or provide the basis for participatory democracy. Consequently, it is insufficient to suggest that participatory democracy can be defined solely by particular organisational structures. Because structure provides potential for either elitist or participationist power relations, it is necessary to examine variations in the organisational environment and members' responses to them in order to explain internal power relations. With this in mind, the discussion can turn to an analysis of how the environment can foster participatory democratic power relations.

INJUSTICE AND MEMBERSHIP CONTROL OF INTEREST AND SUPPORT

The ability of workers to autonomously initiate union or party policy that resists capitalist domination and exploitation depends on the workers' ability to resist the leaders' domination within their own organisations. This ability, in turn, results from the development of class consciousness and collective solidarity at the workplace. The antagonism of interest between labour and employer under capitalism results from non-reciprocal relations of power in the labour process.[6] While the lack of reciprocity in power, rights, and obligations is general to the social structure, its manifestation in modern societies is mainly located in the political economy. In this sphere, the lack of reciprocity engenders feelings and cognitive perceptions of injustice insofar as workers feel capable of expressing their basic human integrity and need for respect.[7] On the other hand, ideological, organisational, and repressive conditions can limit the realization and articulation of unequal social relations. When this occurs, workers are likely neither to develop collective interests nor to organise the collective solidarity needed to pursue them. Recognition of injustice, then, is particularly important to the development of collective organisation because it is the motivating force behind class struggles. Indeed, the struggle for Justice and its constant renewal are the driving power through which classes are, as Przeworski expresses it, "continually organized, disorganized, and reorganized."[8]

Sentiments of injustice motivate resistance to exploitation and provide moral foundations for defining perceptions and bonds of collective unity and prescriptions for action. Feelings of injustice foster common interests in ultimate or substantive values, and it is these values, that is, absolute goals and standards of evaluation, that bind individual objectives into a common pursuit and that compel group members to defend their collective solidarity.[9] Substantive or ultimate goals define workers' interests in opposition to the peculiar rationality of capitalist production, provide a basis of common interests and action, and further contribute to sociability or ideological bonds between members of the group. Substantive or ultimate interests developed in response to non-reciprocal relations of power in the mode of production and patterns of status engender the development of autonomous demands and workgroup organisation. Thus, the *principle of community autonomy* constitutes the first major proposition in the construction of a theory of participatory democracy.

PROPOSITION I

Ultimate or substantive commitments to democratic procedures and equality in social relations can override individual calculations of self-interest, integrate different individuals' judgments concerning the collective interest, and foster community relations (collective solidarity) that provide members with autonomous (non-elite) control of their interests and support.

The development of substantive interests and collectivist organisation among workers depends on factors which undermine material, legal–rational and coercive means of rationalized control and so enable workers to express their claims for greater reciprocity. The extent of collective solidarity and the strength of workplace resistance, then, vary inversely with the extent of rationalization of control. Complete bureaucratization would permit no collective solidarity whatsoever, since personal relations would be rigidly and completely subordinated to impersonal rules. Alternatively, complete absence of rationalization would permit workers to protest or bargain as individuals. In either case, workers' collective action would depend on the pursuit of individual self interest and would require incentives (specific benefits) to collective organisation and action in order to overcome the free-rider problem, since some members could not be convinced to contribute to the pursuit of collective goals when their benefits do not depend on their participation. The moral basis of community and autonomy thus counters the rational-choice theorists' argument that individual self-interest is, to a significant extent, incompatible with the pursuit of a collective or common good.[10] In short, this type of organisation represents group formation on the basis of instrumental values.

The maintenance of leadership prerogative depends precisely on developing and reinforcing effective strategies of rationalization of organisational and workplace practices. Bureaucratically dominated workplace organisation can be fostered from above by management and unions for the purpose of administering shopfloor control. Recent studies of a large British chemical firm reveal that management can effectively shape workplace unions according to this bureaucratic mode.[11] By recruiting a labour force without a trade union tradition and without any community ties, by locating the plant away from an urban centre, by structuring the rewards on the basis of a rationalized company-wide productivity deal based on measured day work and a simplified grading of work, and by sponsoring and manipulating a union, the company inhibited the development of both a factory-level and a wider class consciousness. In these circumstances, groups of workers and individuals found themselves largely in conflict with one another rather than with management and, while workers sometimes put up resistance in the form of sabotage, they generally focused on "getting by"[12] or "making out."[13]

Internal power relations in workplace organisations, thus, involve diverse patterns of resistance and collaboration by workers at the point of production. The potential for working-class power is limited because the conditions that give rise to substantive and ultimate interests and collective organisation are constrained by the peculiar historical features of the labour process, modes of managerial control, and other factors which may influence the authoritative command of labour practices. As one American economist notes, "As the environment for capital accumulation changes from one stage to the next, the limits to and possibilities for trade-union structure and behavior obviously change."[14]

Because non-reciprocal social relations are never eradicated, sentiments of injustice may emerge to support workers' resistance. On the other hand, control strategies of managers, political leaders, and union officials may effectively handcuff disruptive sentiments.

By locating the sources of interests and attitudes toward authority in the emergence of a sense of injustice, this analysis avoids the limitations of objective interest analysis. Because latent interests may only be recognized if stimulated by what happens to individual workers as changes in the labour process foster collective organisation and permit their collective autonomy to be realized, this analysis focuses on subjective, identifiable interests, not hypothetical ideals. At the same time, the analysis recognizes that an objective standard is also necessary in order to eliminate the possibility that workers may be subjectively mistaken about injustice. It does this by locating the basis of political conflict in the lack of reciprocity in social relations and the expression of such conflict in the success or failure of strategies designed to reproduce these structural inequalities.

COMMON INTERESTS AND PARTICIPATORY CONTROL AT THE BASE

What factors, then, foster sentiments of injustice that, in turn, may lead to workers' control over their own interests and objects of support? Factors of workers' political and cultural heritage that determine the potential for class consciousness and collective action include the labour process, the larger factors of the political economy that strengthen or weaken workers' bargaining power, the role and extent of state involvement in regulating workplace power relations, the structure of collective bargaining, a sense of "exploitation" engendered by an unfavourable reward for effort relative to other workers or classes, and the homogeneity of the workplace and residential communities. Variations in these factors foster substantive or ultimate interests in greater equality and collective solidarity among workers at the base, or, alternatively, instrumental relationships which facilitate hierarchical, bureaucratic control.

The class consciousness—the aspiration for liberty and equality— that enables workers to exercise choices over interests and support is most likely to occur when workgroups are organised on the basis of strong collective bonds and managerial control is arbitrary and rigid but allows workers significant control of the work processes. Workers need a substantial degree of control in the labour process in order to develop their own common interests and informal organisation for protecting them. If workers are isolated through the labour process or the career patterns internal to the firm, they are less able to develop common interests, within either the firm or the industry.[15] Moreover, militancy presupposes confidence of continued employment. Full employment, stable product markets, unionization, and welfare state benefits provide workers with the bargaining power necessary for assertiveness.[16] Furthermore, workers' collective organisation which is largely dependent on state legislation is unlikely to have the autonomy to defy employers or the law in pursuit of their claims to justice.[17] Significantly, the centralization of collective bargaining can heighten class conflict, as can sentiments of "exploitation" that arise from differentials between profit levels and real wages.[18] Finally, whereas heterogeneity often undermines class solidarity, residential and workplace ethnic and racial homogeneity reinforce class consciousness.[19]

More specifically, factors which foster class-conscious community at the workplace include large workforces (over five hundred employees) in industries which rigidly structure work;[20] militant traditions;[21] a production system which affords workers a middle range of control, status, and common interests;[22] frequent bargaining and a complicated payment system;[23] a strong collective bargaining position and a stable product market;[24] and a centralized bargaining structure that is based on the substantive interests of workgroups rather than the instrumental interests of union officeholders and bureaucrats.[25]

The environmental factors that contribute to community or collective solidarity at the workplace are those conditions which foster expressions of sentiments of injustice, demands for greater reciprocity, and the participation that is essential to collective organisation. Groups intentionally organised on the basis of substantive or ultimate principles typically govern themselves by informal processes of participatory democracy. Equal status among members, decision-making by consensus, and decision-making in face-to-face assembly characterize these groups and constitute the traits of direct democracy.[26] Because the basis of authority and group power depends on informal and consensual processes of agreement which are fluid and open to negotiation, the external strength of these groups depends on the extent of collective solidarity. As solidarity grows, particularistic initiatives of individual members tend to be limited by the collective definition of the consensus and pressures toward unanimity. Only by appealing to the common interest can initiatives capture the support of the collectivity.[27]

Among shop stewards in Britain, the steward's authority arises from the solidaristic needs of the group or subgroups composing the workplace unit, although stewards' organisations in recent years have been organised from above by management and unions and have consequently been bureaucratized. The traditional steward is, in effect, a delegate or spokesman on behalf of the collective, although the degree to which stewards are capable of giving a lead on particular policy decisions varies. The delegate role emerges as the collectivity recognizes that its objectives can only be reached with the help of a leader who initiates action, develops consensus, and links the workgroup to the management, the union, and other workgroups.[28] Yet, the fluid and consensual character of the steward's authority means that his power depends on mobilizing membership support through persuasion and argument. Even when the steward acts as a leader rather than a spokesman, his power over the membership is limited by this collective consensus. In other words, the more completely and effectively the shop steward reflects his members' collective sentiments, the more support he has from the group.[29] A steward who sides with union officials who ignore the members' interests or with management may cut himself off from the group, since it violates the collective consensus and fosters the emergence of independent action by subgroups.[30] In essence, workgroup leadership is a property of primary group behaviour itself, a theme emphasized by those who have identified principles of workshop organisation. Sykes, for instance, points to two principles of workgroup behaviour in the British printing trade—the right of the group as a whole to make final decisions on all matters concerning work and the commitment to equality among chapel (or workgroup) members.[31] Similarly, Brown singles out the pursuit of unity and equity among members, the maintenance of good bargaining relationships with management, and a reduction of uncertainty as basic principles of workgroup organisation.[32] For example, workgroup solidarity at British Ford in the late 1960s made it impossible for management to tip the balance of power in its own favour by the introduction of a productivity deal. Workgroup solidarity was maintained in part by the active involvement of the shop steward with his membership and in part by a tradition of militancy. While stewards tend to be individuals predisposed to defy authority, the bonds of collective solidarity are what make the shop steward organisation an effective mechanism for the defence of working-class interests, manifest as "factory consciousness" in this instance.[33] In short, class-conscious workplace organisation manifests the traits of direct democracy: equality, intimacy, and unanimity.

To summarize, the sources of membership participation and control in autonomous primary groups at the base can be stated in the following hypothesis:

Workers' participation and control depend on class (community) consciousness (a moral revolt against unfairness and aspirations for liberty and equality) and organisation which arise from labour processes that are exploitative yet permit solidarity among workers, experiences of relative deprivation in consumption, and state repression of civil, industrial, or political rights.

COMMON INTERESTS AND PARTICIPATION IN DELEGATE COUNCILS

Power gained at the workplace need not, however, lead to power at higher levels or enable members to shape decisions on issues, such as inflation or unemployment, of importance to a whole class. Workers may remain divided or be manipulated by ambitious union and party leaders. But, if working-class autonomy relies on the development of common interests and collective solidarity at the workplace, what are the conditions which engender feelings of injustice that may operate to consolidate the solidarity at the base into sectional or even national institutions of working-class power?

The analysis of participatory democracy at higher levels involves delegate councils which, despite overt conflict, safeguard interests by formal commitments to equal protection, majority rule, and impersonal mechanisms of electoral representation.[34] Representation through adversary procedures engenders conflict between the formal bureaucratic nature of large-scale working-class organisations and their substantive basis in common interests and collective solidarity. While representation of working-class interests at higher levels involves the aggregation of collective solidarity, the internal dynamics of broader class formations cannot be like that of primary groups at the base. At higher levels, bureaucratic structures and formal representative procedures are necessary and thus conflict with the substantive goals and collectivist proc-

cases of workplace organisations. Also, broader class aspirations involve a wider scope, transcending the narrower, more limited interests of workgroups. Collective action in large-member delegate councils is even more vulnerable to the free-rider problem mentioned above. In organisations based on class consciousness, however, ultimate and substantive values contribute to creating the community solidarity that provides incentives for collective action. In order for delegate democracy to succeed in pyramidal representative organisations, formality and sectionalism, thus, must be transcended by the consolidation of common interests in substantive and ultimate ends at higher levels.

If these common interests in equality and liberty are to be articulated at higher levels, environmental imperatives must engender shared interests in substantive or ultimate objectives among a broad range of working-class organisations. Three of the factors affecting workplace power relations in particular may contribute to the mobilization of mass solidarity on behalf of wider working-class objectives and the determination of leadership responsiveness in large-scale organisations. First, the solidarity of working-class movements presupposes a high degree of racial and ethnic homogeneity. The predominance of class interests at work and at home reinforces class solidarity.[35] Second, inequitable differentials in living standards can foster a them-versus-us mentality. When effort at work brings relatively little in return and engenders sentiments of "exploitation," workers find common interests in fighting for greater justice and equality.[36] Third, government policies designed to repress or restrict customary rights and privileges of workers can stimulate common interests in defending political and civil liberties and, at the same time, politicize workers' aspirations.[37] While each factor does affect the development of collective solidarity among workplace groups, these three factors play a decisive role in shaping the level and extent of class-based community and so the degree of inter-class and intra-class conflict.

In sum, the following hypothesis posits the basis of common interests and participation in policy-making:

At higher levels, such as delegate councils and executive bodies, in complex mass-member organisations, broad or inclusive issues are needed to transcend narrower group interests and to foster community solidarity and participation.

ABSOLUTE INTERESTS AND MEMBERSHIP CONTROL OF ADMINISTRATION

Even though the non-elite may recognize and assert its own interests, a critique of elite theory is by no means complete because the organisation is still controlled by the officeholders in its day-to-day operations. For the political system, the role of exclusive managerial control over the binding decisions for the community virtually guarantees a significant degree of hegemony for the authorities. Binding decisions by political authorities—outputs, as Easton calls them—afford the leadership a special and irrefutable claim to dominance over the political system. According to Easton, "outputs are indeed a special kind of political behavior or activity because through them persons who occupy the special roles of authority in a system are able *to exercise some control or direction over other members* of the system."[38]

Elite theorists, like Michels, hold this rather special claim to be universal to all systems of effective decision-making. As they see it, even if the leader has no choice over policy and therefore actually does fulfil the desires of the followers' demands for material advantage, he can use the followers' demands to advantage against threats to his authority and power. In other words, the leader can use the followers' demands instrumentally to serve the aims of the leadership section of the organisation. Consequently, the generally unconscious assumption that the leader will necessarily dominate the masses because, by virtue of his control over administrative tasks and duties, he is able to make use of either his own or his followers' demands to further his own organisational interests becomes the crucial question in any challenge to the elite theorists' model of power. It is the elite theorists' answer to this question that gives rise to their claim of the existence of universal elite domination.

Yet, once it is recognized that the environment can determine conditions that permit rank-and-file workers to shape the political agenda, it follows logically that the environment can also structure the internal power relations of trade unions and party organisations. Michels' elite theory assumes that the "rationalization" of administrative and executive tasks out of the need to act involves a process whereby the organisation comes to be regarded as an end in itself. He contends that the ends of efficiency and calculability result in structures of control which are then assessed according to these same standards, not according to whether they yield the original objects, Michels writes:

> To the institutions and qualities which at the outset were destined simply to ensure the good working of the party machines (subordination, the harmonious cooperation of individual members, hierarchical relationships, discretion, propriety of conduct), a greater importance comes ultimately to be attached than to the productivity of the machine.[39]

Yet, the bureaucratic movement toward obsession with efficiency and calculability, which in fact represents a criterion for assessing the effects of policy upon the system's level of support (the officeholder asks how effectively the particular policy helps to promote the persistence of the stratum of which he is a part), is not inevitable.

The elite theorists' assumption of the identity of administration and domination can be questioned by examining the particular types of values shaping patterns of control. Conflict over control, involving different standards for evaluating administrative activities, calls into question the idea that leaders always control policy according to a single standard, namely, their own instrumental interests. How differing evaluative criteria can affect the operation of control in organisations can be illuminated by Weber's discussion of the sources of irrationality in economic systems. Weber accounted for the irrationality of the economic system in terms of a struggle among substantive ends. The substantive conditions that promoted the profit-maximizing, capitalist industrialism were the outcome of power struggles, which meant that capitalism would not be free from interference by "interests" which would impede the operation of processes of efficient calculation and the autonomy of the operation. Weber referred to these antagonistic interests as deriving from substantive rationality in opposition to the dominant formal rationality of capitalism.

> Substantive rationality, rather than restricted to purely formal and unambiguous fact that the action is based on "goal-oriented" rational calculation with the technically most adequate available methods, refers to application of certain criteria of ultimate ends, whether they be ethical, political, utilitarian, hedonistic, feudal (*standish*), egalitarian, or whatever, and measure the results of the economic action, however formally "rational" in the sense of correct calculation they may be, against these scales of "value rationality" or "*substantive* goal

rationality." There is an infinite number of possible values scales for this type of rationality, of which the socialist and communist standards constitute only one group.[40]

The conflict between formal and substantive rationalization produces irrationality in economic systems and fosters political conflict in organisational contexts. Bureaucratic organisation, like capitalism, is not free from conflict between formal and substantive rationality and hence from conflict over the distribution of control.

Insofar as there is conflict between substantive values, there is a struggle for advantage or power at the level of how rewards are to be parcelled out rather than the level of how much is to be allocated. Whether such conflict requires assimilation or accommodation of the control structure of an organisation is basic to the analysis of effective power. Recognition that effective decision-making systems are embedded in a larger environment of discrete subsystems which function to asymmetrically distribute scarce values, and, in so doing, to provide the basis for any system of effective power constitutes a foundation for explanation of a system of effective power in which both the ends and the means emanate from the followers' demands. According to this analysis, it is possible for the followers to be the activators or initiators and the leaders to benefit through collaboration. In short, non-elites obtain "power over" elites by putting pressure on their leaders to act on their substantive interests, and the leaders obtain "power for" but not "power over" their members to the extent that they act on the rank-and-file's mandate. Substantive rationality—Weber pointed to job control by workers[41] and to movements of planned economies[42]—institutes action evaluated and determined by ultimate ends, thereby placing control in the hands of the initiators. Thus, insofar as members autonomously formulate and assert interests involving substantive or ultimate ends, leaders are denied the ability to control the use of policy in their own interests. This is because substantive interests contain within themselves the criterion by which leadership and members alike must assess policy decisions. Thus, the analysis of the standards by which administrative activities are evaluated provides a method for distinguishing non-elite from elite control over policy in organisations. This argument identifies the *principle of participatory control*, the second key proposition in our theory.

PROPOSITION II

Because autonomously created moral ends contain standards by which to scrutinize and assess leaders' policies, members' support for these ends (rather than authority per se) enable them to control their leaders' authority by making their support contingent on leaders pursuing their moral goals.

The fact that substantive and ultimate interests contain criteria for assessing officeholders' decisions calls into question the idea that power is inherently and exclusively hierarchical and cumulative. More abstractly, an analysis of how types of values can organise the distribution of control makes it possible to explain hierarchy itself at the same time that it opens the analysis to the possibility of non-hierarchical power relationships and provides a basis for their explanation. The elitist conception of power limits itself to phenomena included under the locution "power over" and completely ignores events categorized under the very different locution "power for." By a fuller understanding of the political processes identified by the latter locution, the possibility for a conception of power that is both more inclusive and systemic than the traditional elitist conception arises.

PARTICIPATORY CONTROL IN DELEGATE COUNCILS

What, then, is the character of the political process in which officeholders, as representatives of their fellow group members to higher councils, are likely to adopt membership initiatives in order to maintain the support necessary for organisational persistence and leadership stability? Thus far, I have focused on how the environment of trade unions and socialist parties in industrial societies can foster feelings of injustice that result in collective solidarity that, in turn, afford the membership control of their own aspirations and the support they give to their leaders. The next step is to characterize how membership control of interests and the object of their support gives them control of the organisational agenda and the decisions made by officeholders. The solution lies in the way absolute values enable members to control collective decision-making and administration.

First, common interests in democratic and egalitarian ends enable the membership to control organisational agenda-setting. The members' collective control of interests and the use of their support mean that the locus of initiatives is at the base. Leaders are unable to manipulate members' preferences since they are collectively defined in response to the imperatives of the environment. Moreover, collective creation of common interests puts the timing of the initiative in the hands of the group members. Finally, since interests must become accepted by the community, the pattern of issue-formation is a collective process, involving the fluidity and variable momentum that reflect responses to the workers' environment.

Second, the collective consciousness, reflecting a consensus on ultimate ends of equality and justice, that provides members with control of their interests and the object of support, whether at the workplace or higher levels, creates a situation in which workplace and union leadership alike must constantly renew their support in order to prevent isolation and impotence. The extent to which leaders commit themselves to act on behalf of the substantive and ultimate ends specified by their members determines the level of support they receive and hence the degree of power they have to act on behalf of their members. In other words, authority itself rests, not on the legal–rational, material, technical, and psychological foundations typical of large-scale representative organisations, but on a grant of support contingent on the adequate pursuit of membership claims. This, in effect, places formal officeholders in a situation parallel to leaders in direct democracy in that substantive interests and collectivist decision-making processes prevail over particularistic leadership interests. The common commitment to ulterior ends fosters a moral imperative toward consensus and an increased fear of conflict, despite the lack of face-to-face contact found in direct democracy at the base. The resulting organisational incentive conditioning leaders' choices in whether to adopt, reject, or modify the demands of their members is the recognition that a failure to gain the requisite support would produce organisational impotence and invite independent action by component groups. This would threaten the power of officeholders and the stability, if not the very existence, of the organisation.

Participatory democratic leadership, then, consists of either a delegate or coordinator role. Of these, the coordinator role is more important for the concept of participatory democracy in modern organisations. While largely the object of influence, a responsive leader inevitably is also its subject; he will receive and magnify the attitudes of his members, thereby enlarging their collective influence. In exercising influence, however, a leader in participatory democracy does so within the moral imperatives established by the collective consensus. He is neither an initiator nor an energizer. A participatory democratic leader articulates his followers' views, translates them into plans that can be effective, and helps obtain agreement on a single policy out of various alternatives.[43] Because leaders are made responsive by the actions of organised members in pressing forward their demands and focusing their support, the leadership role becomes one of service in realizing members' interests. This conception of leadership demands closer scrutiny of leaders than J. S. Mill's view that representation can involve the delegation of administrative tasks to competent persons, yet is less sceptical than Rousseau's general dismissal of the possibility of representation.[44]

The theory of participatory democracy stresses that the movement away from domination and toward cooperation in policy-making results from the emergence of moral imperatives that shape group solidarity, recognition of common interests, and collective decisions. This adds to the idea of leadership contained in what Pennock calls "organic-pluralistic" theory.[45] Leadership in participatory democracy is distinctive in that it involves facilitating or directing group behaviour when in the first instance it is the group members who determine the common purpose. While common moral ends do make relations between leaders and members reciprocal, the fact that the common purpose is defined by and belongs to the group means that the leader is influenced more than he influences. On the other hand, a charismatic leader who uses a moral appeal to create and hold a community together, mentioned by Barber, would violate group autonomy and undermine the processes of participatory control.[46]

Moreover, the theory of participatory democracy also adds to the attempt to combine the values of participation and competent leadership in a theory of democracy. J. S. Mill and more recently Robert Dahl[47] attempt to unite greater participation and competence in decision-making but leave the balance between participation and competence undetermined. Dennis Thompson offers a solution to this in his proposal that "greater competence in leadership is acceptable to the extent that it also tends to increase opportunities for participation."[48] That moral ends of group members define the common good gives the members the means to assess leaders' moral competence and to ensure their commitment to the general interest. Effective leadership then centers largely on instrumental competence within the guidelines of the members' moral imperatives. Greater participation thus makes members more competent (in the moral sense) and demands greater leadership competence (in the instrumental sense). Because it relies on shared interests with the membership, greater leadership competence in participatory democracy would, at the same time, facilitate a fuller expression of members' interests through greater participation.

In the development of leadership responsiveness to members' interests, the substantive and ultimate egalitarian demands of the membership play a decisive role. Autonomous rank-and-file protest can be disruptive, but in itself it is not sufficient to give the organised membership control or guidance of their leaders' decisions. For, as Michels emphasizes, leaders adopt members' claims as their own and continue to dominate precisely because they retain control over the execution of policy. It is the substantive and ultimate ends that enable the members to effectively scrutinize leadership behaviour, since such ends define standards of action which they use to evaluate the results of their leaders' actions. This enlarges and specifies G. D. H. Cole's insight that "true representation is always specific and functional. . . . What is represented is never man, the individual, but always certain purposes common to groups of individuals."[49] The elitists' identification of execution of policy with domination constitutes a special and putatively irrefutable claim to dominance over the organisation, according to Michels and the proponents of democratic elitism. Yet, insofar as members' demands involve substantive or ultimate values, leaders cannot manipulate policy in their own interests, because these types of issues contain within themselves the criterion by which leaders and members alike must assess policy decisions. Ulterior interests in more equitable social relations thus create a "general will" that defines a community and specifies the principles of group solidarity which enable members to actively assess and respond to officeholders' actions.[50]

Egalitarian demands, moreover, undermine the technical, psychological, material, and legal–rational sources of officeholders' authority, thereby compelling the leaders to continuously re-create the basis of their support. One reason for this erosion of formalized authority is that the assertion of substantive and ultimate demands for equality and liberty by the rank and file undercuts the claims of legal formalism and expediency that justify legal and bureaucratic domination.[51] In Britain, rank-and-file demands for greater justice often arise from workers' grievances over wages and job control and gain legitimacy through the informal traditions of "custom and practice" norms.[52] As a result, leaders of trade unions and socialist parties have no independent ideological or legal source of authority with which to justify their attempts to shape decisions. The narrow technical issues of wage negotiations, for example, are overshadowed by the larger substantive claims for worker control of production and distribution.

A second reason why the substantive and ultimate ends of equality erode the authority of officeholders and bureaucrats is that leaders are unable to engender support by offering specific benefits or claiming general effectiveness.[53] Typically officials derive at least part of their right to make binding decisions from the material benefits that they gain for their members. However, claims for greater social, political, and economic justice overshadow the gratitude that members feel for the material improvements achieved by their leaders. Moreover, rank-and-file demands that contain specific criteria for evaluating policy consequences prevent leaders from determining policies and then convincing the members that it is in their interests to support them. Finally, the leaders' inability to bring about the social changes required to realize the members' aspirations for ultimate ends like greater justice and equality undermine officials' justification for the right to make policy and thereby to exercise control over other members of the organisation.

A third reason why egalitarian demands limit organisational authority is that they dissolve any deference or blind loyalty that officials may enjoy. Whether such loyalty derives from the veneration of a particular leader or the generalized goodwill toward the organisation itself, interests in equality and liberty reinforce the delegitimation of authority that gives workgroups the ability to choose their own ends and to make their support contingent on policy results. The product is an informal policy-making process in which leaders constantly attempt to renew their support and members assert their right to fair and just treatment. The substantive and ultimate demands for justice that derive from workplace, factory, or class consciousness orient the organised members' support toward the ends themselves, rather than toward heroes or institutions. By making members' support for authority contingent on "success," substantive and ultimate interests promote what Habermas calls a legitimation crisis. This involves situations in which members' expectations cannot be satisfied by authorities because there is a lack of the available quantity of either a culturally provided general commitment to authority or specific benefits that conform to the system.[54] The pursuit of substantive ends, then, undermines any feelings of generalized affection toward authority that derive from goodwill toward the organisation or particular leaders and compels officials to adopt their members' demands in order to regenerate their basis of support.

Fourth, the substantive and ultimate interest in greater equality that fosters the solidarity and autonomy of rank-and-file organisation enforces the policy process that undermines and limits officials' power and authority. This prevents leaders from using ideology to gain power and authority. The independent control of aspirations and the use of support that result from a substantive consensus motivate the collective pursuit of common interests and afford workers a basis of unity and action independent of officials. Group consensus and autonomy thus reduce leaders' capacity for coercion and limit their credibility to those issues consistent with the members' self-defined interests. By making it clear, moreover, that independent action in pursuit of their substantive or ultimate ends would ensue if leaders of the larger organisation failed to take up their cause, autonomous rank-and-file organisation constitutes a threat to organisational stability and effectiveness. Thus, the threat of independent action, for example, wildcat strikes, constitutes a powerful sanction that enables organised members to compel leaders to adopt their demands and even to institute significant changes in the structure of organisational authority for the purpose of increasing membership participation and influence.

To summarize, the analysis of the political processes of participatory control suggests the following hypothesis:

Members' participation in trading their support for leaders' pursuit of their moral ends enables them to exercise control of policy substance (moral ends), if not its detail.

IMPLICATIONS

A theory of power relations and participatory democracy based on the examination of the systemic sources of the interests of leaders and organised members and the members' support for policies, officials, and authority-structures offers several key advantages over the cumulative theory of power exemplified in Michels' theory of oligarchy and in democratic elitism. First, this analysis focuses on the exchange of interest and support between leaders and members involved in actual policy-making processes. It avoids the one-sided, top-down perspective of the cumulative theory of power which logically excludes the organised mass from any significant role in policy-making and portrays power as a zero-sum contest in which the aggregation of power resources by those at the top entails the diminution of influence by those at the bottom. As a result, the role of membership participation in policy-making can be appreciated and leadership can be interpreted as a response to the aims of community bonds.

Because all activity by the mass membership relies upon "leaders" to move resolutions, to communicate with employers or trade union officials, and to organise protest actions, there are methodological difficulties in investigating the contribution of the organised membership to union and party policy-making. The theory of cumulative power underlying Michels' law of oligarchy and made use of by democratic elitists precludes rank-and-file control precisely because it fails to fully examine the bases of authority upon which leaders rely. The aggregation of resources, particularly by the leadership alone, provides only a partial account of the complexity and dynamics of the relationship between leaders and members and therefore ignores important ways in which authority is constructed. One advantage of a systemic approach to a theory of participatory democracy is that it does require examination of the bases of authority through relationships of interest and support between leaders and followers. Because such an analysis facilitates the examination of the dynamics of relations between leaders and followers, it makes possible the interpretation of leadership as a product of community processes and needs, reflecting a commitment to collective solidarity in pursuit of ends crucial to the persistence of the group itself. In short, while it is difficult to "get to" the rank and file through their leaders, the study of the sources and types of interests and the possible modes of control between leaders and members provides a method for identifying circumstances in which members subordinate leaders' prerogatives to the ends of the community.

Second, the theory avoids the conundrum of objective interest analysis by locating the sources of interests and control of support in the complex and conditional confluence of factors which foster a sense of injustice and motivate revolt. Because latent interests may only be recognized if stimulated by the way the imperatives of the environment shape what happens to other workgroups, unions, or classes to which comparison is made, this analysis focuses on subjective, identifiable interests, at the same time that it locates conflict in the fundamental structure of social inequalities.

Third, this theory offers the methodological criteria for assessing the sources of policy initiatives and the modes of control. Most analysts of power agree that it is possible to determine the existence, direction, extent, comprehensiveness, and intensity of influence, though the practical difficulties are immense.[55] In large part this is because power is a value-laden or essentially contested concept.[56] As pointed out in the previous chapter, discussions of power by democratic elitists and theorists of objective interests presuppose that power involves contradictory interests, resulting in a myopic focus on the question of who controls the agenda. The theory of participatory democracy, however, argues that leaders and members can share common moral interests defined by community solidarity and that this is arrived at by members defining their own interests and compelling leaders to pursue the common interest. This implies that identifying an exercise of power involves (1) justifying the expectation that leaders would have thought or acted differently from their members (though not necessarily against workers' interests), (2) specifying mechanisms by which workers shaped organisational ends, and (3) showing how processes of decision-making in delegate councils converted members' interests into organisational policy. The first two constitute agenda-setting processes and the third actual decision-making.

Because power involves both moral and instrumental dimensions, the identification of an exercise of power in delegate councils can distinguish the control of moral ends as critical and the shaping of instrumental ends as routine.[57] With an interest in focusing on the important decisions, the first test of power (agenda-setting) is to determine whether the moral ends that foster community solidarity are shaped by the membership or by leaders. This involves showing that leaders would have acted differently from their members and how members defined the agenda. It can be accomplished by examining the organisational locus of initiatives, their timing, and whether the issues involve moral ends that promote workers' general interests in a capitalist society. The pattern of exchange of interest and support by which rank-and-file organisations aggregate pressure for a particular issue and shape organisational agendas also identifies the source of policy. The second test (decision-making) is to specify the mechanism by which the moral ends become organisational policies. This involves assessing the exchange of interests and support between leaders and members in delegate councils that make organisational policy. The focusing of support on policy objectives or authorities, evaluated through threats of independent action, other challenges to the leader's authority, and the justification provided for such actions, provides a way of determining the relations of interests and support between leaders and members. A further complementary test is whether specific policy plans are consistent with the chosen moral ends. In short, the analysis of policy formation and decision-making on key issues affecting members' lives and conditions can help clarify the theory of participatory democracy.

CONCLUSION

The key concepts involved in a theory of participatory democracy, while derived from a critique of Michels' elite theory, constitute the bases for a more comprehensive theory of power in formally representative organisations than that provided by elite theory. The first proposition is that the internal dynamics of effective power is shaped by the conditions and imperatives of its environment. By shaping values and interests, the environment creates incentives for variations in power relations. The second is the principle of community autonomy which focuses on interest formation and community organisation, factors that provide the basis for the exercise of participatory control in policymaking. Non-reciprocal social relations can give rise to sentiments of injustice among workers, which, in turn, lead to autonomous communities bonded together by substantive or ultimate interests aimed at rectifying inequalities of power and reward. Whether these feelings are articulated or provide the basis of collective organisation and action, however, depends on historically determined factors involving the labour process and the overall political economy. Nonetheless, feelings of injustice provide a potential for collective interests and participation that presupposes any assertion of workers' interests in organisational policy-making and action. The third proposition—the principle of participatory control—involves the application of substantive and ultimate interests to the analysis of control in decision-making and administration. Because these types of interests contain precise and definite criteria by which policy is evaluated by members and leaders alike, the ability of officeholders to use them instrumentally to reinforce their own power position rather than to achieve external results is impeded. Organisational policy can be controlled from below when members assert the moral ends that define their common interests.

CHAPTER 3

The Environment of Democracy: Sources of Participatory Power Relations

To test our theory of participatory democracy, we now turn to an examination of policy-making in British workplace organisations, trade unions, and national union and party federations (the Trades Union Congress and the Labour Party) during World War I. This period provides a paradigm for theorizing about participatory democracy because rank-and-file influence in organisational policy-making reached unprecedented levels. While rank-and-file militancy did not explode into revolutionary activity as it did in Russia and Germany during the same period, revolutionary fervour was especially widespread and intense during 1917. Industrial militancy, moreover, reflected and contributed to ideological movements, like guild socialism, advocating greater control of union policy, workshop practices, and Government decisions. The new manifestations of rank-and-file participation at the workplace produced lasting policy and structural changes in many unions as well as the Labour Party. Looking at these exceptional instances of rank-and-file influence in trade union and Labour Party policy-making, then, provides insight into participatory policy processes that form the basis of a theory of participatory democracy in modern societies. The conditions that encouraged and inhibited participatory democracy during World War I exist, if only more moderately, in all modern capitalist democracies.

However, before turning to these case studies of wartime policy-making, an examination of the environment that precipitated participatory democracy is crucial. As we have argued above, the environment determines workers' experiences which, in turn, affect their consciousness of interests and objects of support. Because the environment shapes interest and support, it affects motivations for collective organisation and action, although it does so differentially.

An analysis of the environment is fundamental to an investigation of participatory democracy because it shapes the normative and structural imperatives that foster consciousness of basic moral principles underlying social relations. Recognition of normative principles informs and guides action toward ultimate or substantive ends. Thus, the environment can facilitate the development of class consciousness, that is, perceptions and feelings of injustice, which, in turn, inform attitudes toward interests and the rights of superiors to issue commands. When attitudes combine demands for greater equality and disaffection from authority, workers have incentives for collective organisation and action, a development which affords them the autonomy necessary for group decision-making and the stimulus for individual participation in shaping collective policy.

This chapter, then, outlines the environmental bases of participatory power relations in the British trade union and labour movement from 1915 to 1918. Consciousness of injustice and definition of interests and objects of support depend on variations in the labour process, bargaining power, the impact of state intervention, and the consequences of changes in the standard of living in comparison with that of other social classes. Because the combination of these four factors affects various sections of the working class differentially, the form, extent, and level of collective action in resisting injustice vary. As a result, this study will focus on the leading labour organisations which, despite the fact that they were composed of a minority of all workers, represented the collective power of the working class.

LABOUR PROCESS AND CLASS CONSCIOUSNESS

Certain labour processes facilitate workgroup formation and the development of class consciousness. These are the processes that promote the primary group relations among workmates and the sociability during leisure activities typical of what Lockwood labels the "traditional proletariat."[1] A product technology that fosters common interests, makes operators indispensable, accords a middle range of status, and gives workers substantial control over job performance promotes class consciousness and organisation when linked with rigid and centralized managerial control.[2] These types of labour processes usually coincide with systems of direct managerial control which attempt to discipline labour by coercive threats, close supervision, and prescribed procedures that regulate the execution of tasks.[3] At the same time, a strategy of responsible autonomy, applying mainly to skilled workers, gives workers greater leeway and encourages them to adapt to changing situations in a way that benefits the firm.[4] Both direct control and responsible autonomy give workers a base from which to build collective consciousness, solidarity, and organisation.

The development of direct control of labour in Britain paralleled its course in the United States. In both nations, employers' response to problems of labour productivity from the late nineteenth century through the 1930s involved the use of greater mechanization, greater supervision, larger plant size, decreasing skill differentials, and an increased labour supply.[5] The predominance of highly skilled craftsmen diminished and unskilled labour gained ground as the skill content of many jobs became more complex with the introduction of formal procedures associated with direct control. By World War I, the simple, informal nineteenth century methods of management were giving way to more bureaucratic systems. Increased international competition and concentration of capital, the drive to accumulate more capital, and rising union membership compelled employers to extend formal collective bargaining and dispute procedures in an effort to speed up productivity without making substantial investments in new technology.[6] The war, however, spurred greater mechanization, increased plant size, and further extension of direct control. The result was a more homogeneous pattern of working-class experiences at the point of production. According to Cronin: "In its very essence, the phase of industrialization that gathered momentum near the end of the nineteenth century was inimical to skilled, craft labor, and tended inevitably toward the creation of a different labor force, typified by the semi-skilled machine-tender in mass production."[7] The war accelerated this trend toward homogenization and the creation of the "traditional proletariat."

The overall pattern of convergence in the labour process before, during, and after the First World War was conducive to the development of class consciousness among manual workers, especially in the engineering and related trades. The Government's subjugation of labour to the exigencies of war involved reorganising production so that the contribution of labour to output was reduced. To get the greatest possible result from a limited supply of skilled labour, employers relied on a process called dilution. This involved the upgrading of unskilled and semi-skilled workers to jobs previously performed only by skilled craftsmen, the introduction of unskilled into newly created semi-skilled jobs, and the increased use of "scientific management." Skilled workers were responsible for retooling and training of the less skilled on the more specialized and productive machines. The two million workers affected by dilution also felt the Government's increased control over wages. Piece-rates created incentives for increased production, legislation prevented wage conflicts from disrupting production, and Government policy limited wage increases to at most the cost of living.

The acute shortage of skilled men in the first war years necessitated intensified production under State supervision. Skill substitution involved, for the most part, the process of upgrading: no person could be employed on work requiring less skill or usefulness than he or she possessed.[8] Yet, dilution was in very few cases simply a question of replacing skilled by less-skilled labour. The content of the job and the methods of production changed simultaneously. Skilled turners were required to design and maintain tools for dilutees and to supervise their work. Dilution was limited by the number of qualified men who could supervise, until the Ministry of Munitions found it could train unskilled workers to set up and maintain simple machines in about four weeks. Dilution also required expansion in the ancillary services department of machine shops. With the growth of specialized machinery, the "toolroom" became more significant.

The rationalization and standardization of production techniques associated with dilution represented a direct assault on the self-respect and economic security of the craftsman. The production process supporting dilution efforts threatened his independence in the workshops and pride in his work.[9] The defence of the craft tradition constituted a major source of militancy in the munitions centers.[10] Inherent in craft unionism was a desire to take over the duties of the employer because craft skill was held to be a property, much like the employer's business and capital. Craft solidarity was manifest in the workshop through ceremony and social ritual. Regular social exchanges occurred around the breakfast stoves or in the workshop dining and reading rooms. Even during working hours, men maintained a social existence independent of the employer.[11] Perhaps surprisingly, skilled men during the war earned less than the unskilled, who benefitted from piece-work introduced to speed up production, in spite of being told that skilled work was of greater national importance. Craftsmen also feared that piece-work would be used not only to lower their status but to reduce wages permanently after the war.

The Government's Dilution Scheme, moreover, was foisted on militant craftsmen by means of repressive tactics employed to achieve wartime manpower goals. The Government overcame the resolute defence of the craftsmen's rights fought by the Amalgamated Society of Engineers (ASE) with the help of concessions, but the strong resistance of the militants of the Clyde Workers' Committee (CWC) led to the Government imposing its policy through overt repression.[12]

Dilution in engineering and related trades established a pattern that was followed in other occupations. The downgrading of the traditional craftsman stimulated the skilled and the industrial workers to strengthen their collective organisation in defence of their customs and standards, and the upgrading of the mass of unskilled and semi-skilled workers provided the latter with a new basis for collective solidarity and organisation. While the integration of the less skilled into the labour process generated new sectional consciousness and produced conflict with the skilled craftsmen, the narrowing in skill differential drew the two groups together because it wiped out distinctions between different occupations in the same works.[13] Dilution opened new channels of mobility absent for the less skilled in the prewar period, raising their expectations as they gained greater status, economic reward, and confidence to assert their own claims.[14] Moreover, more homogenization in the labour process created more group consciousness at the workplace, and workers' collective subjection to the monolithic authority of the state and employer fostered a broadening of class consciousness and common goals.

LABOUR SUPPLY AND COLLECTIVE POWER

The unlimited demand for labour during the war increased the workers' bargaining power dramatically but produced feelings of injustice when Government actions placed restraint on unprecedented opportunities. Marxist and Keynesian economics supports the proposition that full employment erodes employers' ability to discipline workers.[15] Full employment permits workers to move easily to a better position, to refuse extra work or harsh conditions, to increase real earnings, and to successfully pursue industrial action in order to redress grievances. Workers' bargaining power is further enhanced by the importance of their productive contribution. During wartime, critically needed workers found their bargaining position strengthened substantially. Especially, workers with strong, stable "product markets" were in a better position than those with declining, unstable ones.[16] As a result, monopoly, state, and competitive industrial sectors identify those locations which distinguish workers' bargaining capacity. Workers in the monopoly sector generally enjoy a strong and stable product market, workers in the public sector enjoy a measure of security from political forces, and those in the competitive sector suffer from unstable and uncertain fluctuations in product markets. During the war, the infinite demand for war material created stable product markets that strengthened workers' bargaining power.

Moreover, collective organisation can strengthen workers' bargaining power. Unions can undermine managerial prerogatives by making wage determination more susceptible to political pressure than to impersonal market forces.[17] Further, government action that curtails market freedoms politicizes industrial conflict and provides incentives for united action by diverse groups of workers. As the Government replaces the market as the source of job allocation, it becomes the target of intense resistance and political conflict. Workers' recognition that industrial action (strikes) can yield results also contributes to incentives for developing collective organisation and pursuing collective action.[18] In short, workers' confidence fostered by the existence of full employment heightens their incentives to act collectively against injustice.

With the drain-off of men into the military and the surge in the production of war material, the domestic labour market became favourable to the individual wage-earner, making the allocation of civilian manpower to munitions work more difficult. Yet, unemployment rose to 3.3 percent in 1914 because of the dislocation of business, especially in the export trades. (See Table 3.1)

But employment dropped rapidly when a labour shortage developed following the rival claims for manpower between production and military service. After conscription was introduced early in 1916, every physically fit man between eighteen and forty-one, unless he was engaged in work of national importance, had to join one of the fighting forces. As a consequence, some eight hundred thousand women entered

Table 3.1
Working Population, Employment, and Unemployment (Thousands)

Date	Total in civil employment	Armed Forces	Total in employment	Unemployment	Working Population	% Unemployed
1913	19,910	400	20,310	430	20,740	2.1
1914	19,440	810	20,250	660	20,740	3.3
1915	13,400	2,490	20,890	200	21,090	1.1
1916	17,700	3,500	21,200	70	21,270	0.4
1917	17,100	4,250	21,350	100	21,450	0.6
1918	17,060	4,430	21,490	140	21,630	0.8
1919	19,030	2,130	21,160	660	21,820	3.4
1920	20,810	700	21,570	430	22,000	2.0

Source: C. H. Feinstein, National Income, Expenditure and Output of the United Kingdom, 1855-1965, (Cambridge: At the University Press, 1972), Table 57, p. T126.

the labour market, especially in metal-working trades and Government factories, to replace recruits and to sustain family standards of living which were deteriorating as a result of the rapid rise in the cost of living.[19] In short, the trade-off between military and civilian manpower served to give the civilian wage-earner considerable market power that, from the point of view of the war effort, meant that an efficient allocation of manpower was not possible.

The high demand for skilled labour gave the workman so much market power that dissatisfaction with the job would provide him with cause to move on to another employer, putting the worker beyond the control of employers or union leaders and disrupting munitions production.[20] The employer could get neither enough nor the right kinds of workmen. Efforts to import skilled labour proved abortive, being opposed by employers and unions alike.[21] The possibility of strikes threatened production, and the manufacturer could not change men from one occupation to another or put semi-skilled men into skilled work as a result of trade union restrictions and regulations. As the men woke up to their economic power and as prices started to rise, wage conflicts erupted and employers bid against one another for the available men. As the capacity of the market to secure control disappeared, skilled workmen escaped the control of their employers and union leaders.[22] The Government saw that these conditions were inhibiting production and that it would be necessary to ensure uninterrupted work, to utilize the full energy of the workman, and to mobilize and place all available manpower as efficiently as possible.

The voluntary agreement to remove union restrictions, on the one hand, and to limit profits, on the other, proved insufficient and led in July 1915 to its statutory embodiment in an expanded Munitions of War Act applying extensively to workers in munitions and partially to those in mining and transport. Sir Llewellyn Smith argued that non-economic control over workmen was necessary to increase the production of war material.

The ordinary economic control over the individual workman had broken down, the question is whether some exceptional form of control or motive not of a purely economical character can be effectively substituted.[23]

Industrial conscription was ruled out, although it was preferred by influential leaders in the Government. Lloyd George held the "conviction that the war could not be won without the sacrifice of individual liberty to the needs of the State, which involved a much wider measure of State control over labour."[24] While he believed the state had the right to commandeer labour, he recognized that organised labour would not submit to it and that the Munitions Act went as far as labour would tolerate. The Government initiative to subordinate labour through an extensive reform of industrial relations passed into law with the consent of the patriotic union leadership, desiring to help the national war effort but knowing fully the explosive nature of rank-and-file opposition to industrial conscription.

Giving an overt appearance of equality of sacrifice on the part of employer and worker, the Munitions Act, in fact, constituted an effective attack on the industrial customs and liberties of the wage-earner, while placing only indirect and imprecise constraints on employers. According to the official *History of the Ministry of Munitions*, "The general purpose of the Munitions of War Act was to carry the progress of Government control over the workman's normal freedom . . . as far as the exigencies of war production demanded and the state of feeling in the Labour world would allow."[25] In the designated munitions firms, lock-outs were prohibited and profits were limited, though guaranteed at a prewar level. Craftsmen and other munitions workers, on the other hand, lost their right to strike, their traditional conditions of labour, their right to choice of contract through the notorious Section 7 (which required a worker to have his employer approve his leaving for another job), and their right to bargain collectively.[26]

Conscription provided another mechanism for counteracting labour's new-found bargaining power. The inability of union leaders to win any concessions, other than a promise that there would be no industrial conscription, seemed to prove the disregard of labour's interests and the unilateral authority of Lloyd George, Lord Kitchener and the Tories.[27] The Trade Card Scheme and the List of Protected Trades[28] that superseded it created dissatisfaction with conscription and contributed further to rivalries between occupations. Skilled workmen complained of dilutees getting protection from induction into the military that was intended for them. Married workers engaged in essential war work complained that the single, skilled men should not get protection that they were receiving. Moreover, the calling-up of physically unfit men and the formation of "Labour Battalions" composed of drafted skilled men were sources of grievance. Yet, because military conscription meant the loss of liberty to the workingmen, regardless of different skills, ideals, and incomes, it created a political issue and consequent unity among them that overshadowed differences between them. The Military Service Act strengthened their determination to resist industrial conscription. As Wrigley pointed out, "Every turn that is given to the screw of the MSA swells the ranks of the movement and hardens the animosity of the extremists."[29] Workers' resentment grew because an employer could deny them a military exemption as a result of his right of dismissal, a situation which enabled him to hold the threat of conscription over them. According to the Commission of Industrial Unrest,

It is said, and occasionally it is no doubt true, that tactless foremen or managers occasionally intimidate men with threats of the Military Service Acts, and there is a feeling abroad that compulsory industrial service is being enforced, in the guise of exemption from compulsory Military Service.[30]

In such circumstances, the Conscription Acts were tantamount to industrial compulsion.

Finally, the demand for labour had a different impact on the material and psychological circumstances of various sections of the working class and on its aspirations for political power. Those central to the war economy felt the impact of state controls most directly, benefitting from the tight labour market but being less free because of Government restrictions. Already highly organised before the war, the craft and industrial workers in munitions work, mining, and transport experienced injustices that led to collective resistance. The number of metalworkers rose from 1.8 to 2.4 million during the war—or 12.3 percent per year as compared with 3 percent per year before the war.[31] The expansion of wartime engineering production also required the addition of large numbers of less-skilled workers, lowering the proportion of skilled workers in the industry from 60 percent in 1914 to 50 percent in 1921.[32] The number of miners, by contrast, fell at the beginning of the war as many left the pits for the trenches. Similarly, of about 650,000 railway employees, 184,000 railwaymen joined the armed forces.[33] Altogether these workers represented 25 to 30 percent of the civilian working population of about 17 million during the war. The remaining groups of workers, less affected by state regulation, worked in industries doing war and civilian work, such as building, construction, paper, printing, and woodworking, or in the industries more peripheral to war production, such as textiles, food, clothing, and agriculture. These industries experienced a loss of manpower to those producing war materials and to the military. Because the most advanced sections of organised labour were located in the industrial sectors central to war production, the impact of the demand for labour on these workers helps explain their capacity for collective resistance.

WAR AND STATE INTERVENTION

While prewar state involvement in industrial problems had been increasing, its expansion during the war exacerbated conflict between labour and capital. S. M. Lipset argues that a long and intense period of state repression of working-class economic and political rights heightens class consciousness and organisation, often leading to revolutionary movements.[34] Long before the war, the British working class had won considerable power and representation, even though some industrialists, like the railway owners, refused to recognize unions until just before the outbreak of war and even though the working classes were not fully enfranchised until 1918. More specifically, state intervention during World War I confirms a related Lipset hypothesis: "The denial of political rights in a situation in which a social stratum is led to claim such rights will increase its feelings of deprivation and increase the likelihood of a favorable response to revolutionary and extremist doctrines."[35] The imposition of a loss of rights and customs was at first accepted by patriotic workers but increasingly led to suspicions about the future of labour. As the abuses mounted, workers became more and more disposed to demand a return and often an extension of their prewar rights. In short, the exigencies of war and the lack of precedent for state involvement in industrial relations led to a repressive strategy that exacerbated and politicized class conflict, particularly in the industrial sectors crucial to the war effort.

In order to secure the scarce resources necessary to win the war and to divert the manpower and capital required, the state became, according to Tawney, not merely "a protective agency, but . . . an organizing, directing, and sometimes managing authority."[36] It assumed responsibility for prosecuting the war, for organising and maintaining the production of war materials and goods for home use, and for controlling public opinion in order to maintain the legitimacy of the war effort. Significantly, the emergence of these "affirmative" functions led to profound changes in the relation of the state to labour and capital. At the initiative of Government officials, capital became a virtual arm of the state, blurring the distinction between private and public spheres. At the same time, wage labour, an indispensable scarce commodity, was unilaterally subordinated to the direction of employers and Government authorities. These changed roles led, in turn, to a more extensive and complex system of control over labour. The intimate collaboration between Government and industry that guaranteed the strengthening of industrial and financial capital at a time when Government policy systematically subjugated labour politicized basic norms of social reciprocity on which attitudes toward social justice were founded. This produced widespread and serious concern over the fairness of labour's contributions to the war effort and uncertainty about the position of wage labour in Britain's industrial society.

First, the extension of the state's power to wage war made its appearance in a series of Defence of the Realm Acts, marking a new departure in Government control over the management of the war. The first Defence of the Realm Act, passed on August 8, 1914, empowered the Government to make regulations for public safety and national defence. The second, passed twenty days later, extended these powers to include control over munitions factories and workers. In November 1914, this was widened further to allow the Admiralty and Army Council to requisition land and factories and to require manufacturers to produce goods for military and naval purposes.[37] A third Defence of the Realm Act, the most significant, passed in March 1915 and gave the Government full legal power to take over any factory and to control its processes and output in addition to the right to cancel any contracts which might hinder the production of war material.[38] The immediate result was an "Armaments Output Committee" under Lord Kitchener of the War Office and a Munitions of War Committee under Lloyd George of the Treasury.[39]

Second, wartime industrial policy involved Government cooptation of and support for industry. By June a single Ministry was formed to direct all aspects of munitions production, taking over functions from the War Office, the Admiralty, and the Board of Trade. The new Ministry of Munitions fulfilled the trend toward state control and was shaped by the personal views of Lloyd George and its other top administrators. For example, William Beveridge, an administrator, favoured unlimited extension of state power during war, believing that the interests of the state and community took precedence over the individual.[40] Bureaucratic incompetence gave way to an infusion of businessmen of exceptional drive and organisational skill. Headed by Lloyd George who had un-flagging confidence in the ability of business organisations to win the war, the Ministry of Munitions brought in more than ninety well-known directors and managers from larger firms for the duration of the war, many of whom were kept on the firms' payrolls.[41] Further, employers directed the production of war material. The District Armament Committees were mostly made up of executives from the largest engineering firms.[42] Turning the war effort over to the business community was done hurriedly and unguardedly, "trusting to the integrity, to the loyalty, to the patriotism of the businessmen to do their best for the Government and to do it on fair terms."[43] The intermeshing of business and Government personnel freed the munitions industries from military direction and restrictions of Government routine, and advanced efficient production as a result of businessmen's familiarity with industrial operations at the same time that it united in a common system the interests of business and Government.

The first Munitions of War Act gave the Government the power to make firms "controlled establishments," which allowed it to organise and control production and to limit profits to a maximum of 20 percent over profits earned during the boom year of 1913. The Ministry of Munitions became the largest employer in the country before the war was over. By then, 218 national munitions factories and about 20,000 controlled establishments employing over 3 million workers in munitions production were in operation.[44] In privately owned firms producing munitions, the Government bore the cost of needed extensions and adaptations to war work.[45] In short, the Ministry was fundamentally a business organisation, dominated by recruits from the business world and linked to all the essential industries.[46]

Moreover, the Government's policy for industrial mobilization transformed those industries essential to the war effort—munitions, shipping, coal, and transport—into virtual monopolies with generous profits. Reluctant to use the Defence of the Realm Act's provisions in regard to control over industry, the Government offered private businesses generous rewards to encourage them to switch to war production in the interest of national survival. It followed the imperatives of private capital in strengthening the employers' capacity to realize their class interest by guaranteeing handsome profits and large orders and reducing the risk of private firms in turning to war work. Government purchasing agencies established criteria for standardization and quality control in cooperation with trade and employers' associations, providing incentives toward horizontal and vertical mergers.[47] The Excess Profits Duty provided a concession to trade unions in the bargain over the Government's manpower policies and an encouragement for new investment that would increase the efficiency of production. With only approximately 34 percent of the Excess Profits Duty collected, private enterprise clearly took full advantage of this opportunity to renovate their plants.[48] With the excessive demand for war material exceeding the output capacity of the firms, their monopoly position allowed them at first to charge to Government "unduly high" prices. Following investigations, the Government set the price by assessing the actual cost of manufacture, with the unit cost of the least-efficient firms setting the level, and offering "a fair percentage of profit."[49] Profits soared, while ownership and managerial control were untouched.

The Government, moreover, encouraged reorganisation of production in an effort to increase output and maintain continuous production. It initiated longer hours of labour and more intensive work, better organisation, equipment, and scientific management. When efficiency declined from overstrain, disease, and drink as a result of overwork, the Government stepped in to improve the welfare of the labour force.[50] The acute shortage of materials, fuel, machinery, and labour led the Government to introduce improved processes, saving labour and material, the use of scrap metals, standardization of components, reorganisation of factory layouts, combination among manufacturers, and the determination of wages and conditions by national, rather than local, agreements.

Third, wartime labour policy restrained the rights and market power of workers. As we have already seen, from the conversion of the Treasury Agreement into the Munitions Act of 1915 and the introduction of conscription for military service the next year, the state controlled the labour market through anti-strike legislation, restrictions on the mobility of labour, and military conscription. The Government's partiality toward private enterprise was manifested also in its policy on wages. While there was a free market in prices, the Munitions Act restrained the power of labour to get the full return that the market would bear. As wage grievances accumulated in the face of rising costs during 1915 and 1916, the workers found themselves facing an embargo on wage rises. The Government's declared policy, promulgated in November 1915, cited the need for economy in refusing to permit general wage advances.[51] For their part, employers contended that they were pressed to economize by the Government, that only large earnings must be considered when setting higher wages in relation to the increased cost of living, and that the workers needed to keep better time.[52] The employers argued that the wage increases in 1916 and 1917 "were to be regarded as Government imposed, unrelated to the real profitability of industries, and open to revision after the war's end."[53] While the Government provided incentives to reap generous profits, its policy assumed that labour would absorb the rising cost of living as a minor sacrifice to the war effort. By 1917, the Committee on Production had centralized wage reviews for munitions workers, granting advances three times a year according to the rise in the cost of living.[54] It was only after the May 1917 strikes among munitions workers when the Industrial Unrest Commission revealed that the working class' grievances derived from "high food prices, low wages, and unfairness of the call-up" that the War Cabinet decided a more contented working class was needed for the prosecution of the war and fixed the price of essential foods.[55]

From the beginning of 1915, wage restraint made profits a matter of serious concern to some important groups of workers. Many of the rank and file in the war industries, as well as those in industries suffering dislocation, were not getting an increase in pay at a time when it was clear that some employers were beginning to make large profits. In spite of the duties on profits, the workers' aggravation remained, since they saw many instances of excessive expenditure, evasion of duties, and waste.[56] Their suspicion of employers' mercenary motives served to undermine their commitment to the war cause, to arouse their anger, to inspire them to demand higher wages and better conditions, and to question the existing modes of control in those enterprises for which they worked. Thus, the issue of profiteering came to have a high priority among workers who noted the contrast between their own standard of living and that of the owners and managers of industry. As a result, discontent with the *status quo* rose.

In order to control unrest, the Government enlisted the union leadership to assist in the formulation and implementation of its manpower policies. The Treasury Agreement led to the creation of the National Labour Advisory Committee and subsidiary local committees, on which sat representatives of the Trades Union Congress (TUC) and the Labour

Party (LP).[57] This Committee consulted with the Government on matters arising from the latter's interference in industrial relations. The Munitions Act instituted tripartite representation between the Government, employers, and trade unions in local Munitions Tribunals set up to resolve breaches in the Act and to minimize industrial stoppages. Union leaders were also given powers to issue exemptions under the Trade Card Agreement of November 1916.[58] When the Agreement proved ineffective, the union leaders, after consultation, agreed to the new Scheduled List of Occupations Scheme and were given powers to interpret conscription regulations in Local Labour Enlistment Complaint Committees.[59] Increasingly, national organisation leaders became national figures.[60] The inclusion of Henderson in Lloyd George's War Cabinet as head of the new Ministry of Labour charged with managing industrial unrest represents an important example of Lloyd George's strategy of fostering industrial stability through cooptation. But ironically, by identifying themselves with Government policy, Labour leaders undermined their credibility with their own members and, in effect, encouraged the rank and file to organise and act independently.

Fourth, wartime financial policies served to generate rapid price increases, placing the already harassed working class in an even more undesirable condition at the same time that profits soared. Taxes on consumption, which fell most heavily on the working class, proved less able to meet the increasing need for war finance, since the workers had little margin for "luxury" spending on sugar, tobacco, or beer. Rather, the workers demanded higher wages.[61] Consequently, the main additional tax burden fell on direct taxes. Income tax was raised from 1s. 2d. per pound sterling in 1913–14 to 6s. in the years 1918–19 and 1919–20; at the same time, the exemptions were lowered from £160 to £130 in 1915. As a result of wages and prices doubling by 1918 and trebling by 1919–20, the number of wage-earners paying tax rose from 1.13 million in 1913–14 to 3 million in 1917–18 and 3.9 million in 1919–20.[62] Taxes on excess profits contributed little to wartime finance. The Munitions Levy, assessed at 100 percent on all profits above a prewar standard plus 20 percent, was mostly evaded by capital expenditure, depreciation allowances, and other methods. The Excess Profits Duty, introduced in late 1915 in order to assuage complaints of widespread profiteering, averaged 63 percent of excess profits over the prewar 1913 standard, although the amount collected was only 34 percent as a result of capital expenditures and other evasive practices.

Because normal types of taxation were inadequate to finance the war effort, the Government turned to a combination of credit expansion, war loans, and borrowing from abroad. The owners of the means of exchange reaped huge returns on their capital. The "ransom" paid to private capital is estimated to have doubled the Government's expenditure during the war.[63] The financial pressure groups had a friend in Lloyd George, Chancellor of the Exchequer before he became Minister of Munitions and then Prime Minister, who favoured their advice over that of industrialists or landowners.[64] He regarded any effort to abolish profiteering and to usurp capital as the end of the capitalist system and the heraldry of the unimaginable "equalitarian state."[65] The failure of the Government to consider seriously an attempt to finance the war at the expense of the rich testifies to the entrenched domination of private capital and the success of its legitimation.

THE STANDARD OF LIVING AND CLASS CONFLICT

Though the income of unskilled workers improved relative to those of skilled and industrial workers, all incomes still lagged, though to different degrees, behind the rise in the cost of living from 1915 to 1918.[66] The differentiated decline in workers' living standards, judged largely in terms of their real incomes and levels of food consumption, resulted mainly from the panoply of Government policies that strengthened the advantages of capital over labour. Despite important sectional differences between the skilled and the less skilled, the result of this overt collaboration was a greater tendency for key groups of workers to compare their situation to that of businessmen and the rich and to perceive themselves as part of a section of the larger community who were treated unfairly. This was especially true of industrial workers in mining and on the railways and the craftsmen in the engineering trades, the most prone to develop collective resistance. To illuminate the attitudes that promoted greater class consciousness during the war, the Commission on Unrest in 1917 can be cited:

Statements of prices and profits in the newspapers, admissions made in Parliament, their own sources of information and their personal and family experience make them [the workers] feel, to use their own language, they are "being bled white." . . . The feeling just mentioned is intensified by the belief, which is general among the workpeople, that a large proportion of these high prices is due, not to the necessities of the case, but to "Profiteering." The sense that many individuals are benefitting through the war at the expense of the community, and especially of the poor, generates a bitterness which intensifies the unrest.[67]

According to Runciman, the essence of class consciousness is "that the class-conscious person takes his normative reference group from his equals and his comparative reference group from his superiors."[68] A comparative reference group is the group whose attributes a person contrasts with his own, whereas a normative reference group is that from which a person takes his standards.[69] In short, the coincidence of a rise in profits and a decline in real earnings heightened the contrast between workers and capital and provided workers with an incentive for common identification and collective solidarity.

As a result of the deterioration of most workers' standard of living from 1915 to part of 1918, in contrast to the large profits enjoyed by capital, the workers felt that a minority was unjustly taking advantage of their wartime sacrifice for its own private gain. While the war did benefit the poorest and least skilled, the inability of the majority of the most powerfully situated and organised craft and industrial workers to keep up with the rising cost of living while huge profits were being made reinforced the sense of subjugation perpetuated by the Government's manpower policies. The Right Hon. G. N. Barnes, M.P., in his summary to the *Commission of Enquiry into Industrial Unrest* of July 1917, wrote:

All the commissions put in the forefront, as the leading cause of unrest, the fact that the cost of living has increased disproportionately to the advance in wages, and that the distribution of food supplies is unequal. Commissioners are unanimous in regarding this as the most important of all causes of industrial unrest in itself, but its existence in the minds of the workers colours many subsidiary causes, in regard to which, in themselves, there might have been no serious complaint; and the feeling exists in men's minds that sections of the community are profiting by the increased prices.[70]

Estimates of the movement of wages in comparison to the cost of living indicate a declining real income between 1914 and 1918. Rates of wages increased less rapidly than the cost of living in the first three years of the war, although in 1918 wage rates rose more rapidly than

Table 3.2
Indices of Wage Rates, Wage Earnings, and Retail Prices

	Average Weekly Wage Rates (1)	Average Weekly Wage Earnings (2)	Retail Prices (3)	Wage Drift (Earnings minus Wages) (4)
1913	100	100	100	0
1914	101	101	101	0
1915	108	117	121	+9
1916	118	133	143	+15
1917	139	170	173	+31
1918	179	211	199	+32
1919	215	241	211	+26

Source: C.H. Feinstein, National Income, Expenditure and Output of the United Kingdom, 1855-1965 (Cambridge: At the University Press, 1972), Table 65, p. T140.

previously.[71] Similarly, earnings, reflecting the introduction of piece-work systems and overtime that created substantial "wage drift," moved up faster than wage rates but did not surpass the rise in prices until 1918. (See Table 3.2.) The Minister of Labour, G. H. Roberts, informed the Cabinet in October 1917 that it was "extremely improbable that the increase in total earnings is more than double the increase in rates of wages, as it would need to be if it were to be made commensurate with the increase in the cost of living."[72] Purchasing power was 10 to 15 percent lower than before the war.

The argument that counterbalancing factors, such as higher employ-ment, fuller employment, and more profitable employment, kept work-ers' incomes up with inflation can be questioned when the differential

Table 3.3
Movements of Wage Rates for Industries Central to War Production

Year	Engineering Artisans	Coal Miners	Railwaymen
1914	100	100	100
1915	110	115	110
1916	111	129	120
1917	134	136	155
1918	173	187	195

Source: A.L. Bowley, Prices and Incomes in the U.K., 1914-20 (Oxford: At the Clarendon Press, 1921), pp. 105, 150. See Table III.1 for retail prices. (1914 = 100)

impact of extra exertion, functional importance of the trade group to the war effort, and skill differences are taken into account. While unequal sacrifice contributed to a heightened sense of working-class solidarity and exacerbated the tendency for workers to contrast their situations with the privileges of capital, these variations help to explain different potentials for class consciousness and collective action.

First, industrial and craft workers in mining, railway, and munitions industries that were crucial to the war effort and most capable organisationally of advancing their earnings in a tight labour market lagged well behind the rising cost of living. The movement of time-rates gives a rough indication of the increase in income when it is recognized that overtime certainly increased earnings significantly, but probably no more than 40 to 50 percent. (See Table 3.3.)

Even in the most essential type of work bringing the greatest reward, workers' earnings only approached the rising cost of living because of increased exertion under great pressure and discipline. In the first year of the war, excessively long hours became common, with men working seventy and eighty hours a week.[73] Data for Clydeside skilled workers reveal that those who worked the longest hours increased their earnings proportionately; yet, in only one case did this result in additional earnings that nearly matched the increase in the cost of living. (See Table 3.4.)

Second, while opportunities for overtime made it possible, though

Table 3.4
Overtime Hours and Earnings

Trade	% Increase in Earnings 1914 to June, 1914 (rank)	% Increase in Average No. of Hours Worked (rank)
Fitters	43.5 (1)	14.2 (2)
Turners	34.6 (3)	12.3 (3)
Shipwrights	20.7 (5)	4.2 (5)
Joiners	17.6 (6)	2.3 (6)
Woodworking Machinists	15.0 (7)	2.3 (7)
Painters	2.0 (8)	-7.3 (8)
Shipsmiths	30.7 (4)	7.5 (4)
Drillers	37.3 (2)	17.3 (1)

Source: History of the Ministry of Munitions (London: HMSO, 1920-24), Vol. IV, Part IV, Ch. VI, p.128. Based on the Report of the Ministry of Munitions Wages Section for the Clyde District, June, 1916. The official cost of living index rose 45 percent over this period.

improbable, for workers in the war industries to keep up with the rising cost of living, workers in trades functionally peripheral to the war economy who did not have the benefit of extra work suffered in the face of rapid inflation. Consequently, they failed to maintain their prewar levels of consumption. According to a Board of Trade report,

Certain classes normally in regular employment, whose earnings have not risen in the same proportion as the cost of living—for example, the cotton operatives

Table 3.5
Movements of Wage Rates for Industries Peripheral to War Production

Year	Bricklayers	Compositors	Cotton Operators	Agriculture
1914	100	100	100	100
1915	102	100	103	112
1916	108	105	107	---
1917	122	120	119	---
1918	157	156	157	189

Source: Bowley, Prices and Incomes in the U.K.,
pp. 105, 113, 160, 179. (1914 = 100)

and certain classes of day-wage workers and labourers—are hard pressed by
the rise in prices, and actually have to curtail their consumption, even though
the pressure of high prices may have been mitigated, in some cases, by the
employment of members of a family in munition works, and by the opening
of better-paid occupations to women. Many people in receipt of small fixed
incomes necessarily also feel the pressure; and it is obvious that while the total
receipts of families past school age may have greatly increased, a family of the
same class in which children are within school age may suffer exceptionally.[74]

The increase in time-rates and piece-rates for workers in some trades
peripheral to the war economy reveals the disadvantage experienced by
them in comparison with those in the war industries. (See Table 3.5.)

Third, there was a relative improvement in the earnings of the less
skilled in comparison with the higher skilled. This resulted from wage
settlements designed to benefit the less skilled at a time of rapid inflation
and from the recruitment of many less-skilled piece-workers in munitions plants. The latter received perhaps the highest wage increases of
any group, since many were recruited from lower-paid work and benefitted from long hours and the piece-work system. The resulting increases in earnings caused considerable discontent among the craftsmen
tied to time-rates that were outstripped by the rising cost of living. The
levelling of the differential between skilled and unskilled is illustrated
by comparing piece-rates and weekly time-rates for engineering labourers with those of the skilled engineers and bricklayers' labourers
with those of bricklayers. (See Table 3.6.)

Table 3.6
Movements of Wage Rates for Skilled and Unskilled Workers

July	Engineering Artisans	Engineering Labourers	Bricklayers	Bricklayers' Labourers
1914	100	100	100	100
1915	110	---	102	103
1916	111	---	108	115
1917	134	154	122	134
1918	173	213	157	185

Source: Bowley, Prices and Incomes in the U.K., p. 105 (1914 = 100)

While not taking into account overtime and other factors, these estimates do provide evidence of the increase in wages and earnings of the unskilled relative to the skilled and their ability to keep pace with rising inflation.[75]

The effect of the workman's being rewarded for his patriotism by ever-increasing sacrifice was felt most saliently in regard to food consumption. Expenditures for food in the working-class budget were high, 60 percent, while rent, including rates, was 16 percent; clothing, 12 percent; fuel and light, 8 percent; other items, 4 percent.[76] Food underwent the most drastic price rise, climbing faster than the general cost of living. As a consequence, the working class was forced to cut back on food consumption and to change its diets. In short, increased expenditures on foodstuffs lagged behind the prewar standard by as little as 20 percent and as much as 28 percent.[77] Such a rise suggests a considerable decline in workmen's standards, producing misery and bitterness, particularly in view of the fact that the prewar standard did not itself allow much, if any, room for belt-tightening.[78]

The workers' wartime experience, moreover, involved a deterioration in quantity and quality of foodstuff consumed. Consumption of meat, eggs, butter, sugar, and tea declined by about 40 percent by 1918.[79] Bread, flour, bacon and margarine consumption increased significantly to fill the gap. Bread and flour became the primary source of calories and nutrients. Bread prices doubled by mid-1917, at which time a subsidy was introduced to bring the four-pound loaf, of poorer quality, within reach of wage-earners. On the other hand, the reduction of overall consumption and the substitution of lower-quality foods resulted in only a slight decline in the prewar calorie levels. The increased life expectancy of civilian workers and the decline in infant mortality reflect the greater integration of the population into the labour process and increased social awareness rather than an improvement in the overall standard of living, at least before mid-1918.[80] Thus, the larger number of family members requiring substantial food because of increased exertion and the lack of a well-balanced diet point to the likelihood that members of the working class, particularly skilled and semi-skilled war workers, were under considerable mental and physical stress.

CONCLUSION

This chapter has argued that the environment was conducive to participatory democracy in working-class organisations from 1915 to 1918. The wartime political economy stimulated attitudes of injustice that gave workers the incentives to take advantage of conditions that facilitated collective organisation and action. Labour processes were supportive of workplace solidarity and organisation among skilled and less skilled alike, and the demand for labour gave workers the bargaining strength to assert their demands and to develop collective power. State intervention, moreover, favoured capital and restrained labour, fostering multiple sources of class antagonism. The failure of workers' earnings to keep up with or exceed the rapidly rising cost of living also contributed to feelings of unequal sacrifice. With this context in mind, we can now turn to an examination of participatory power relations in workplace organisations, trade unions, and the national federations, the Trades Union Congress and the Labour Party.

CHAPTER 4

Democracy at the Base: Direct Democracy and Rank-and-File Organisation

Even the most spontaneous working-class action requires the skills of leaders. Shop stewards, movers of resolutions, participants at rank-and-file conferences, constitute a minority of workers. During the First World War, these active few reflecting the attitudes of the majority in the most politically advanced unions led the battle against overt injustices toward organised labour and the working class. Expressing a diffuse and intensified class consciousness derived from a sense of injustice, we need to examine whether these active few translated the preferences of large numbers of discontented workers into workplace policy. In other words, did the policy-making processes of workplace organisations in the major unions—the Miners, Railwaymen, and Engineers—resemble direct democracy?

To document the nature of democracy in typical rank-and-file organisations during the war, we need to explore two important questions that help illuminate whose interests are being served. First, who controls the issue-agenda in workplace organisations? Even if it can be argued that, at least in the case of the most class-conscious unions, the active few among the rank and file articulate genuine mass rank-and-file grievances, it is still possible that they dominate the mass of workers through their ideological influence and control over the mass consciousness. Second, who controls the substance, if not the details, of policy outcomes? Do workplace activists constitute an out-elite, manipulating and taking advantage of mass discontent in their own self-interest, that is, in an effort to displace existing officials at higher levels? If the active few at the rank-and-file level do constitute such an out-elite, then it is they, not the bulk of the rank and file, who are exercising power over the national and district officials. Or do the activists represent the interests of the rank and file, thus reflecting direct democracy? The latter is crucial, for participatory democracy at higher levels ultimately depends on the participation of autonomous workgroups in influencing representatives to delegate assemblies and elected executives.

COMMON INTERESTS AND WORKSHOP ORGANISATION

While it may be argued that early trade union development was based on workshop organisation far more than it is today, the growth of industrialization and the spread and strengthening of trade unionism that brought about collective bargaining did not displace workplace organisation completely. In fact, since World War I, organisation at the point of production has been reestablished as the most important source of rank-and-file control in relation to their national leaders, their employers, and increasingly the State. By contrast, branches involve organisation by place of residence and include members employed with many different firms. The rise of branch organisation is associated with the establishment and extension of "collective bargaining." What collective bargaining, based on branches, sought to achieve was the principle that, over a whole territory, certain standard rates of wages should be paid, that certain recognized hours and conditions of labour should be respected, and that these wages, hours, and conditions should be determined by negotiation between the concerned trade unions and employers.[1] Under these circumstances, the need for workplace organisation was neglected and was sometimes treated with hostility. Employers were to be allowed no recourse that would permit the evasion of uniform conditions. Thus, collective bargaining emerged out of the growth of national trade unionism in response to the growth of large-scale capitalism and its concomitant methods of rationalized industrial relations.

Even so, not all workers were brought completely under the process of collective bargaining. The Miners, for example, organised their unions around a particular pit or group of two or three pits associated with a single mining village. Organisation and policy-making centring around the pithead has always been a feature of unionism in the mining industry.

Where trade unionism was organised around the point of production, there developed close contact between the men themselves and between the men and their spokesmen. Representation of the workers' problems tended to fall naturally upon the workman who oversaw the shops or works operation, the checkweightmen in mining and the shop steward in engineering. On the other hand, branch organisation put representation into the hands of union officials who were responsible for developments area-wide, and thus tended to diffuse conflict. Even in engineering where collective bargaining had won the day before the war, there were union officials—the shop stewards—on the shopfloor. They were assigned relatively minor duties and did not involve themselves in any real bargaining or representational activities. These shop stewards were assigned the tasks of inspecting members' cards and collecting dues. They also spoke to new workers for the purpose of enrolling them in the union. Aside from these activities, the shop stewards were expected to be alert to members' complaints and to make reports to union officials.[2] There was little full-blown workshop organisation before the war, and that which did occur was limited to skilled workers, who were the most strongly organised and exhibited the most solidarity.[3] World War I changed all this. The industrial developments necessitated by World War I led to extensive workplace conflict that inevitably encouraged workmen to organise and act in solidarity with their fellow workmen at their places of production.

As dilution spread during the war, the tasks and numbers of shop stewards grew rapidly. The wartime steward, as authorized by his union district council, became a negotiator on workshop grievances, representing the workers by whom he was elected.[4] The changes in the methods of production necessitated by the need to step up production created friction on all kinds of issues, some trivial and some involving basic trade union principles. According to G. D. H. Cole,

More and more the shop stewards undertook the handling of these daily problems of workshop administration, calling in the Union officials only when they were unable to bring about a direct settlement by formal or informal negotiation.[5]

The hastened appointment of new stewards also meant that shop steward organisation had to be improvised and that the appointees were of unequal calibre. The need for stewards often opened the door to recognition by the end of the war from employers and the Government, just as the need for dilution itself promoted their proliferation and strengthened their new role.

Shop steward representation involved both matters of day-to-day administration and ideological significance. In the absence of guidance from the national unions, the left-wing unofficial shop steward organisations influenced the development of the duties and expectations of this important new position. As G. D. H. Cole notes, the immediate effect was to

give the shop stewards a conception of their office as one of the means to the gaining of "workers' control" in industry, and to make them envisage the problems of dilution as part of the bigger problem of the transformation of production under the influence of large-scale capitalist organisation.[6]

Nonetheless, for the most part, the shop stewards' work involved dealing with the details of workshop adjustment in regard to problems of dilution, wage claims, and the safeguarding of threatened rights. Furthermore, as problems arose and became more numerous and serious under the Munitions Act, it became necessary for shop stewards to devise a system to regularize coordination and cooperation within each department and within the whole firm. The upshot was shop steward committees and workers' committees on a considerable scale. The stewards in a particular shop would appoint from amongst themselves a secretary or convener, who possessed the power to call meetings of all the stewards in the shop.[7] Thus, while workshop organisation became a seedbed for propagandistic efforts by industrial unionists and Marxists, it provided an effective channel for resolving day-to-day problems and for expressing larger grievances.

Even though the men on the shopfloor may support a shop steward unstintingly in his efforts to satisfy their consciously intended aims, it may still be claimed that there is room for an ideologically committed militant to control the members by planting the ideological seeds of their discontent. The possibility of ideological militants riding to power by taking advantage of deeply felt grievances by formulating and heightening discontent is suggested by elitist and democratic elitist analyses.[8] Leaders take the initiative on issues in order to secure their hold on elective office. The question of this section is whether this process applies to wartime workshop politics in Britain or, alternatively, whether there is evidence of membership control of key issues. Fortunately, it is possible to clarify the matter by comparing the stated ideological aims of the Engineering militants with their actual policies in response to pressures from the workplace, and by assuming the situation in engineering applies to rank-and-file organisations in other industrial sectors where important wartime development occurred, such as the railways, mining, printing, building, and cotton.

The stewards' ideological militancy varied from area to area and in the degree to which their activities were integrated into official trade unionism. In Sheffield, for example, workshop organisation only broke the bounds of the official structures of the Amalgamated Society of Engineers District Council in late 1916 and established the Sheffield Workers' Committee in January 1917. The Amalgamated Society of Engineers District Council accommodated the craftsmen's militancy up to then and remained in intimate relation with the unofficial organisation. In the May strikes of 1917, the Sheffield District Council was suspended by the Amalgamated Society of Engineers Executive for its close association with the strikers. The Sheffield Workers' Committee leaders apparently were less ideological because they were well integrated into the Sheffield labour movement. On the other hand, the Clyde Workers' Committee, the other leader in the Works Committee movement, was far more ideological and cut off from the semi-skilled and unskilled sections of the Glasgow labour movement. Hence, ideological militancy is bound up in the extent of the shop stewards' integration into an area's labour movement, itself a product of local patterns of industrialization.

On the Clyde, the revolutionary shop stewards at the helm of the Clyde Workers' Committee were unable to forge a militant mass movement because the grievances of most of the men arose from the narrow, sectional concerns of skilled craftsmen. For all their militancy, the skilled munitions workers were concerned to protect their job control and status whenever they were under attack. This meant that militant ideology had to be abandoned in favour of practical solutions to problems of dilution, rents, conscription, free speech, and anti-war politics, as each at its own time became the focus of activity. The militant skilled workers were, therefore, less likely to take the initiative on issues of concern to the semi-skilled and the unskilled. For example, the Clyde Workers' Committee failed to take the lead in the rent strikes of Fall 1915, which were led in large measure by women's housing committees.[9]

The militants, nevertheless, sought to influence the men through education and propagandistic activities. The Clyde Workers' Committee drew its membership from a group that were both shop stewards and members of socialist parties to the left of the Independent Labour Party, the socialist society which had worked with the trade unions to create the Labour Party. Among the leading shop stewards, only Kirkwood and Messer were associated with the Independent Labour Party, while the bulk were from the Socialist Labour Party, which was marxist and Industrial Unionist in orientation, and from the marxist British Socialist Party. Willie Gallacher, the Committee chairman, was a member of the British Socialist Party and an associate of propagandist John McLean, who dominated a section of that Party. McLean agitated through organising and lecturing to classes in Marxian economics and gained a considerable following, despite the fact that the socialist parties in the Clyde remained small. Gallacher attributes success to McLean's work. According to Gallacher, McLean taught by showing that increased prices and higher rents revealed the "truth of Marxism" and that "the boys at the front were being slaughtered for profit, and the very slaughter of the workers at the front was being used for increased robbery of the workers at home."[10] Eventually this propagandistic work, according to Gallacher, turned the men's minds to focus more on the "war against profiteers" than the war against the Germans. If Gallacher overdramatized the effects of McLean's activity, it is because he refused to see that the day-to-day experiences of a large number of skilled workers led them to the same conclusion. In fact, the craftsmen's experiences of increasing exploitation sent them searching for explanations. If discontent is the breeding ground for advanced ideological causes, increased conflict at the point of production fosters the development of class and sectional consciousness rather than ideological conversion. Again, the efforts and achievements of the revolutionary leaders reveal just how much they relied on the support of the rank-and-file Engineers to give militant demands and threats credibility—support which was always contingent on the workers' subjective concerns at a particular moment.

Typical of the inability of the militant shop stewards to have their ideological stance translated into policy is the Hargreaves strike in Sheffield in late 1916. This example is important for several reasons. First, it reveals how skilled workmen's pragmatic class interests took precedence over the ideological militants' commitment to all-class unionism. Secondly, it affords an opportunity to see how well militancy can be accommodated within official trade union organisation and how its rigidity results in unofficial organisation. In short, the strike reveals the structural rather than ideological causes underlying the wartime development of workgroup organisation.

The Sheffield leaders learned their political skills in the Amalgamation Committee Movement, of which Jack Murphy had been the secretary since its foundation in the Spring of 1914. The Amalgamation Committee adhered to the "syndicalist socialism" of Connolly, Tom Mann and the *Miners' Next Step*.[11] While Murphy claimed to have initiated the introduction of workshop organisation shortly before the war, his claim remains unconfirmed because there seems to have been little workshop organisation in Sheffield prior to 1915.[12] Nonetheless, the conditions of war, particularly the problems arising out of dilution, were conducive to the militants introducing the idea of independent rank-and-file organisation to Sheffield. Dilution problems and other matters, such as the unskilled earning wages higher than the skilled, led to many complaints among the skilled munitions workers. Murphy states:

The great influx of unskilled and semi-skilled workers under the dilution schemes roused the skilled workers to great activity. Every trade union branch meeting saw scores of complaints brought forward, all of which were forwarded to the district committee of the unions. These were literally overwhelmed with complaints.[13]

Murphy claimed that the study of these experiences led him to "bring forward proposals for workshop organisation."

These proposals were first discussed in the amalgamation committee. They were then brought forward in the Sheffield No. 8 Branch of the Amalgamated Society of Engineers. This was necessary in order to get the matter raised before the district committee of the union.[14]

Because the militants could work inside the offices of the Amalgamated Society of Engineers and because they were well integrated within the Sheffield labour movement, unofficial rank-and-file organisation seemed unnecessary. The militants' proposal for workshop organisation called for the District Council, based on a complete roster of its members' place of employment and the numbers of shop stewards, to establish shop stewards in each factory. Adopted by the Amalgamated Society of Engineers' District Council and endorsed by the union's National

Executive, the proposal resulted in an organisational campaign by the Engineers that was imitated by other skilled workers' unions in the area.[15]

The Sheffield rules for shop stewards were broadened to include negotiation with management, though it was restricted by the Procedure for Avoidance of Disputes. Failure to resolve disputes at the shopfloor level had to be taken up to the national level through this procedure; otherwise any strike action would be illegal. The ease with which these syndicalist proposals made headway within the official union structure constitutes evidence that workshop organisation in Sheffield was an idea of practical significance rather than a manifestation of ideological diffusion and conversion. In fact, the campaign fell on exceptionally fertile soil because it was carried on while the Munitions and Conscription Acts were being implemented and stepped up. Even conservative trade unionists came to recognize the need to elect shop stewards. According to veteran engineers, "The rank and file knew they were divorced from the officials and that the officials were linked with the government so far as the war was concerned. The rank and file wanted to express themselves and this was their medium."[16] In the Autumn of 1916, a local Engineering Shop Stewards' Committee was formed to link up stewards in the different factories.[17] Thus, to November 1916, the Amalgamated Society of Engineers was able to absorb the militants by officially accommodating workshop organisation, and giving expression to the rising tide of discontent among many of the rank and file.

The discontent over conscription of skilled workers, reflecting a militant defence of craft privilege and rights, rose to a peak in the Fall of 1916 and provided the basis, again in contrast to class-inclusive syndicalist propaganda, for the emergence of the unofficial Sheffield Workers' Committee. Throughout the Summer of 1916, the local Amalgamated Society of Engineers had been harassed by the constant conscription of its members. Some three hundred call-up papers had been processed by the Organising District Delegates by the end of August. Aside from being irritated, the workmen were concerned that employers were using conscription as a disciplinary weapon. This tension provoked a crisis in October when a young Engineer, Leonard Hargreaves, was conscripted into the army, because he missed his chance to appeal due to the firm having withheld the papers that would have secured his discharge. To many Sheffield Engineers, this apparent connivance between employer and the Government smacked of industrial conscription and an assault on the craftsman's right to exemption.

The incident was reported to the shop stewards and spread through the shops "like wildfire." It was reported to trade union branches, the District Council, the union's Executive, and other skilled trade unions. The results of ordinary methods of grievance resolution were nil. Consequently, on November 8, 1916, the District Council of the Amalgamated Society of Engineers and the shop stewards called a mass meeting of the Engineers and other skilled workmen. At this meeting, the District Council deferred to the unofficial Shop Stewards' Committee. As Murphy reported:

Whilst the district committee of the Amalgamated Society of Engineers was present in full force, it retired from the leadership on the grounds that the district committee as a part of the union machine was bound by the agreements as to strikes, etc. They passed the control into the hands of the shop stewards committee. This was possible because the majority of the members of the district committee were also shop stewards.[18]

This assumption of responsibility by shop stewards meant little change in personnel, because most shop steward leaders were on the District Committee. It did, however, facilitate the creation of a joint committee of all the unions.[19] After several leaders at the mass meeting appealed to the men to turn the issue over to the trade union official on patriotic grounds, rank-and-file members voiced their attitudes.

We feel we have been betrayed and are being betrayed. We accepted the proposals of the Treasury Agreement reluctantly and because of the written pledge of the Government both as to the position of the engineers in the war and after the war. We are not unpatriotic. We have seen thousands of lads senselessly recruited for fighting when they were needed here. We have trained thousands to take their places. But if the Government is allowed to tear up its agreement now, as the German Government tore up its agreement, how can we face the lads when they come back?[20]

No amount of flag-waving could derail the men. In the end, it was resolved to give six days' notice to the trade union Executives and the Government that unless Hargreaves were returned to the shopfloor at Vickers, the Sheffield Engineers would go out on strike.

Efforts to develop further workshop organisation among the craftsmen flourished. Up to the time of this incident, some sixty shop stewards had been elected. Up to ten days before the strike, the number of stewards elected rose to more than three hundred.[21] Murphy reported: "If there were any engineering workshops in Sheffield without shop stewards before that time, there were none known to us six days after the ultimatum had been delivered."[22] The skilled men were aware of the forces that they were up against and knew that there would need to be perfect solidarity. According to one of them,

We knew what we were up against—that three-quarters of the country would be solid against us; that the employers, the military authorities and the Government would stop at nothing to crush this "rebellion"—if they saw even a suspicion of weakness or hesitation on our side. So we took care that our plan of action was complete.[23]

Moreover, given the press censorship, delegates were appointed at the mass meeting to inform other centres of what was taking place and to arrange for joint action.

After the six days passed, the Sheffield Engineers still had no response from their union or the Government. The union's Executive did not get around to asking the District Council for further particulars of the case until the day before the strike was due to start. On November 15, a mass meeting decided to carry out the strike threat on the next day. The skilled workmen resolved to stay out until Hargreaves was returned to Sheffield in person, being suspicious of offers to arbitrate the issue. Even the union Executive's telegram that Hargreaves was being released did not get them to call off the strike. For as the men suspected, they were being misled. Not until the strike started was the War Office forced into releasing him. By November 16, there were about twelve thousand men, constituting probably the complete membership of all the skilled engineering unions in Sheffield, out on strike.[24] The skilled men made their determination to resist the imposition of conscription abundantly clear.

Two days later, the Government capitulated to the strikers' demand. The strikers stayed out until Hargreaves appeared at their mass meeting. The rapid resolution to the conflict resulted not only from the solidarity of the vast majority of skilled workers, but also from the willingness of the Government to yield on this issue, given some interdepartmental ambivalence on the question of conscripting skilled workmen. None-theless, the enthusiasm and prestige gained by the shop stewards' com-mittee were great. Murphy reported:

For the time being the shop stewards committee became the dominant authority. The men felt that it was only through this new form of organisation that the unions could now justify themselves in the least as defenders of the interests of the workers.[25]

In early January 1917, the unofficial shop stewards' committee was given formal recognition and efforts were made to extend the organi-sation to the unskilled workforce.

Yet the revolutionary aims of the militant leadership were never able to take precedence over the pragmatic responses to the craftmen's sense of injustice. More often, workshop organisation in engineering grew out of deep-felt concerns of the skilled workmen in the face of the pressing problems of rising prices, dilution in the munitions factories, and conscription. The craftmen's seriousness was confirmed by their willingness to strike in order to preserve or to recapture what they believed to be their rights and standards. As Murphy suggested, "Work-ers don't throw up their jobs and face loss of wages without strike pay just for fun."[26] In short, their willingness to strike and their solidarity testified to the depth of their grievances.

, While the craftsmen's interests often collided with those of the un-skilled and the semi-skilled over income, exemptions from conscription, and control over certain jobs, the sense of inequality of sacrifice that wartime state capitalism fostered brought many Engineers into alliance with class-conscious Miners, Railwaymen, and Transport Workers over the key issues of inflation and profiteering, industrial relations restric-tions, and military and industrial conscription. The impact of the war by no means dissolved sectional conflict. It did, however, bring to the forefront of the labour movement the issue of injustice—an issue around which major groups of workers central to the wartime effort and the future of the Labour Party found common grievance and cause for large-scale collective organisation and action.

The shop stewards, in contrast to the national or local union officials, were able to respond to workshop members' feelings and aspirations because they were embedded in the workmen's day-to-day experiences and struggles. Being a member of the workgroups, stewards in these class-conscious workshops were sensitive to the needs of their fellow workmates and subject to the pressures of the collective consensus. The shop steward typically worked alongside his mates and was distinguished only by his responsibility—a responsibility delegated by his fellow workers—to oversee the operations and report any grievances. With the development of shop steward organisation, however, he took on new tasks of representing, advising, and negotiating on behalf of the men in his shop. Still, shop stewards, while gaining some prerogatives and resources through this leadership role, remained part of the productive unit in the factory, thereby sharing the grievances and aspirations of the workgroup and subject to its informal power relations. If they fail to be responsive, the rank and file can withdraw their collective support, rendering stewards ineffective. Trade union leaders, on the other hand, are often separated from the men because they function in the environment of union bureaucracy, employer, and state officialdom. Perhaps the most crucial single element in the social position of the union leader, a factor that sharply distinguishes him from the rank and file, is that he is no longer personally involved in the conflicts and group pressures that arise at the point of production. The responsiveness of union officeholders can only be assured through the active pressures of workgroup representation. The shop steward directly representing his class-conscious group, thus, is far more likely to be responsive to the substance and the movement of shopfloor sentiment.

PARTICIPATORY CONTROL IN WORKSHOP ORGANISATION

The ability to exercise final decision-making power, elite theory argues, enables leaders to "usurp the exclusive right to decide on behalf of the rank and file."[27] A second key question, then, is whether shop stewards' decisions are responsive to the wishes of the membership. In this section, we argue that in class-conscious workplace organisations, the group consensus on substantive and ultimate ends produced a process of participatory control that compelled leaders to serve their members' interests.

Workgroup policies were resolved and carried out, and could only be, with the support of the men on the shopfloor, a situation which inhibited the centralization of power in stewards' hands. This can be illustrated by the support given to the shop stewards' organisation in the battle to get employers to recognize the rights of the head convener, the top steward in a plant, to enter any department in the works for the purpose of obtaining information or dealing with any grievance which may have arisen. In March 1916, this issue led to conflict when Beardmore's at Parkhead in Scotland decided to refuse David Kirkwood the rights normally accorded to a head convener. After two weeks of negotiation, the Parkhead Engineers decided to strike. Several days later, they were joined by workmen at the North British Diesel Engine works at Scotstoun and the gun shop at Dalmuir, where the men had been given gun work belonging to Parkhead.[28] This incident precipitated the arrest and deportation of Kirkwood and other Clyde Workers' Committee leaders from the Clyde area by a Government fully intent on breaking this stronghold of opposition to dilution and conscription.[29] The crackdown brought about an extension of the strike as well as further Governmental repression, constituting a series of events that became a national issue. Nonetheless, the point is that workmen were willing to go out on strike, risking their own future, in order to obtain the kind of workshop representation they desired.

These features of participatory control are further exemplified in the first unofficial shop stewards' committee which emerged out of the Engineers' strike on the Clyde in early 1915. This strike arose out of a demand made in a resolution of the Amalgamated Society of Engineers' District Committee in June 1914 for a rise of 2d. per hour to take place in January 1915, when the three-year agreement of 8$^1/_2d$. an hour was due to terminate. By an agreement, shop disputes in Engineering could not eventuate in a work stoppage before they had been considered first by a local conference, and secondly, after fourteen days' notice, by a central conference.[30] The North Western Employers' Association, after receiving notice of application for the 2d. per hour increase from the District Council, took advantage of a slight technical breach to withhold its reply until December 30, when it refused the demand as unreasonable. The delay effectively deprived the men of one month's benefit regardless of its amount. As a result, the District Council immediately instructed its members, failing a satisfactory reply from the employers, to "come out" on January 20. A special conference on January 19 averted the strike and, when the Conference was convened again on January 22, the employers offered $^1/_2d$. per hour. The Engineers refused, and the matter was referred to the February conference for further negotiation.[31]

At this point, a spontaneous rank-and-file movement emerged to take up the issue. A Committee of Shop Stewards at one of the factories called a mass meeting of some four or five thousand operatives which passed a resolution in favour of the abolition of overtime until the employers agreed to consider the case. Against the orders of the District Council and the Executive Council of the Amalgamated Society of Engineers, overtime ceased in about fifteen shops. The Executive then called a mass meeting for February 7, and its representatives advised the men to resume overtime work on Government work for reasons of national and self-interest. Despite pressure from the National Executive Council, the men adhered to their resolution to stop overtime.

When an offer of $^3/_4d.$ advance was made at the February conference, the Executive Council recommended acceptance and balloted the men. Discontent rose still further: first, because delay meant that already two months' bonus would be lost; secondly, because it was likely that if the proposed $^3/_4d.$ were rejected, there would be further delay.[32] On February 16, discontent broke into open revolt as operatives at one factory struck; by the end of the month, over five thousand men were out. At this point, the Shop Stewards' Committee was enlarged to include shop stewards representing all the shops involved. This body became the "Central Labour Withholding Committee," and it continued to press for the $2d.$ advance, holding itself and not the Amalgamated Society of Engineers to be responsible for the claim.

The cause of the spontaneous emergence of the informal shop stewards' movement on the Clyde was the workers' conviction that their employers were economically exploiting them. Rank-and-file Engineers were increasingly bitter over the increasingly heavy personal sacrifice they were forced to endure while employers were allowed to profiteer. As reported in the *Herald*,

The persistence of the rank and file is due to the feeling that they are being cheated. All through the war frequent appeals have been made to their patriotism; they have been told that, at a time like the present, they have no right to consider their own profit or convenience. At first they were gullible enough to take the fulsome professions of national solidarity at their face value; but six months' experience has taught them to know better. They have seen prices rising, and they know that the rise is due largely to the shameless exploitation of the situation by "patriotic" persons of the employing class; they have seen the motto "business as usual" turned into a justification of every enormity of profiteering in the sacred name of the law of supply and demand.[33]

After only six months of war, the rising prices and trade union reluctance to press home the craftsmen's wage claims resulted in shop stewards spontaneously mobilizing through in an effort to realize economic justice.

Just as the men's support could flow toward unofficial leaders who chose to take up their cause, a shift in the rank-and-file's consensus on policy would find support flowing back to the officials of the Amalgamated Society of Engineers. In the face of the workers' rejection of the proposed $^3/_4d$. advance in balloting, the union recommended a return to work, while the Central Labour Withholding Committee recommended a gradual return and a continued slowdown. After the return to work had been accomplished, the union balloted the men as to whether they should turn the matter over to the newly appointed Committee on Production for arbitration. This time, the men followed their officials and the matter went into arbitration. The outcome was an award of $1d$. an hour on time-rates and 10 percent on piece-rates. Throughout this series of events, the men regarded the union's moderate action as "pusillanimous." Moreover, the Committee on Production's award refused what the men considered a long overdue advance and so left a legacy of suspicion and ill-will which was to lead to new problems in the future.

The Central Labour Withholding Committee was a spontaneous organisation that was informal in membership and structure, general in aims, and responsive to shopfloor concerns. It was a convention of delegates from the shop stewards, works, and workshop committees throughout the Clyde area. It appointed its own Executive apart from the official District Councils of the various unions to which its members belonged and from the District Committee of the Federation of Engineering and Shipbuilding Trades, the official organ for coordinating opinions and policies of skilled workers on the Clydeside. The Socialist Labour Party militants who encouraged and developed the organisation stressed the importance of workshop organisation as a means not only of more successful bargaining with employers, but of obtaining the "control of industry." Yet, their leadership was dependent on the members' collective viewpoint. They were a militant minority whose authority rested on the informal support of the non-ideological majority. Consequently, they could wrest the authority of the unions from their hands when a particular grievance was strong. Their success depended upon sensitivity to the sentiments of the skilled munitions workers. As G. D. H. Cole wrote, the "Clyde Workers' Committee had carefully to watch its opportunity to place itself upon the crest of the wave of unrest, and to risk the loss of its influence if it failed at any time of action to carry the main body of Trade Union opinion with it.''[34] Membership in the Central Labour Withholding Committee, and later the Clyde Workers' Committee, was loose and open. Funds were raised by voluntary subscription in the workshops. In short, unofficial workshop organisation, of which the Clyde Workers' Committee is exemplary, was spontaneous and informal, based upon the need to resist injustice.

Workshop organisation was directly responsive to the workgroup because it was composed of elected delegates who were under pressure to respond immediately to specific issues aggravating their members. The Clyde Workers' Committee believed itself the true representatives of the Clyde munitions workers. Composed of delegates from all trades in the Glasgow area and ''open to such *bona fide* workers,'' the Clyde Workers' Committee felt autonomous. As the activists Gallacher and Messer asserted,

We will support the officials just so long as they rightly represent the workers, but we will act independently immediately they misrepresent them. Being composed of delegates from every shop and untrammelled by obsolete rule or law, we claim to represent the true feeling of the workers. We can act immediately according to the merits of the case and the desires of the rank and file.[35]

At the same time, the openness of the Clyde Workers' Committee did not mean that it was made up of unrepresentative ideologues.

When the men in the workshop agreed to affiliate to the Clyde Workers' Committee, they usually sent their shop stewards as their representatives, so that as a fact, being a shop steward was one of the qualifications for being the representative of the Committee. Where they previously had sent their shop stewards to the Society to report to their District Committee, the shop stewards were sent to the Clyde Workers' Committee.[36]

However, it was not absolutely necessary to be sent by one's shop. ''If you went there you could only speak for yourself if you were only representing yourself, but if you represented the department you could speak for the department.''[37] Thus, being a part of the workgroup and directly responsible to it, the leaders of the shop stewards' movement could only lead the majority of the rank and file where it in fact wanted to go and as fast as it desired. As Pribicevic concluded,

The power of the movement did not depend on the number of members, on contributions, or on solid organisation—all of which were decisive in the case of trade unions—but rather on the capacity of the local leaders to interpret the desires, demands and grievances of the main body of the workers. To ascertain when this main body of workers wanted action on any particular issue and then to place themselves at the head was the correct policy for a movement of this kind.[38]

The political process of wartime workshop organisation in the radical sections of the labour force involved the mobilization of support for a particular rank-and-file claim through an elected representative chosen from amongst the men on the shopfloor. Being participant in the actual work situation as well as the workgroup that it gave rise to, the shop steward accurately reflected the rank and file's attitudes and, at the same time, was held accountable to its wishes. Wartime workgroup leaders in engineering, in mining, or on the railways were not an out-elite manipulating the rank and file in a bid for power. The responsiveness of workgroup leaders derived from the bonds of equality and collective solidarity shared by the shop steward and the other workgroup members, the men's collective but autonomous support of their delegate's actions on behalf of their claims, and the ease with which the rank and file monitored and assessed its representative's actions. There was, thus, little room for the workgroup representative to take advantage of rank-and-file discontent for his own ends.

To sum up, this chapter has shown that direct democracy can prevail in formally and informally organised workgroups at the base of trade union organisation. The principles of community autonomy and participatory control can be seen working in the processes that afford members control of group ends and policy actions. Because group members shaped group objectives in response to their environment, leaders were influenced more than influencing, despite their best efforts to influence workers' consciousness and actions. Leaders, while often sharing workers' conception of an objective general interest in a more cooperative and just society, were compelled to act in accord with their members' sense of particular collective objectives.

CHAPTER 5

Trade Union Politics and Delegate Democracy

In large-scale working-class organisations, participatory democracy must involve some form of delegate representation. Trade unions and large shop steward organisations are prime examples of organisations in which direct democracy must blend with representation through delegates. The main reason is size.[1] An organisation that represents the interests of all miners in Great Britain, for example, cannot maintain the intimacy of face-to-face decision-making. Nonetheless, similar environmental imperatives may foster common interests in absolute goals that maintain commitments to collective solidarity and equality. Conditions that create class consciousness produce demands for greater reciprocity in social relations and equal status and participation in collective resistance to injustice. The ultimate ends of class consciousness assure an equal status among groups and decision-making by consensus. A highly developed sense of solidarity limits the ability of individual leaders to centralize power, since it violates the collective definition of the common good and concomitant pressure toward unanimity. If such solidarity is to develop in larger unions, environmental forces must engender common interests in substantive and ultimate ends among members of a broad range of workplace organisations. Yet, perfect unanimity may be unrealistic, and differences may flourish within an overall commitment to a common good.

Even if a loose but strong collective consensus is possible at higher levels of a working-class organisation, does the need for representative decision-making processes—conferences, executive meetings, elections—still make participatory democracy impossible? Michels argued that in large-member organisations nominally committed to democratic procedures guaranteeing membership influence, technical and psychological factors would enable leaders to appropriate decision-making and agenda-setting power to themselves.[2] In other words, while direct democracy may be possible in small, face-to-face organisations, oligarchy inevitably emerges in all forms of delegate or representative democracy. The source of this collapse into oligarchy is that the division of labour prevents a large membership from being intimately and technically involved in legislating, in deciding general policy, and particularly in implementing policy. Members must permit their conference delegates to make important, if often general, decisions, while entrusting responsibility for policy implementation to elected executives. Elections, generally held by democratic theorists to be the main instrument by which members hold their officials accountable, are easily manipulated by officeholders through policy initiatives and the resources and symbolism of authority at their command. Moreover, elections do not permit continuous assessment and are limited to selecting personalities to fill offices rather than actually choosing policy.

Formal democratic procedures, then, are not in themselves sufficient to assure leaders' responsiveness to members' interests. What can make leaders accountable is the formal and informal mechanisms through which the exchange of information about members' interests and support for specific policies takes place. The participation of workplace organisations, branches, and regional divisions in the presentation of policy demands and the offering or withdrawal of support contingent on leaders' adoption of these initiatives can compel officeholder responsiveness. This process of widespread and active involvement in organisational agenda-setting and support-granting makes collective decision-making inclusive and egalitarian, subject to popular control, and gives meaning to the idea of popular supervision of policy implementation.[3] Insofar, then, as conditions foster workgroup initiatives and autonomy, organised members can effectively participate in union decision-making.

Before going on to analyse policy-making in trade unions, it may be useful to outline the historical context of the Railwaymen, Engineers, and Miners and their leading role in the labour movement. As already discussed, the response of the working class to the changed conditions of political and economic life varied considerably. Sidney Webb accused trade union leaders of failing to pay attention to "the three-quarters of the whole who are outside trade unionism," including the low-paid labourers and women.[4] Clearly, trade unions represented only a minority of the working civilian population, while the Trades Union Congress (TUC) and the Labour Party (LP) represented even smaller subgroupings of the organised movement. During the war years, trade union membership rose significantly, from 23 percent of the workforce in 1914 to 36 percent in 1918. Of this much enlarged and more privileged section of the whole working class, the proportion belonging to the TUC rose from 65 to 81 percent. While the TUC included a majority of organised labour, the Labour Party affiliated a large minority of the total union membership, although a majority of those belonged to the TUC.[5]

The general unions, benefitting from increased employment in low-skilled war work, grew faster than the industrial and craft unions at the centre of the war economy. This disproportionate growth, however, did not undermine the predominance within the Labour Party of the Miners, Railwaymen, Engineers, and other craft unions, measured in terms of their leading role in influencing policy of smaller organisations, the number of members affiliated, and votes at LP Conferences. The Miners Federation of Great Britain controlled about 25 pecent of the conference votes, and the industrial and craft unions together controlled over 40 percent of the total conference votes, compared to approximately 15 percent for the general unions.[6] Other sizable unions whose workers were in trades intermediate or peripheral to the war economy included the Boot and Shoe Operatives, Carpenters and Joiners, and the large textile unions. Together these composed another bloc of votes comparable to that of the general unions. The proportion of trade union votes at Labour Party Conferences dropped from 91 to 89 percent between 1916 and 1918, but the significance of the socialist societies diminished due to the rise in the numbers of members in the Local Labour Parties and Trade Councils. The Labour Party during the First World War was clearly a party in the hands of those industrial and craft unions most affected by and necessary to the war economy.

While workplace organisations rose to prominence in some general unions and even among some unions at the periphery of war production, they did not generally take on the role of a militant alternative authority capable of shaping policy of the national officials in the same degree that is found in the industrial and craft unions.[7] One example of a general union which benefitted dramatically from the war at the same time that it remained firmly in the control of right-wing officials is the Workers' Union, a general union organising the less skilled. By 1920, it grew to ninety times its 1910 size.[8] Its two most notable leaders, Beard and Duncan, supported the Government's war policies, denounced left-wing policies and shop stewards' organisations, and crushed left-wing opposition in the union. Their continued domination arose from the fact that the Munitions Acts were advantageous to its lower-skilled members, bringing them employment if not necessarily wage rises that kept pace with the cost of living until after 1917, a loss of members as a result of conscription, and a lack of activists since most had been easily incorporated into the union's fast-growing organising staff.[9] A second example involves the semi-skilled workers of the National Union of Boot and Shoe Operatives. Branch autonomy and success in negotiating high wages allowed little room for the emergence of militant shop stewards. The benefits that the war brought to the rank and file led the branches to take control of wage movements away from national officials during 1915 and 1916, while a minority of active rank and file complained of the "secrecy and aloofness" of officials.[10] On the other hand, the Dockers, while organising the unskilled, were an industrial union at the center of the wartime economy. The outbreak of war brought them great benefits, but inflation denied them any gain in their standard of living and the centralization of matching men to jobs available, or decasualization, threatened their rights and customs. As a result, rank-and-file Dockers grew more class conscious and militant, forcing leaders on the defensive and moving union policy leftward.[11]

The war clearly had differential effects on various strata of workers, depending on their centrality to the wartime political economy and the impact of industrial rationalization. The experiences of the Dockers paralleled more closely that of the Railwaymen and Miners than other groups of unskilled workers. The unskilled and the semi-skilled often benefitted from the war relative to the skilled Engineers and the bulk of the workers in the industrial unions. As a result, evidence suggests that it was the major industrial unions and the skilled craftsmen, not the general unions or those less central to the war economy, which experienced the greatest sense of inequality of sacrifice. The rank-and-file protest in defence of their rights and standards in these large unions centred largely on workplace unionism and played a disproportionate role in shaping the development of the Labour Party during the war.

In the following sections, three case studies in trade union policy-making will reveal the power relations between active workplace organisations and delegate councils. By examining policy processes which enabled the membership, acting through delegates, to shape key policies of the most important industrial and craft unions, our conception of participatory democracy in modern working-class organisations gains support and clarification.

WAGE GRIEVANCES AND POLICY IN THE NATIONAL UNION OF RAILWAYMEN

The war brought more work and more responsibility to the Railwaymen without a corresponding increase in real wages. A number of war-related developments account for this turn of events. First, the National Union of Railwaymen (NUR) entered into an "industrial truce" with the railway companies, agreeing to adhere to all prewar contracts and conditions of service and to refrain from making new arrangements. This official abdication of rights to improve the Railwaymen's conditions remained operative until November 12, 1918. Secondly, thousands of patriotic Railwaymen flocked to recruiting stations in the early days of the war, leaving a shrunken workforce behind. By the end of September 1914, the Cabinet put an end to the enthusiastic rush to the colours by declaring that no Railwayman could enlist without the permission of his company officials. Third, the war brought an increased amount of work for the depleted labour force. Goods and passenger traffic increased greatly in most regions.[12] For most Railwaymen, then, the war brought longer hours, greater responsibility, and a hopeless struggle to maintain an adequate standard of living in the face of escalating inflation.

But a large number of Railwaymen reacted to their dramatically contracting living standards by vigorously organising pressure for wage rises that would remedy the situation. Their lead in wage demands surged ahead both of the Executive's tendency to anticipate desires and of its capacity to realize wage increases that would dissipate rank-and-file pressure. The mounting pressures from key areas of militancy forced the Executive into action during 1915 and the following year led to a renewed wages movement alongside a constitutional initiative to place control of wage settlements in the hands of the active rank and file rather than the Executive. By 1917 the development of mass-based rank-and-file organisations in the major industrial centres reached a point where they were able to dominate the National Union of Railwaymen's policy-making functions and, at times, to threaten the very existence of the union itself. The story of wages policy in the National Union of Railwaymen during the war is one of struggle for justice and equity by a plurality of the rank and file in key workgroups combining with a militant few to shape the agenda and increasingly to control union policy and its administration.

As the cost of living shot up during the first year of the war, increasing numbers of the rank and file initiated efforts to obtain wage rises that would sustain a minimum standard of life. Yet, despite one bonus in 1915, their situation remained dire. In September 1915, a member of the Crewe Branch No. 1 wrote that the extreme difficulty of meeting life's necessities strained his patriotism.

After over a year of war we are not able to supply our children with that which is so necessary to rear them up strong and healthy, while to see one's wife growing paler and thinner through lack of nourishing food makes one pause and wonder whether it is possible to carry patriotism too far.[13]

In the face of the severe contraction of an already minimal standard of life, of which this Railwayman was characteristic, the bulk of rank-and-file Railwaymen began to take action.

Already by late 1914 and early 1915, active rank-and-file pressure, even though limited to a few militant workgroups, forced the Executive Committee to negotiate an increase in wages. With the Board of Trade figures showing a cost-of-living rise of about 20 percent by January 1915, resolutions from the most discontented groups of Railwaymen began to flood the union's newspaper, the *Railway Review*. In January 1915, the *Railway Review* reported discontent among the militant Liverpool branches as indicative of the growing dissatisfaction among the union's ranks. Because most members of Liverpool No. 3 were disturbed with the "industrial truce," they issued a strong protest against the rising food prices, among other items, and warned Cabinet Ministers that if they did not act to protect the people's living standard, "we will do so drastically." Liverpool No. 5 reported that distress was "becoming more acute" as a result of the rising prices.[14] Likewise, the Llanelly Branch in South Wales passed resolutions requesting the Executive Committee to give six weeks' notice to the Government-regulated railway companies and then to demand a general wage advance of 15 percent in addition to asking the Government to take control of shipping in order to stop the rising prices at their source.[15] The South Wales Railwaymen in early February were reported asking themselves whether they were patriots or fools, as increasing prices were causing such "endless suffering." The men in South Wales were in a defiant mood and gave notice that "unless effective steps [are] taken immediately [to end a] glaring anomaly by higher wages and lower profits . . . some people will have trouble of no ordinary kind."[16]

Support for ending the "industrial truce" came from all parts of the country and from the district councils, whose role as organising and propagandistic agencies had quickly become transformed into melting pots of agitation. A meeting on January 10 of the Yorkshire District Council had a well-sustained discussion concerning the position of Railwaymen and the future of the National Union of Railwaymen's national program. "There was a general feeling representative of the whole of the Northern districts that the Executive Committee should demand a substantial part, if not all, of the programme." In the end, it was decided to ask the Executive Committee to terminate the truce and to put forward the national program in its entirety. Copies of the resolution were sent to other District Councils in an effort to generate nationwide support among the active rank and file for the Yorkshire position.[17] Moreover, the Bristol District Joint Committee unanimously supported Avonmouth's resolution calling for an end to the truce, as did the Midland District Council. Dissatisfaction with the Executive's truce was widespread, and it was quickly becoming a "truce" in name only.

The rising cost of living generated numerous branch resolutions calling upon the Government to take action to end the inflationary trend. The Sheffield and Chesterfield District Council called upon the Government to control all food supplies and stop the "scandalous inflating of prices by private enterprise to the detriment of the poor and needy."[18] A resolution from Birkenhead Branch No. 2 revealed a sense of inequality of sacrifice. It urged the National Union of Railwaymen Executive to send a deputation to the Prime Minister to impress upon him the one-sidedness of the bargain unless purchasing power of the workers' wages were also (like profits) guaranteed to be as great in wartime as in normal times.[19] Similarly, Glasgow and West Scotland District Councils expressed their dissatisfaction at the unequal sacrifices emanating from the wartime arrangements in their call for the "Government to take over control of the necessaries of life and so prevent the exploiters growing fat.''[20] These forms of pressure from branches and district councils throughout the kingdom typify a growing cry from an increasingly active rank and file for better wages and conditions in the face of huge profits on the part of some sections of industry.

By February 1915, the overwhelming pressure for a national wage increase forced the Executive to act. As early as November and December 1914, the South Eastern and Chatham Railway had granted war bonuses to meet the increased cost of living. Seeing the wages movement coming, J. H. Thomas, at the time an assistant general secretary of the National Union of Railwaymen, picked up the idea of a war bonus as a solution to the rising tide of demands. Recognizing the companies' recalcitrance, Thomas helped arrange for the Government to underwrite three-fourths of the cost of a wage bonus. The day before the negotiations began, a special Executive meeting instructed its representatives to demand a flat 5s. a week increase in wages for all grades of workmen. Yet, the companies refused to concede that figure. A resulting compromise provided an arrangement giving 3s. to those earning less than 30s. per week and 2s. to those earning more than 30s. per week. The settlement, then, was designed to help the lower-paid and less-skilled Railwaymen most.

Not surprisingly, instead of passively accepting the bonus, militant rank-and-file organisations protested against the work of the National Union of Railwaymen's President and General Secretary and reasserted the demand for the full 5s. increase. Severe criticism continued to fall on the heads of the Executive from late February into March and April. By that time, criticism of the February settlement became lost in a new movement calling for a significant rise upon current earnings. The Executive had made every effort to justify the settlement to the men. J. H. Thomas explained the February settlement to a mass meeting at Stratford in the following terms:

There were in many parts of the country murmurings of a strike. I said then that if people wanted to strengthen our efforts on their behalf we must base our case not upon a sudden stoppage but upon the grounds of justice, equity, and service rendered.[21]

Yet, the majority in many branches felt that justice and equity had not been achieved by the agreement. Caerphilly Branch expressed its regret that the Executive Committee was not able to get 5s. and decided to seek cooperation with other trade unions to hold protest meetings against the high price of food.[22] Liverpool No. 3 resolved to ask the Executive to insist upon all members getting the bonus,

as we are not even satisfied with bonus doles of 5, 10, and 15 percent whilst food and other commodities have increased 33.25 percent, and demand the national programme be submitted, Government to pay three-quarters of bonus.[23]

In similar fashion, Acton and Ealing No. 1 Branch in West London condemned the Executive Committee for the agreement on the war bonus, since it did not include all grades, and suggested a protest demonstration, "as this bonus is totally inadequate to meet increased cost of living."[24] Later that month, Yorkshire District Council members resolved that it considered that "the time is opportune to ask for the extra 2s. per week and asks the Executive Committee to press the matter at an early date."[25] Nonetheless, during April a new drive to raise wages to meet the continuously increasing costs of living began to take shape. The Southeast Essex District Council decided that "owing to enormous rises in the cost of living branches should request our Executive Committee to open negotiations with railway companies and demand a further increase of 5s. to include all railway workers."[26]

From May 1915, the surge of new pressures on the Executive from the branches and district councils expressed a deeper and more political concern with the hardships caused by the rapidly rising cost of living. More and more of the rank and file pressed their workgroup leaders to express their demands for wage rises as a result of the continuing profiteering and the Government's unwillingness to control prices. The Birmingham and District Council carried a resolution at its May meeting calling upon the Executive Committee to press for increased bonuses for all, "in view of the ever-increasing cost of living and fabulous profits of shippers, coal, and other merchants, apparently to be allowed to go on unchecked."[27] Moreover, in the face of widespread profiteering that increasingly agitated the workmen's minds, rising prices increasingly became a political issue. The Newcastle and District Council decided to request branches to pass resolutions concerning the rising food prices and forward them to the Prime Minister, Chancellor of the Exchequer, the Labour Party, and others, calling upon them to raise the issue in the House of Commons.[28] Likewise, Sheffield and Chesterfield District Councils carried a strong resolution on disclosures of certain milling firms' profits, "calling on the Government to at once take steps to regulate the prices of food commodities and prevent the cornering of the people's food by profiteers."[29] The North London District Council carried a resolution strongly protesting against rising food prices and instructed its Secretary to forward the resolution demanding that the Government take control of shipping and food supplies.[30]

The upswing in the active rank-and-file's insistence on Government action to prevent inflation and profiteering increasingly made such action the condition of future support for the war effort. At a well-attended meeting, the Bristol and District Joint Committee agreed

that this Joint Committee, representing over 3,000 members of the National Union of Railwaymen call upon our Executive to make a supreme effort to stop the gambling with the necessaries of life; we call upon them to approach the Government and point out to them the hardship that exists among the rank-and-file owing to the abnormal high prices of food, etc.[31]

They further asserted that "if we are to remain loyal to our pledge we must demand from the Government that they will take steps to protect us from exploitation by the capitalists."[32] Such expressions of a threatened withdrawal of loyalty reflected a real undermining of uncritical deference to authority. By making their loyalty to trade union and Government officials contingent upon those authorities carrying out their demands, the militant workgroups were expressing their accumulating distrust of, alienation from, and bitter hostility for officialdom. Similar sentiments came from Liverpool, where decisions were made to demand wage rises, to vigorously press home the food prices scandal, and to demand a general election, in view of "much dissatisfaction with conditions of service."[33]

During August and September 1915, the upsurge for improved wages intensified as demands for more militant action swelled. A meeting of the Manchester and District Council gathered to consider a circular from the powerful but unofficial Liverpool and District Vigilance Committee calling for a war bonus of 5s. and double-time for Sunday work. Throughout the long discussion, the anger of the bulk of those present was difficult to contain. According to a report of the meeting,

things began to look warm at times, as everybody in the room appeared to want more wages, and it was high time the Executive Committee was beginning to look into the matter and withdraw the truce, as foodstuff is so high at the present time that it takes a man with a family all his time to exist.[34]

And the South-East Essex District Council, representing two thousand organised Railwaymen, decided that

owing to company failure to keep the truce and the Government's failure to control the prices of commodities, which is equivalent to a reduction in wages, we demand our Executive Committee to end the agreement with the companies and insist on the national programme being put in operation at once.[35]

Similarly strong demands for wage increases in face of the spiralling cost of living came from leading areas of discontent, such as South Wales and Liverpool, in addition to more moderate groups of Railwaymen, such as branches like Paddington No. 2 and Poplar Nos. 1 and 2 in London. Workers in the Glasgow area joined in the call for a rise in wages to meet the cost of living and readied themselves for industrial action.[36]

The growing unwillingness of increasing numbers of workplace groups to accept the words and deeds of the Executive took shape in efforts to develop and sustain an independent rank-and-file organisation. The most militant of these unofficial rank-and-file organisations was the Liverpool Vigilance Committee, although there were many others throughout the nation. The district councils absorbed many of the functions of an independent and militant rank-and-file organisation, focusing much discontent within the constitutional structure of the union. In Autumn of 1915, the Liverpool Vigilance Committee initiated a campaign to gather support for a 5s. rise in wages. By early September, reports indicate that the Liverpool Vigilance Committee's circular had been discussed at many branches and that most of the rank and file agreed with its claim, although some disagreed with its methods. The large reservoir of discontent over wages documented above only needed to be given direction. When the Liverpool Vigilance Committee met in late September to consider the Executive Committee's reply to its 5s. rise demand, they found hundreds of positive replies and only ten antagonistic responses. They reported: "Very keen feeling demonstrated and drastic resolution handed in."[37] After a deliberative meeting, the Liverpool Vigilance Committee found the Executive Committee's reply unsatisfactory, but decided to give the Executive an opportunity to make good their expressed intentions. This action, however, was taken with much difficulty due to the impatience of the men.[38] For example, a resolution from the North Lancashire, Cumberland, and Westmoreland District Council, in addition to calling for an immediate advance of 5s. per week to meet the cost of living, gave warning "that we consider we are entitled to the advance asked for and that any delay in negotiation is dangerous to the organisation."[39] Meanwhile, the *Railway Review*'s "Topic of the Week" column attempted to dissipate the spreading belief that the Executive was being passed over by asserting that it was on top of the wages question, saying that the Executive Committee would have taken up the issue at that week's meeting as a result of an Annual General Meeting resolution. Nonetheless, the intensity of feeling among a plurality of the rank and file forced the Executive Committee to the wall on the issue. "The resolutions from branches indicate that there is considerable unrest amongst certain sections of railwaymen, which has been spreading within the past few weeks."[40]

When the Executive was able to settle for only a 2s. rise instead of the full 5s. demanded, there was a great deal of dissatisfaction among the membership. The depth of the men's discontent is revealed by the subsequent initiation of a movement to withdraw the power to make a settlement from the Executive Committee and place it in the hands of a national conference more representative of the rank and file. The move to change the Constitution of the National Union of Railwaymen was a direct upshot of the bitterness over the October settlement. In late October, a Liverpool branch reported "much dissatisfaction with the settlement." At Newcastle, the predominant feeling amongst the members was that "our liberty of action had been bartered for a mess of pottage." Carlisle City reported that the settlement "received the emphatic condemnation of all the members present and the discussion revealed a depth of bitter feeling of antagonism to the signatories of what is without doubt the weakest settlement in trade union history."[41] It was then suggested that the Constitution be changed so that settlements like that just concluded could not be made without rank-and-file sanction.[42] There is no doubt that the attitude of a radicalized majority of the rank and file was expressed through the decision of the Bath Annual General Meeting in 1916. Delegates representative of rank-and-file workgroups voted by thirty-eight to nineteen for a resolution that stipulated that arrangements with reference to the questions of hours and wages or machinery for settling wage movements considered by the

Executive Committee and railway company representatives be ratified by the Annual or Special General Meeting. This important constitutional change was reconfirmed at the 1917 Annual General Meeting and clearly reflected the intent of a plurality of the organised rank and file to exert greater control over their union's policy.

The increased activism of rank-and-file organisations restricted union officials' flexibility and prerogatives. Branches and the district councils, as well as various unofficial bodies, increasingly made acceptance of Executive Committee actions subject to the Executive fulfilling further rank-and-file stipulations. The dissatisfaction lingering from the October settlement, for example, resulted in a situation in which the men acquiesced only on the condition that the Executive Committee prod the Government into regulating food prices. After the settlement, H. Ellison, a member of the National Union of Railwaymen Executive, spoke to a mass meeting of Liverpool militants, which in the end carried the following resolution:

This mass meeting of Liverpool and district railwaymen, while expressing regret at the action of the Executive Committee in acting contrary to the wishes of the members by asking for war bonus instead of wages, decides to accept and loyally abide by the settlement, providing (1) that the Executive Committee get the settlement applied to all railway workers . . . [and] (2) that the Government take drastic steps to prevent any further advance in the cost of living.[43]

The contingent awarding of loyalty and the focusing on control over Government policy marked the increasing radicalization of large groups of Railwaymen.

The upsurge in pressure from the active workplace organisations for higher wages, or alternatively Government control of prices, is more significant when viewed against the restraint imposed by the Railwaymen's patriotism. During the first eighteen months of the war, patriotism often took precedence over class interests, except where hardship was particularly acute or exploitation egregious. The Munitions Act aroused discontent mainly over the leaving certificate provisions, since the introduction of dilution only took place during the first half of 1916. It was really with the passage of the conscription legislation in early 1916 that there was a significant shift in the orientation of the consciousness of the bulk of the labour movement. The problem suddenly was to regain lost privileges and standards developed over the course of many years of struggle. Large sections of the working community turned their attention increasingly to the political and economic issues arising out of the war insofar as they had a detrimental effect upon their political and economic interests and, in turn, to "after-the-war" plans designed to regain and improve upon the conditions and power of the organised workers. At the same time, this new consciousness inspired a keener sensitivity to the march of exploitation that was being so immediately and deeply felt. The upshot was that 1916 was a year of increasing unrest and developing autonomy of increasingly large groups of organised rank and file most directly bearing the burden of wartime restrictions.

This changed industrial context from 1916 onward produced greater efforts by active Railwaymen to control union policy. One tangible change was the modification in the National Union of Railwaymen's constitution. On the wages issue, unofficial organisations took on the task of formulating and mobilizing support for a demand that became the official union policy. In April 1916, the unofficial Liverpool Vigilance Committee, now representing over thirty thousand workmen on the railways, reported that local agitation demanded a substantial rise.

This district is seething with discontent, and a most difficult position exists. The present bonus is totally inadequate to meet the rising prices of commodities. Many of the representatives dealt with the fact that no tangible effort has been made to restrict and reduce the high prices, and expressed the opinion that drastic steps should be adopted. After a full discussion during which the subject was dealt with from every aspect, it was decided that an initial step be taken, and the following resolution [was adopted and sent out]: That this representative meeting calls upon our Executive Council to at once make arrangements to negotiate for an immediate advance of 10s. per week in wages.[44]

This was the beginning of a nationwide campaign to mobilize the members' support for the demand.

While grievances over low wages were plentiful and intense, the mass of the rank and file as expressed through resolutions and other actions of their delegates were still inclined to prefer the State to control prices to the more difficult route of a wage movement. Demands often gave priority to the necessity of the Government taking control of supplies in order to curb the inflation. For example, Bishop Auckland District Committee, in a unanimous resolution which was forwarded to the Prime Minister, the Labour Party, and the Press, protested "emphatically'' against the decisions of the Committee on Production's meagre wage rises.

> In view of the very serious increase in the cost of living, due in a large measure to the rapacity of the shipowners and other profiteers, we feel that the time has arrived for the whole forces of organised Labour to demand that the Government shall take over the control of all food supplies, such control being in our opinion necessary in order to enable the poorest of the workers to obtain the necessaries of life.[45]

Similar demands came from many other district councils and branches. Almost all of them called upon the Government to stop the profiteering of those who controlled the means of production and supply. Some called upon the Executive Committee to work through the Triple Industrial Alliance, an organisation of the National Union of Railwaymen, the Miners, and the Transport Workers. Still others insisted that the Executive Committee work through the Labour Party, deploring the lethargy of the Government and urging their elected representatives in Parliament to attend to the matter.

By July 1916, resolutions demanding an advance and instructing the Executive Committee to open negotiations immediately became far more numerous. The focus on getting a rise came not only in response to the rising cost of living. It came also from the failure of the national Labour leadership, in response to pressure by the workers in all sectors of the economy, to get the Government to commit itself to stopping inflation. As a result, the Railwaymen were eager for action. The London District Council recommended affiliated branches to instruct the General Secretary to summon a Special Executive Committee Meeting to give effect to the Annual General Meeting decision carried only a few weeks earlier, which stated that if efforts to get the Government to curb rising prices failed, the Executive Committee should open negotiations for a wage rise equivalent to the rise in the cost of living.[46] Other District Councils similarly joined in the call for a 10s. rise.[47] As demands flowed in, an increasing militancy was apparent. When the South Wales and Monmouth District Council met on July 30, Swansea Branch No. 1 brought up the issue of the high cost of living. According to the report, this issue set the delegates in a fighting mood and only the chairman's skill managed to maintain some semblance of commonsense, with the result that the Executive Committee, together with the railway companies and the Government, were given another chance. This time, however, the demand stipulated a time limit and a call that nothing less than a 10s. all-round advance would prevent trouble, as the "position has now become unbearable and more than human nature can bear."[48]

By the Autumn of 1916, then, the role of unofficial rank-and-file organisations in pushing forward the demand for a rise in wages was greater than ever. The Spring campaign of the unofficial Liverpool Vigilance Committee, in which it circularized the branches in order to generate support for a rise of 10s., had mobilized massive rank-and-file pressure on the Executive Committee for action. By the time the issue had come to a head in September, the *Railway Review* reported that eighty-three branches, district councils, and vigilance committees from all over the country had sent resolutions expressing overwhelming sentiment in favour of a 10s. rise to the Head Office.[49] The previous week it was reported that twenty-four branches and the South Wales District Council sent in resolutions supporting their demand for a 10s. increase.[50] Thus, it was the initiative of the Liverpool Vigilance Committee in mobilizing a multitude of wage claims into a national movement that brought pressure to bear upon the Executive to fulfil their commitment to seek a wage rise, provided they failed in their bid to secure Government action to control prices and the distribution of necessary commodities.

Moreover, the increasing militancy of the majority of the rank and file in the branches of the main centres was evidenced by the tendency to back up their demands that the Executive Committee push the railway executives for the full 10s. per week by threats of strike action. In late August, all branches of the Liverpool Vigilance Committee met and had a "keen" discussion on the 10s. wage demand. Because of delegates' reports that trouble in the district was certain should weakness be shown by the Executive, the Vigilance Committee passed a resolution instructing the Annual General Meeting delegates to insist on the 10s. increase "even to the extent of a withdrawal of labour."[51] In September, the Liverpool Vigilance Committee renewed its threat of industrial action if the 10s. rise were not granted. Similarly, at a crowded meeting of the Bristol and District Joint Committee, the men resolved that nothing less than the 10s. rise would be satisfactory and called upon the Executive Committee to declare a national strike unless the demand were conceded. Growing impatience with the Executive Committee and its delay in considering strike action resulted in the men from the South

Wales District deciding to strike on their own if no settlement were reached by September 24. This was not only a threat of independent industrial action; it was also a threat to break with the National Union of Railwaymen and negotiate an agreement locally In any case, the South Wales threat was not taken lightly. Faced with possibly disastrous consequences, the Government stepped in and gave J. H. Thomas, now the General Secretary, the authority to promise improved conditions if the South Wales men would suspend their decision and give the Special General Meeting another opportunity to reach a settlement. The result added 5s. to the war bonus, beginning from September 16, 1916.[52] Such threats of breakaway industrial action had become a major problem confronting the National Union of Railwaymen leadership as it attempted to translate the discontent of the bulk of the Railwaymen into effective policies.

During 1917, pressures from activists representing the rank-and-file workgroups threatened the organisational stability and persistence of the National Union of Railwaymen to a greater extent. As grievances intensified due to the continued rise in the price of necessary commodities as a result of the all-too-apparent profiteering, so the active members became more disaffected from their trade union officials. The district councils and vigilance committees more than ever took the lead in initiating policy and organising mass rank-and-file pressure upon the Executive Committee. For example, in early March 1917, the London District Council organised a meeting at Albert Hall of ten thousand members, resulting in a unanimous demand that the Executive Committee negotiate a 10s. wage rise. In arguing for the rise, a representative from South Wales District Council spoke of the "smouldering anger of the men against the rapacity and greed of the food profiteer." He went on to give the Board of Trade figures to prove that food prices had risen by 95 percent since July 1914, whereas the Railwaymen's total increase was only 10s. per week or less than 40 percent above the average prewar wage. The ensuing wage movement, however, netted only a 5s. advance, because of the reluctance of a majority of delegates to call a railway strike while the country was at war.[53]

While the war continued to act as a damper on the extremes to which the bulk of the membership would have liked to see their claims pushed, the increasing hardship due to rising prices and shortages of commodities led to renewed efforts of the unofficial organisations to redress their grievances. The effect was that independent rank-and-file organisations shaped the National Union of Railwaymen's wartime industrial program in a wholesale and direct fashion. And the wages issue became part of this larger active rank-and-file effort to develop a more advanced and comprehensive response to the effects of the war. The increasing ability of the militants to marshal support for their policies was revealed at the Annual General Meeting in June 1917, when twenty "progressive" delegates met informally to coordinate their votes on each important item on the agenda. Again, in August, the representatives of the district councils and vigilance committees held a conference in London of some fifty-five delegates. They resolved to demand an end to the National Union of Railwaymen's industrial truce and press the Executive Committee to open negotiations for a 20s. per week rise in wages. Significantly, this unofficial conference called for a new national program, eventually translated into official National Union of Railwaymen policy at the Leicester Special General Meeting in late November. And indicative of their disaffection from the official National Union of Railwaymen channels, the unofficial conference urged branches to work up the new policy program completely within the unofficial organisations.

The rank-and-file activists' movement for a totally new industrial policy emerged from the politicization of the drive for a wage rise. In July, the *Railway Review* reported the Sheffield and Chesterfield District Councils' resolution to support the London District Council in a move for a further increase in wages in order to bring the members' standards up to the 1914 level. The West Midlands District Council urged the "Executive Committee to use every means to decrease the rate of profit on all commodities to at least the prewar rate of plunder."[54] And in response to replies from a large number of district councils regarding attitudes toward a national agitation for a further increase in wages, it was decided by the London District Council to convene a national conference of all district councils and vigilance committees.[55] This unofficial conference moved onto other issues besides the wages question. In addition to calling for an end to the truce and a 20 percent wage rise, it suggested that the branches instruct the Executive Committee in other policies that would assure Railwaymen greater justice. These included the demand that the Annual General Meeting or Special General Meeting delegates not accept less than the 20s. advance without first taking views of members by local meetings, a call for a cooperative trade union movement effort to control all foodstuffs and to effect an equitable distribution at fair and reasonable prices, and a claim for equal representation upon the Railway Executive Committee by the National Union of Railwaymen. The militant minority who organised and attended this unofficial conference was representative of the large body of progressive rank-and-file attitudes and succeeded in initiating closer coordination among radical Railwaymen in different parts of the country.[56] By late October, many branches, responding to informal workplace groups, had taken formal action to this initiative. The *Railway Review* reported such a large number of war and after-the-war programs submitted for consideration at the Leicester Conference that "they cannot publish them all, especially since those already published exhaust the possibilities."[57]

The wages question became critical at the same Leicester Special General Meeting that formulated the National Union of Railwaymen's after-the-war policy in late November 1917. Despite the 20s. claim by the unofficial organisations, J. H. Thomas and the Executive, in tough negotiations earlier that month, had sought to persuade the railway managers to concede a 10s. rise. To make matters worse, Thomas was forced to inform the sixty delegates on November 22 that they could not get more than 5s. The Meeting then decided that the employers' offer was unacceptable and instructed the Executive Committee by a vote of fifty-one to eight to resume negotiations for a "substantial increase." The Government refused to intervene in order to restart negotiations. It was the companies' fear that union matters would tip into the hands of the radicals in the district councils and out of the hands of the more moderate Thomas and the Executive Committee that eventually brought them to agree to resume negotiations on November 26.[58]

Before negotiations had hardly started up again, news that the Railwaymen from Liverpool and Birkenhead had started a "go slow" movement and issued circulars to all branches to persuade others to follow suit interrupted the Executive Committee's efforts. Further evidence of rank-and-file militants' dissatisfaction with the Executive Committee's progress is indicated by the London District Council's action of organising a mass meeting for a 20s. increase in wages and publication of a circular calling for "drastic action" from December 3 if their demand were not met. The result was a crisis of unity for the National Union of Railwaymen. The Executive recalled the Special General Meeting to London only six days after the Meeting on the national program at Leicester had rejected a resolution condemning the unofficial activities of the district councils and vigilance committees. In a debate over the new Executive initiative to force the upstarts into line, the General Secretary, J. H. Thomas, argued that "either you have to repudiate Liverpool . . . or you are going to say that Liverpool is going to run the Society. Either the Executive Committee and yourselves have to control our union or there is going to be chaos."[59] The Special General Meeting then proceeded to carry a resolution by fifty to ten pressuring the militants back into line. They decided

that this Special General Meeting repudiates action of our Liverpool members in their decision to "go slow" as a result of which our negotiations with the Railway companies are broken off, and we hereby demand that normal working be resumed in order that we may resume negotiation with them [railway companies].[60]

The Special General Meeting also referred to the Executive Committee's responsibility for discipline in regard to the London District Council's call for industrial action.[61] Nonetheless, the Executive Committee was well aware that it was constantly on the verge of losing the ability to focus rank-and-file grievances into effective policy, as it was increasingly caught between the insistent demands of the bulk of the members and the intransigence of the railway companies. In any event, the Liverpool men returned to normal work while negotiations resumed. A final settlement of 6s., only one shilling more than the companies' original offer, brought little satisfaction to the Executive Committee, nor did it bring much support from the rank and file for its dismal result.

Thus, the drive to resist a deteriorating standard of living proved to be the source of increasing pressure from informal workplace organisations and unofficial rank-and-file movements that were mediated through official branches, effectively shaping National Union of Railwaymen policy. While the workplace representatives utilized constitutional channels during 1915, they increasingly turned to local rank-and-file organisation to determine the course of union policy thereafter. By 1917, the official leadership lost effectiveness because it could not contain workgroup militancy and successfully channel it into a national movement. These developments occurred in response to the growing flood of grievances the leadership had to deal with at the same time that most members were becoming disaffected and hostile toward constitutional authority as a result of its association with Government policies that promoted increased subjugation. While patriotism dampened militancy during the first eighteen months of the war, it lost ground more and more to the rank-and-file drive to assert their class interests as hardship and inequality of sacrifice fostered both a greater self-reliance and a greater aspiration to control Government policies. Workgroup pressures played a key role in fostering participatory democracy within the formally representative arrangements of the National Union of Railwaymen (NUR). By defining issues to be dealt with, workplace organisations set boundaries on leaders' autonomy and compelled them to formulate solutions to their policy demands in a context of complex political and institutional pressures.

The evidence of this case, in sum, supports our argument that participatory democracy depends on an environment that creates community autonomy and fosters participatory control. As a result, workgroups arising in response to grievances over unfair and imposed sacrifice of living standards caused by the wartime system of production were able to channel and mobilize interests and support through official organisations and to develop alternative organisational instruments when official channels proved ineffective. The social pluralism evidenced, however, does not in itself produce responsiveness. Rather social pluralism, the institutions and procedures of the formally representative constitution of the NUR, and elections combined to facilitate the mobilization of collective action aimed at achieving specific policy ends. With the ultimate and substantive objectives of greater equality predominant, the members' ends enabled them to enforce leadership compliance and to inhibit leaders' self-interested action. The result was not an instance of direct democracy but of the organised membership participating in shaping the relationship between interests and support so that officeholders in delegate councils felt compelled to exchange their service on behalf of the initiatives of their members in return for the support required for effective power. In short, through rank-and-file organisations, members determined major issues and set the guidelines which compelled elected officials to choose policy solutions responsive to their articulated interests.

THE MUNITIONS ACTS AND POLICY IN THE AMALGAMATED SOCIETY OF ENGINEERS

While wartime policy-making in the NUR involved increasing influence of unofficial rank-and-file organisations, the efforts of craftsmen to amend the Munitions Act provide a case of policy-making that remains within official union channels. A statutory version of the Treasury Agreement, the Munitions Act of mid-1915 curtailed the bargaining power of the skilled workers in the munitions industry in order to expedite production in the face of the increasingly apparent fact that the war was to be won in the shops rather than on the battlefield alone. Most craftsmen were apprehensive about the imposition of the Act because it would restrict their ability to safeguard the conditions of their work. Craftsmen also feared that their traditions and rights of control in the shops would be broken down, permanently undermining their high status and remuneration. The Engineers' vehement objection to the leaving certificate and hostility to dilution evoked widespread demands for restoring lost rights and standards. Working largely through official branch and district organisations, this organised rank-and-file protest compelled officials to attempt to modify the Act and shaped the substance of the proposals to better safeguard the traditions, customs, and rights of the skilled craftsman.

The introduction of the Munitions Act immediately led to discontent. One of the main grievances against which the workmen's furor was directed was the leaving certificate, which signified that a worker had his employer's approval to go on to another firm. The effect of this was to tie a man to his employer when he might well get better wages elsewhere. District Organiser W. Brodie of the Glasgow area wrote in his monthly report that "we are still having trouble through the application of the Munitions Act, many of our members being almost in revolt at being bound over to one employer."[62] Reactions elsewhere were similarly hostile. From Halifax District came the Organising District Delegate's report that "correspondence arising out of the Munitions Act is increasing to such an extent that if prompt answers have to be made at all it will shortly mean nearly day and night shifts for the single organising District Delegate."[63] J. Binns, Organising District Delegate for Division No. 6, commented that

the developments of Government intervention and changes arising therefore [i.e., the Munitions Act] are daily in evidence, causing in many cases unnecessary irritation to both firms and workmen by the method of introduction and want of consideration displayed.[64]

And by December 1915, R. O. Jones, the Organising District Delegate for Division No. 3, which included Liverpool, wrote of the hostility of most skilled munitions workers toward the Act:

There has been so much discontent and unrest caused by its administration that the temper of Labour has been thoroughly aroused. Expressions of opinion have been freely indulged in. The outcome has been that an attempt will be made to amend the Act within the next few weeks.[65]

The irritation and anger that the operation of the Act produced led after only a few months to a surge of pressure from a majority of the rank and file to amend its more intolerable points of inequity.

The rank-and-file Engineers' desire to amend the Act derived from the widespread feeling that the Act was being used by employers to exploit their talents. The unfair advantage that the Act gave to employers allowed them to work men at modest wages when they could have obtained higher wages by changing employers, and under conditions that demanded greater exertion than was common before the war. This irked even the most patriotic men. This theme is well stated by A. B. Swales, Organising District Delegate for the London area, in his November report:

Some employers are taking full advantage of this Act to reduce their workmen to slaves, and for all manner of offences are hauling them to the Munitions Tribunals, where the word of the employers is accepted in almost all cases as beyond all question. Employers may discharge workmen when and how they like, but refuse to give a clearance when they have obviously made up their minds to dispense with men, but keep them walking about for a number of weeks, and then at the Court agree to let the men go. . . . There is a growing and justifiable dissatisfaction throughout the division against the actions of employers using the Act to impose working conditions upon men which in other times would be strongly resented. I feel sure that in each branch there are cases that justify the members sending them to the Executive Council and demanding the influence of the society be used to stop these persecutions.[66]

The advantage to employers in control over the productive process granted under the Act hinted at industrial conscription and was felt to be an unjustifiable sacrifice. The workmen's rights and standards were flouted, while the employers' rights and profits were assured.

No doubt, like the Miners, the Engineers would have refused to sign the Munitions Act had they not felt that it was necessary for the protection of the national interest. Engineering played the key role in the production of war material, and, while the ASE gained concessions from the Government by refusing to ratify the Act immediately, the operation of the Act brought the Engineers' patriotism into direct conflict with their class interests. In response to the discontent resulting from the introduction of the Munitions Act, an Organising District Delegate from Smethwick argued that the national purpose took priority:

I am frankly of opinion that we have about exhausted the possibilities of useful discussion on general principles. We are faced with the alternatives of sacrificing for the time being certain principles and activities which are of vital importance to us in normal times, or of sacrificing the lives of our comrades and endangering the success of the allied troops by a rigid adherence to such principles and activities and I am confident that for the vast majority of our members the former alternative is the only possible one.[67]

The patriotism of the Engineers goes a long way in accounting for the ability of the Government to constrain their market power and direct their labour on the shopfloor. Nonetheless, the Engineers, like other sections of the trade union movement, tolerated increased subjugation only insofar as they felt that they were being treated on equal terms with other members of the community.

Refusal of large numbers of Engineers to endure the most oppressive consequences of the Act would produce a breach between employers and workers that required Government intervention to resolve. When the organising district delegate was unable to get a solution to the problem with the local employer, the matter would be sent to what was called the Central Conference, made up of representatives of employers and trade union officials in the district. If the Central Conference failed to arrive at a satisfactory outcome, the matter would be referred to the Minister of Munitions, or later to the Committee on Production set up by the Ministry of Munitions. Arthur Shaw, the Organising District Delegate for the Sheffield District, gave a typical account of this process, backed by the workmen's resolve:

I regret that after a Second Central Conference on the question of withdrawing of the obnoxious shop rules, the employers decided that they could not recommend to the Sheffield employer the withdrawal of same. It has now been decided that the whole matter shall be brought before the notice of the Minister of Munitions and backed up by the whole of the societies represented at the conference. I may say that the Sheffield members are as determined as ever that they will not work under the proposed rules, and there is sure to be serious trouble if they are persisted in.[68]

Local disputes under the Act went into compulsory arbitration. Despite a commitment to avoid striking, this possibility always remained an important alternative in the event that the dispute was not resolved quickly enough or with satisfaction.

The determination of the employers to utilize the Munitions Act to manipulate and discipline the munitions workers led to an uprising of the rank and file aimed at amending the Act in order to check despotic employers. The growing discontent over the operation of the Act was many-sided. There was the lack of equity embodied in its clauses, the opportunities it afforded to Munitions Tribunals to oppress by coercion rather than to win confidence by cooperation, the power it offered to the opportunistic employer to introduce rules and fines for non-compliance, the burden on the trade unionist of having to prove the unreasonableness of the employer's withholding release certificates, and the practice of employers using release certificates for the purpose of conveying adverse opinions upon workmen's abilities to intended employers.[69] The real problem was the wholesale imbalance of sacrifice called for under the Act. The powers afforded to employers, particularly in regard to the proposals for dilution, produced much concern among the Executive Council and the organising district delegates. From their discussions it became clear that widespread rank-and-file discontent focused on the belief that the provisions declaring the Engineers' rights of redress and guaranteeing the restoration of privileges surrendered for purposes of speeding up production should be compulsory for employers rather than merely recommendatory.

By the end of November 1915, the Executive Council responded to widespread rank-and-file discontent by attempting to amend the Act. According to an Executive report,

Both District Committees and branches have been urging your Executive Council to demand a drastic reconstruction of the whole Act, and for the purpose of ascertaining the support we could secure from the engineering Trade Unions two conferences were called by your Executive Council.[70]

At those conferences, rank-and-file support was obtained for proposals dealing mainly with an alteration of the basis of the Munitions Tribunals, ''which have managed to earn for themselves in their very short career the utmost detestation of the whole Trade Union movement.'' When the Government announced its Amended Munitions Bill in late December, it was clear that most of the points raised in these proposals were not incorporated in the Bill and that the most essential point insofar as it affected the "dilution of skilled labour scheme" was not accepted by the Government. This latter provision would have given power to the Ministry of Munitions to make mandatory upon all controlled establishments Circulars L2 and L3, which stipulated the terms upon which women and unskilled men might be employed in work previously performed by skilled men exclusively.

At the end of December 1915, the Executive Council convened a further conference in an effort to gather more support for its amendments to the Government's Bill. Criticizing those "MPs whose duty it is to watch and safeguard the interests of labour," the Executive Council moved in regard "to the welfare of our members and the pressing urgency of the situation" to hold a National Conference of the Society in London on December 30 and 31. The Conference was fully representative, including one hundred and ten district committee representatives, the Executive Council, organising district delegates, full-time district secretaries, the General Secretary and general assistant secretaries. The purpose of the Conference was to discuss the policy of the Executive Council concerning the "Dilution of Skilled Labour Scheme" and their action in regard to the War Munitions Act, as well as the Amalgamated Society of Engineers' amendments to the War Munitions Act, 1915, Amending Bill.[71]

This Conference revealed both the exercise of membership initiative and control over ASE policy as the skilled workman acted to protect his craft traditions. After the Chairman made his introductory remarks indicating that the "tyrannical" decisions of the Munitions Tribunals had caused great unrest which, in turn, had resulted in the decision to attempt to amend the Munitions Acts, discussion took place among delegates. They stated their approval of the Executive Council's convening the Conference, and asserted that without the amendments to the Munitions Act, "which were the minimum of our requirements, they should have nothing to do with the dilution of labour scheme."[72] It was then moved and seconded that

this conference, while supporting the policy of the Executive Council as expressed in the amendments to the Munitions Act, desires to dissociate itself from the proposed new schedule (Schedule 3) suggesting the embodiment of the dilution of labour scheme, and furthermore resolves to use every means to oppose its introduction until same has been submitted to the vote of the members.[73]

The delegates went on to argue that the Munitions Act was introduced to defeat the operation of the law of supply and demand for labour, no doubt objecting to the way in which the Act curbed their bargaining power in a time of high demand. Moreover, they complained that the Executive Council had not submitted the Dilution Scheme to a vote of the members. Despite a defence of the Executive Council's actions, the Conference felt that the Executive Council had improperly moved without the guidance of the membership.

Next, a discussion took place among delegates in regard to the necessity of the amendments being inserted into the Act. They all indicated that "their districts insisted on the amendments being inserted in the Act," in addition to suggesting that there should be proportional representation on the local advisory committees. The "insistence" of the districts was then backed up by the following amendment: "That if the amendments proposed by the Amalgamated Society of Engineers are not incorporated in the Amending Bill the Amalgamated Society of Engineers will refuse to further discuss the dilution of labour scheme."[74] This amendment carried on a convincing vote of sixty-five for and twenty-seven against, and the original resolution supporting the Engineers' amendments but opposing the introduction of a Dilution Scheme without the vote of the members was carried by sixty-five to forty-four. Responding to the discontent among the majority of workgroups in the districts, the delegates strengthened the Executive Council's policy on dilution.

After a discussion the next day in which the "strong feeling in the rank and file against" the Dilution of Labour Scheme was emphasized, the major resolution of the Conference in support of the Executive Council's amendments to the Munitions Act was carried unanimously:

That this conference, representative of 205,000 operative engineers, are of opinion that the suggested amendments of the Amalgamated Society of Engineers, endorsed by 55 Trade Unions at the conference on November 30th, 1915, are essential as an element of justice in the administration of the Munitions of War Act, 1915, and should be incorporated in the amended Act *if we are to maintain our influence with our members* in securing the high standard of production required. Further, that a committee representative of the conference be instructed to wait upon the PM and the Minister of Munitions and intimate the decision of this conference is the basis of our continued cooperation.[75]

This was a forceful appeal to the Government, implying that the rank and file rejected the inequalities imposed by the Act and were losing confidence in their trade union. The appeal for inclusion of these provisions to the Amending Act reveals their importance to the Amalgamated Society of Engineers' officials as a means to maintain the support of their members so that they could effectively continue to carry out their function as leaders. Again it is clear that the Amalgamated Society of Engineers' leadership was responding directly to the substantive demands of autonomous workgroups which also threatened to withdraw their support if their interests were not safeguarded.

While the main purpose of the Conference was to reconfirm and strengthen the support for the amendments to the Act, there was a strong desire among the delegates to deal with the Scheme of Dilution. Apparently, they felt that the proposed safeguards should be a subject of legal enactment. The Conference report stated:

Behind the whole thing there is a fear—and a justifiable fear—that somehow, notwithstanding the solemn undertaking of the Government to fully restore the concessions we have made at the end of the war, that something will arise to mar the promises given.[76]

Anxiety was being aroused already by elements in the press who were suggesting that the prewar operations would not be restored after the war. The fear was that the gains won by skilled workmen would be lost and that their labour power would be reduced severely in value. It was more, then, than merely a fear of a decline in status accorded craftsmen; it was an apprehension of an impending decline in job control and was experienced as an intensification of the work process without compensation.

After January 1916, the Government decided to push forward with its dilution plans, in spite of the opposition among the majority of Engineers that had caused it to be held up. In early February, the introduction of the new Scheme proceeded by a plan to initiate the Scheme in a few large firms with the intent of convincing the employers of its value and to break the men's opposition to its working.[77] This strategy met with success insofar as dilution was implemented. But the

Government strategy was costly in terms of the massive unrest it aroused. In order to proceed with dilution in the Glasgow area, the Government determined to break the opposition of the militant workgroups mobilized in the Clyde Workers' Committee, the powerful unofficial shop stewards' organisation. The Government's strategy to break the Clyde Workers' Committee met with mass strikes and down-tools when it was put into action in February 1916. By Spring, discontent with dilution was still rife despite its effective introduction, due to a delay in an acceptable interpretation of Circulars L2 and L3 dealing with women and unskilled men. Moreover, the handing-over of Engineers' work to other tradesmen without firm understandings that the work would revert back to the Engineers after the war appeared to pose a problem of considerable irritation to the craftsmen. While the Government had suppressed the most militant workshop leaders, dilution continued to arouse considerable discontent among the bulk of the rank and file.

To summarize, this episode of ASE policy-making also confirms the importance of delegate democracy to an adequate conception of participatory democracy in large-scale working-class organisations. The election of delegates to conferences, substantive discussions, workgroup and branch resolutions demanding specific policies, and voting as a means of deciding policy in delegate councils can serve rank-and-file interests only if workgroup pressure, in this instance in defence of liberties and fairness of sacrifice to the war effort, pushes issues onto the agenda and threatens a withdrawal of support that necessitates Executive Council and conference action consistent with members' demands. The exchange of support for service on behalf of the organised members' specific substantive interests is the *quid pro quo* that underlies leadership responsiveness in delegate forms of participatory democracy. This process underlies the creation of the collective power necessary for the effective pursuit of equality.

CONSCRIPTION POLICY IN THE MINERS' FEDERATION OF GREAT BRITAIN

Whereas the restriction on industrial rights and customs imposed by the Munitions Act applied mainly to skilled munitions workers, conscription affected most of the working class. The attitude of the Miners to conscription represents the response of increasingly class-conscious, semi-skilled industrial workers at the centre of war production. At the same time, the national miners' union, the Miners' Federation of Great Britain, was formally subdivided into regional federations composed of local organisations centred around the workplace or pithead. As a result, the Miners' union was able to easily integrate participatory democratic processes into its formal system of representative democracy. An examination of Miners' policy-making on conscription, then, reveals the democratic internal power relations of a third union in the vanguard of developments in the larger labour movement.

Conscription, the statutory requirement that specified persons serve in the armed forces, was unknown to Britain before World War I. While it had been adopted in most European countries, Great Britain had always relied upon the huge Royal Navy as its main military force, supplemented by a small professional army. Public opinion leaned against conscription, despite increased advocacy for its implementation after the Boer War (1899–1902). When war broke out in August 1914, Lord Kitchener, the Minister for War, and the Cabinet turned to a voluntary enlistment system, fearing the disrupting effects that imposing conscription would cause. The voluntary response to the call to the colours was overwhelming. In less than six months a million men had voluntarily enlisted.

By the Summer of 1915, the inflow of voluntary recruits was not keeping up with the ever-increasing demand for military manpower. The conservative Northcliffe Press pushed hard for conscription, but strong opposition was voiced by those in the labour movement who believed conscription to be precisely one of the features of militarism over which the war was being fought. In September 1915, the Trades Union Congress unanimously protested against any proposals for conscription. In the face of labour's stand, the introduction of conscription could only proceed if the opposition could be divided or worn down. The intermediate step toward conscription took place in October 1915, when Lord Derby, who took charge of the War Office after Kitchener died, introduced a new recruiting scheme, attempting to give voluntarism one last chance. Throughout October and November 1915, pressure for compulsion by conservative and moderate opinion swelled until it was clear that legislation introducing conscription was inevitable. The Asquith Government eventually introduced its Military Service Bill in Parliament on January 5, 1916.

Despite the fact that there was a very short time between the announcement of the Government's intention to introduce conscription and the placing of the Bill before Parliament, the Miners' Federation of Great Britain, among other unions, was not caught unaware. In his Presidential Address to the Annual Conference in October 1915, Robert Smillie indicated his awareness of increasing pressures for conscription. He found renewed efforts to impose conscription suspicious, given the impressive results of the voluntary recruiting campaign.

At such a time an agitation for conscription seems sadly out of place; an agitation for conscription at such a time without any authoritative statement from those who know best as to the needs of the nation.[78]

His fear was that the push for conscription belied an attempt to impose authoritarian control over the labour force.

It has behind it conscription of industries, workshops, mines, and railways in this country. It has behind it the desire to set up what our lads believe they are fighting against, to establish here militarism as existent in Germany. I sincerely hope that we shall be strongly opposed to any attempt to establish militarism in this country.[79]

Nonetheless, if conscription were to become a military necessity, Smillie asserted that it should be accompanied by conscription of land and capital, to maintain some semblance of equality of sacrifice:

Personally I feel that if conscription of the Army or conscription for munitions purposes or industrial purposes is required, it is not only people of the working classes who should be conscripted. I deny, and will fight as bitterly as I possibly can, the right of one class to conscript into the industrial movement my class, or to conscript for military purposes my class until they have first conscripted the land of the country and the capital of the country and put everything into it.[80]

Thus, Smillie, always sensitive to the mood of his members, put forward the view of the most class-conscious members of the union hierarchy and the rank and file who wanted to prevent the institution of military or industrial conscription of any type.

When it became obvious that conscription was inevitable, the Miners' Executive met and summoned a National Conference of the Federation for January 13, 1916. The Executive Committee had been committed by a resolution passed at the previous Annual Conference to call such a Conference immediately when it became evident that conscription would be introduced. The Annual Conference did not empower the union's officials to call the Conference, but rather put it in the hands of the Executive, which had representatives from each of the federated districts.[81] The Conference was to discuss the Government's Conscription Bill and the districts were expected to come instructed to vote according to the decisions of their rank and file. In such cases, it was left to each district to survey the attitude of its men according to its own methods, methods usually of long-standing practice. The Executive proposed that reports be taken from the districts and that if the reports showed that "an enormous majority" were instructed to vote against the Government Compulsion Bill, it would be of no benefit to discuss the principle of compulsion itself. At its meetings on January 5 and 6, the Executive decided not to discuss the issue of conscription and "that no lead be given to the districts" on the question.[82]

The Miners' Conference on January 13 took place against the background of a national Labour and Trade Union Conference which had met to consider the wider movement's attitude toward the Bill. The Labour Conference carried an amendment submitted by the National Union of Railwaymen calling upon the Parliamentary Labour Party to oppose the Government's Bill in all its legislative stages and to vote for complete withdrawal of the Bill. This amendment, which displaced the Labour Party Executive's more moderate resolution which protested against conscription but failed to commit the Party to opposing the impending legislation in Parliament, carried amid much enthusiasm and self-confidence. Yet, the Miners' Conference probably did not take a lead from the national Labour Conference, since the former was genuinely representative of rank-and-file sentiment that in some cases had been tested prior to the movement's Conference and could have been expressed there a week earlier without any change. The absence of the Miners' Federation resulted from the Miners' refusing to attend any Conference where the conservative General Federation of Trade Unions, with which they were in dispute, was officially represented. In any case, a week's time would not have changed the Miners' votes, regardless of the outcome of the Labour Conference, as evidenced by a resolution of the South Wales Miners' Federation Executive Council. In view of the mounting campaign for conscription throughout October and November 1915, the Council on December 30, 1915 carried the following resolution:

That this Council, representing practically the whole of the workmen employed in the S. Wales coalfield, strongly resent the sinister efforts that are in operation by certain party politicians and a section of the Press, to impose upon the people of this country a system of compulsory military service, and desire the officials of the Miners' Federation of Great Britain to at once call a national conference to again enter the protest of the miners of the country against any legislation that may be proposed for this purpose.[83]

The same day that the Military Service Bill was introduced into Parliament (January 5), the Welsh Executive Council resolved "to continue our uncompromising hostility to the action of the Government in attempting to pass a measure for enforcing compulsory military service."[84] The Executive also called for a Conference of the Welsh District one week later, and one day before the Special Conference of the Miners' Federation of Great Britain in London, for the purpose of "confirming our [South Wales'] decision to continue to oppose to the uttermost extent this interference with the civil rights of the people."[85] At the Welsh District Conference on January 12 in Cardiff, 281 delegates attended, representing 133,340 workmen. They listened to Acting-President James Winstone, submitted numerous resolutions from the lodges, and had a long discussion. In the end, the delegates voted by a 6–to-1 majority against the Compulsory Service Bill, by a 2–to-1 majority for a down-tools policy if the Bill passed, and, finally, by 127 to 109 in favour of taking a ballot of the men before implementing a down-tools.[86] The militant South Wales Miners were among the groups most hostile to the Government's Bill and, as shown here, adamant in their determination to prevent conscription. The independence and bloody-mindedness of the South Wales Miners would hardly have been moved by actions or beliefs of outsiders. The South Wales actions were inspired by their own radical class consciousness.

At the Special Conference of the entire Miners' Federation in London on January 13, the delegates expressed rank-and-file views after being instructed by each of their districts. Being organised around the pithead, the official organisation in most mining districts tended to be remarkably representative of rank-and-file opinion. Robert Smillie, in the Chair, called for reports from the districts and asked that personal opinions be put aside. The Yorkshire Federation, the first to report, represented the method of surveying rank-and-file opinion used in most districts. Herbert Smith from Yorkshire indicated that as soon as the Executive decided to have the Conference, and the Yorkshire Executive Council had been informed, a circular had been sent to all branches, calling upon them to have branch meetings and send delegates mandated to vote to a Council Meeting at Barnsley, and "after discussing the matter it was decided to oppose this Bill by a large majority." He continued, saying that

we asked the branches to call meetings of their men and delegates to come prepared to vote for or against this Bill. I may say that we had 1,265 votes against the Bill and 685 for the Bill. Those figures represent one for each fifty members.[87]

Lancashire and South Wales followed a similar method, and both had strong votes against the Bill in their delegate conferences. Derbyshire varied somewhat.

We first of all called a Council, or rather our ordinary Council, and we had a thorough discussion on the Bill, and we then sent it back to the whole of the lodges with instructions to have meetings. Some have had pithead meetings, and I understand, through correspondence from the branches, that where they have three shifts they have had as many as three pithead meetings, which have been very largely attended, and they have gone so far as to take a ballot.[88]

Derbyshire had 12,283 in support of the Bill and 26,869 against.[89] Scotland was another major district which varied in its representative method. According to a Scottish representative,

I had better explain to the Conference that Scotland, while it is represented at this Conference as a National Union of Scottish Mine Workers in Scotland, it is composed of eight districts. We had a Conference in Glasgow, and representatives from these eight districts were present, representing 80,000 out of 90,000. Council Meetings had been held in the districts, and at that Conference delegates were instructed to attend here and oppose the Bill. I may say that one of the districts representing 20,000 had had no opportunity of putting it before a meeting of that district, but were included in the majority opposing the Bill. The figures, so far as we can give figures, are 80,000 out of 90,000 against the Bill, including those who had not had a Council and consulted their men, leaving 10,000 in favour of the Bill.[90]

The larger districts were all against the Bill, with varying degrees of intensity.

There were, however, nearly forty thousand votes in favour of the Bill, as representatives of Nottinghamshire, Leicestershire, and the Forest of Dean voted in support of the Government's legislation. Nottinghamshire summoned a Special Council Meeting as soon as it was learned that a Conference had been called to discuss the Bill. At the Special Council Meeting, the Bill was debated "at very great length." The Council decided to send out a recommendation to the local districts, and

when the vote was taken on the recommendation thirty-five out of forty delegates voted in favour of recommending the acceptance of the Bill. General meetings have been held at every lodge in our county, and the returns have come in which show a vote of three to one in favour of the Bill.[91]

The result, then, was three-fourths of thirty thousand for the Bill.[92] Leicestershire, on the other hand, had no lodge meetings because they failed to get instructions from the National Federation. As a result, the Executive took action and unanimously decided to support the Bill. The issue was never taken up by the men or by their delegates in the Council. How representative the Executive was is simply a question of how closely in touch with the rank and file they were and how willing they were to express their perception of their men's opinion. These questions are unanswerable given their meagre report. Forest of Dean Federation reported having held five meetings of the men in order to assess their feeling, and, after a meeting of the Executive Council, they came out in favour of the Bill. Finally, it should be noted that four other small districts remained neutral, generally because they failed to obtain a suitable evaluation of the men's attitudes.[93]

The Miners' massive opposition to conscription expressed on January 13 preceded the enactment of the Government's Bill, imposing compulsory military service on unmarried men between 18 and 41, on January 27. The overwhelming vote against the Bill, therefore, took place in a context where varying degrees of opposition could be neglected. The Conference's purpose was to state the Miners' position in protest of the Government's intention; it had no instructions to decide upon a course of action to prevent the carrying of the Bill into law, such as striking or slowing down work. The Conference involved simply identifying and gathering rank-and-file support solely for or against the

Conscription Bill. By putting off questions of protest action, division within the Miners' Federation of Great Britain remained latent

Once the Bill had become law, the Miners' Federation faced a different problem: it had to decide a policy toward an Act that it had bitterly and forcefully opposed in principle in order to prevent injustice in fact. Various differences of opposition to conscription now became centrepoints of conflict and threatened the unity of the Federation, which would weaken its ability to represent the bulk of the Miners effectively. The strength of the Miners, after all, was a solidarity built on sensitivity to the needs and wishes of the membership. Therefore, faced with a much more difficult task, the Miners met in Special Conference in Lancaster on February 8–9, 1916, to deliberate and adopt a policy resolution on the Conscription Act that would be submitted to the rank and file for approval or rejection. Again they were meeting after an expression of the national movement's position on the Act. The Annual Labour Party Conference, meeting during the last week of January, accepted the Act under protest. Unlike the situation early in January, the later Labour Party Conference decision limited the options of the Miners. The Labour Party had decided against conscription and against the Act just passed in the House of Commons. But it also revealingly decided that there should be no campaign to get it repealed, largely as a result of the Miners' neutral stance on the votes for agitation to repeal the Act. If the Miners, therefore, resolved to agitate for repeal, as put forward by South Wales, it might threaten the solidarity of the whole labour movement. More importantly, the Miners were themselves deeply divided on the Conscription Act. The complexity of the conscription issue created division among the rank and file that was replicated among their delegates, a development that paralysed the Miners' Federation itself.

At the February Conference at Lancaster, the delegates had an open and free discussion as to what the Miners' Federation's policy should be toward the Conscription Act. Assuming the lead given by the Conference would be affirmed by the vote of the rank and file, which it in fact was, it is still possible to detect the influence of the bulk of the rank and file in shaping the various positions taken by the representatives and in the way in which the delegates converted their different policy positions into policy of the national Federation. From the lengthy discussion, it is clear both that conscription in principle was anathema to almost all rank-and-file Miners and their leaders and, at the same time, that none wanted to see Great Britain lose the war to German imperialism. As a result, a considerable proportion of delegates were unwilling to support any action to repeal the Act because it might harm the national interest or undermine the solidarity in the Labour movement and the Miners' Federation itself. On the other hand, a large body of delegates opposed the Act, viewing it as the thin end of a wedge that would lead to full-blown military and industrial conscription, abrogating the last vestiges of workers' rights and liberties. There was a tension between these two concerns—patriotism and class interests—throughout, with every delegate aware of and more or less sympathetic to his colleagues' claims for support, but, nonetheless, giving emphasis to the aspect he felt to be most representative of his membership.

The debate concerning how the Miners' Federation ought to act in regard to the Conscription Bill presupposed a near unanimous hostility to conscription. A Bristol Delegate, Whitefield, argued that no delegate present at the Conference favoured conscription. He cautioned the Conference against taking a ballot on whether or not there should be a strike against the implementation of the Bill. Such a move would result in disaster because the rank and file might be in favour of the Bill under present conditions, while opposed to conscription in principle. If that were the case, then a rejection by the rank and file would be interpreted by the Government as acceptance of the principle of conscription, which was far from the truth.

I know sufficient I think of the men and what we hear in the districts, when you take a ballot the men will vote in favour of the Bill, doubtless, in my opinion, there would be a majority. What would the Government say to that? They would say: Here are the miners in favour of compulsion.[94]

Other delegates pointed to the opposition to conscription in the sense of absolute military domination involving the elimination of all civil rights. The question was whether the Conscription Bill involved the irretrievable loss of citizens' rights or was simply a temporary means of assisting the Government in prosecuting the war.

While none of the four resolutions put before the Conference made any attempt to advocate approval of conscription in principle, the most moderate one recommended acceptance of the Act. J. Robson, on behalf of the Durham Miners' Association, submitted to the Conference a resolution stating that "this Conference adheres to the findings of the

Labour Party Conference held at Bristol, namely, to offer no opposition to the present Military Compulsion Act.''[95] After ascertaining the views of the Durham Miners, Robson felt confident in putting forward this resolution:

There is no man in this meeting representing a body of men unless he is in a measure representing their views; and when he gets outside the limits of their views, then the membership is not long in reminding him of it. We had reached a point in Durham when we had a desire to know where the 120,000 men whom we represented were in this business. We put it plainly and unmistakably before them: Are you in favour or against the Bill? We have got our answer.[96]

He then justified the Durham decision:

Our men are beginning to realize that it is not right that these sacrifices should fall upon a few; that it ought to be equally distributed over the different families right throughout the United Kingdom. These things are influencing the minds of our people. . . . I believe that we underestimate the intelligence of the rank and file of our members as to the issues that are at stake. It is clear to them that this Bill has been brought in in order to compel a section of men, and I believe that this class of men are not men from our own ranks. There are a lot of men who are well to do who refuse to acknowledge their national obligations and responsibilities in this great crisis, and our men are anxious that they should.[97]

While many of the Durham Miners believed the Act would promote equal sacrifice, the results of the voting revealed significant opposition to the Act. Nonetheless, we see here a strong indication of the egalitarianism and patriotism of the rank and file and its representation in the national Miners' Conference.

Another resolution, submitted by Northumberland, also responded to the patriotic mood, yet exhibited a more vigorous and pronounced opposition to conscription. This resolution read as follows: "That this Conference expresses its opposition to the spirit of conscription, and determines to exercise a vigilant scrutiny of any extension of the Military Service Act.''[98] Weir, speaking on behalf of Northumberland, emphasized that the main goal was to win the war and that it would therefore be appropriate to go along with the Asquith Government Coalition. He stated:

In order to prevent any division in the Labour forces we ought at least to have some consideration for the Coalition Government, and I do not know that any member of this Conference agrees entirely with conscription It is because we all agree and have one object in view, that the war has got to be won, or we would have got opposition to the principle in this Conference today.[99]

Yet, while most Miners would gladly have sacrificed dearly to the war effort, there was a limit beyond which it would have been imprudent to pass. Pointing to apprehension concerning the possible extension of the Act to cover married men and to include industrial conscription, Weir pressed the need to assess constantly the sacrifice of liberty to the war campaign.

I said at the commencement that we were out to win this war, but we ought to measure the cost even now, and from the very commencement to see what it is going to cost us to win it. We have to consider all the conditions, and all we have complied with up to now. Let us so far as possible measure the cost; do not let us lose that which our lads have gone into the trenches and died for, in order to maintain the freedom of the land, and God grant that many of our young men may not return to find in the homeland established what they went into Flanders to prevent.[100]

In the interest of fairness, then, and the protection of rights and liberties won by the workpeople, Weir thought that any attempt to extend the Act should be met with "a thorough scrutiny."

While fully supporting the goal of an Allied victory, other areas of the Federation were more concerned with the effects of the Conscription Bill on subordinating the workers to the interests of the military and industrial classes. James Winstone indicated that he would put forward a resolution from the South Wales Miners' Federation "because [he was] carrying out the wishes of the men [he] represent[ed] in Wales." He stated that the "Executive Committee [should] be instructed to arrange for a ballot vote of the workmen to be taken for or against the repeal of the Military Service Act."[101] Arguments advanced by Winstone in favour of the Welsh resolution were based on a rejection of conscription in any form as a threat to civil liberties and an apprehension concerning eventual industrial conscription. Giving assurances of patriotism, he said, "I have never yet been able to bring my mind to believe that there are any men in Britain today who are anxious that Germany should win this war."[102] Yet he was adamantly opposed to conscription. He asked the Conference to take seriously the clauses in the Act that imposed compulsory military service, to ask just what civil rights anyone would have once they had been brought under the Act's domain. Further, Lord Derby, the War Minister, had made clear that so far as he was concerned Britain would have compulsory military service after the war in any event, and he objected to helping Lord Derby establish compulsory military service in the nation. Earlier in the Conference, T. Richards, M.P. and South Wales Delegate, indicated that Wales believed that the Miners' Federation was not bound by the Labour Party decision, given that the Miners' neutrality determined inadvertently the outcome of the Party's vote, and given that the Miners' votes could have tipped the Labour Party Conference either way. Therefore, he argued that the Miners should, without hesitation, agitate for repeal of the Act.

Until it is removed we should do all that we can legitimately without endangering the success of the war in any shape or form. We ought to continue this agitation, that is if we desire. There are men who do not desire it. I do not complain. There are some who believe that it will be a dead letter, and in a short time all the men provided for in the Act will be on the Statute Book of this country, and I say this country will never be safe from general conscription whilst we have this Act of Parliament.[103]

In support, Barker and Hodges, also representing South Wales, spoke, urging that the Miners' Federation act to bring about the repeal of the Act since, after all, they had rejected the principle of conscription at the last Conference. South Wales, asserting its patriotism by claiming that the nation was best defended by "freemen," put liberty in the forefront. This position was widely espoused among large groups of the Welsh rank and file.

The last resolution put forward for consideration at the Conference came from Yorkshire and, like that from South Wales, called for repeal of the Act. Herbert Smith suggested that Yorkshire felt just as strongly about conscription as did South Wales, but that it objected to the idea of a ballot as an "unnecessary agitation" of the rank and file. The aim of the Yorkshire resolution was to record "its strong protest against any Compulsion Bill and that we resist any further attempt to extend it further."[104] Smith felt it important to place their resolution before the Conference: "That this Federation press for a deputation to be appointed to interview the Prime Minister to request the immediate repeal of the Military Service Act."[105] The reason for supporting repeal was that

we have given three men in the Cabinet an absolute blank cheque to do anything they like, and it is because I want to save if possible the destiny of this Federation and trades unionism generally that I want to put this resolution on record.[106]

Even though Smith disliked the idea of a ballot of the men, he felt that he accurately reflected their attitudes. He continued,

But if I am told I do not represent the men then I had better get to know whether I am or not, that is the position. I have heard so much about consulting the rank and file this last three months that after this war we shall consult the rank and file, and there will be something more in store for some of us than we have had before. There are people today talking about the rank and file who did not talk about it before the war, they have suddenly developed the idea, and I am going to inquire into it. I can tell you I like to speak for the rank and file. I do not like to be here not speaking for the rank and file.[107]

Smith's reference to increased talk of consulting the rank and file suggests that the leadership was more than ever under pressure from their members and, therefore, more concerned to justify their policies as representative of the attitudes of the rank and file.

At the end of the long discussion concerning these four resolutions, the delegates were still divided, but there was a feeling that the Conference had to reach a decision or lose prestige and power as the leading trade union in the nation. After adjournment overnight, the delegates reassembled to cast their votes. The outcome was a small majority in favour of the Northumberland resolution expressing opposition to the spirit of conscription and committing the Miners to a "vigilant scrutiny" of any proposed extension of the Military Service Act.[108] The closeness of the vote—365,000 for the Northumberland resolution to 349,000 for the Durham one—reveals the strong feelings of patriotism among the Miners who at the same time felt intensely committed to defending and developing their industrial and political interests.

In April, the Government began to take initiatives to extend the Act to married men, a little over a month after the first Act had gone into operation. Faced with the extension of conscription, the Miners' Federation decided to reassess its policy. While the South Wales Miners had lost their appeal at the Lancaster Conference, pressures in the ranks were mounting for a more drastic policy than the nominal commitment to "vigilant scrutiny" against the further extension of the Conscription Act. The South Wales Annual Conference in Cardiff on April 17 opposed the National Conference resolution by 153 to 101, and adopted the following resolution:

That this conference reaffirms its opposition to compulsory military service and demands the Government to repeal the Act now in operation, that steps be taken to get this adopted as a national policy by the miners and the trade union movement as a whole, and that in the event of the Government proceeding with the suggested extension of the scope of the present Act, a coalfield conference be immediately called to consider the situation.[109]

When the Miners' Federation met in Special Conference in London on May 9–10, 1916, it was South Wales' initiative to rescind the Lancaster resolution and agitate for outright repeal of the Conscription Act that provided the pole around which the debate turned.

While the South Wales initiative failed to get the backing of the Special Conference, it was clear by May 1916 that the Miners had become more concerned about the dire prospects of conscription than they had been at Lancaster. The voting on resolutions revealed this increased apprehension in terms of a commitment to a more militant opposition to industrial conscription. Whereas the Lancaster Conference had been closely divided as to whether or not to support "vigilant scrutiny" or acquiescence to the Government's Act, the London Conference revealed that a great proportion of delegates favoured a stronger opposition to conscription and the use of the Federation to prevent its further encroachment. Delegates supporting the Conscription Bill, and thereby conscription in principle, were few. The large districts of Durham (120,000) and Scotland (90,000) moved to the more militant position. On a final ballot, the Yorkshire resolution, derived from its district conference that was representative of its own rank and file, carried by 476 for to 107 against. Resolute in resisting conscription, South Wales refused to register its 135,000 votes on the grounds that both alternatives on the final ballot accepted conscription, if not in principle, then surely in actuality. This vote, in short, did more than simply reaffirm the Lancaster Conference's policy of "vigilant scrutiny." The sentiment of the London Conference was clearly more enthusiastic and assertive in its determination to resist industrial conscription in however subtle a form.

The delegates at the Lancaster and London Conferences did not act in a vacuum; rather, they sought to maintain credibility with their rank-and-file members, which is borne out by their elaborate efforts to justify their policy stances in reference to the rank and file. The need to maintain credibility and support was even more evident in militant sections like South Wales. If South Wales delegates surrendered their mandate, they faced the prospect of spontaneous and unofficial action by lodges (pit-head union organisations), an event that would bring chaos to their union and the industry. If leaders were to keep the rank and file behind them, it was necessary not only to give voice to their substantive claims, but also to give effect to them in a way that would make it possible to get results. If the Miners' Federation were to oppose the principle of conscription, it had to aggregate power enough to effect its policy. In the end, the tension between the rank-and-file miners' patriotism and defence of civil, political, and industrial rights prevented the development of a clear mandate for the leadership to oppose the operation of the Conscription Act.

Of course, the history of the Miners' opposition to conscription did not end in mid-1916. The same tensions were expressed during 1917 when military necessity forced the Government to attempt to conscript miners. It met with increased resistance from militant workgroups, especially in South Wales where most of the men were determined to resist. In September 1917, various lodges struck sporadically in South Wales and threatened a general strike of the South Wales coalfield.[110] Much of the resistance in late 1917 arose as opposition to the war itself became widespread. Once again, rank-and-file action in defence of civil, political, and economic rights threatened the organisational persistence of the Miners' Federation, shaped the lines of conflict, and determined the course of policy execution itself.

In sum, the Miners' policy on conscription, representing a defence of liberty and an assertion of the right to fair treatment, provides further evidence for a conception of participatory democracy that incorporates delegate decision-making. Many of the delegates to the Miners' Conferences were member–representatives of pithead organisations and subject to consensus-making processes of direct democracy. Others were full-time elected officials. The formal electoral procedures involved in consulting the membership were extensive and were reinforced by ideals of equal status and inclusive decision-making. The commitment to collective solidarity provided the incentive to protect collective unity without violating the diversity of value priorities among the rank and file. To ignore diverse attitudes on this crucial issue would itself threaten collective solidarity. The substantive interests in greater equality and power that were defined by a community solidarity among Miners provided the incentive for action that gave priority to the conscription issue and enabled members to participate in shaping the outlines of policy. At the same time, the formal mechanisms of electoral competition and decision-making facilitated and guaranteed that participatory control would involve the expression of diverse workplace interests and the working-out of the policy consensus.

CHAPTER 6

Delegate Democracy in the National Federations and Domestic Policy

While workplace organisation can directly affect trade union policy-making through formal and informal channels, workers at the base can have only indirect influence in the national delegate councils that attempt to represent the whole of organised Labour. The Trades Union Congress (TUC) and the Labour Party are federated Labour organisations consisting of national trade unions in the former and trade unions, socialist societies, and local Labour Parties in the latter. In these national federations, delegates to conferences and executive members, while subject to periodic election, are clearly removed from workplace pressures and experiences. Unlike leaders from trade union affiliates, top TUC and Labour Party executives are not likely to be confronted by representatives of rank-and-file organisations on a daily basis. As federation executives, they are two steps removed from rank-and-file organisations in terms of both their distance from the work situation and the substance of their daily activities which regularly involve them with Government officials and employers. Even so, not all TUC and Party decision-makers were totally isolated from the collective solidarity of Labour organisations and the specific pressures of union concerns. Many officials and most delegates to decision-making assemblies were themselves trade union officeholders, subject to immediate pressures from below, while a few were rank-and-file activists. Still, the shaping of policy by the organised members at this level can be expected to be either unlikely or extremely difficult. Certainly the rational-choice theory of collective action suggests that membership influence is unlikely since widespread and intense participation in collective action on issues of broad scope cannot be expected from rational self-interested members. In short, because federation officeholders are removed from the workplace, interact daily with Government officials and employers, deal with larger issues rarely the concern of workplace groups, and can claim to act in the general interest of millions of trade unionists, the Trades Union Congress and the Labour Party would appear to be even more susceptible to the law of oligarchy than the trade unions.

This chapter examines the policy-making processes that produced the TUC's and the Labour Party's commitment to socialism to see if the internal policy processes in the national federations provide evidence supporting our theory of participatory democracy. The central analytic and historical focus will be on how relations between interests and support from the various constituents of these federations create imperatives that compel leaders to adopt members' initiatives and to make decisions within the moral boundaries set by their expressed interests. This, of course, assumes that these affiliates are themselves responsive to their own organised members in the fashion we have documented for the Miners, Railwaymen, and Engineers. While clearly not applicable to all union affiliates or on all issues, this assumption is probably accurate for more class-conscious unions on major issues. Whether TUC and Labour Party policy is responsive to members' interests, then, depends on the leverage members exert on their trade unions and, in turn, the pressure union officeholders bring to bear at the federal level. Ultimately, membership and union leadership pressures are a response to the environment, mediated by organisation and plans of action informed by consciousness. The way in which pressures from below affect top leaders depends on how formal electoral and representative mechanisms enable the plural communities among the membership to check and override leadership prerogatives so that participatory control can operate in making federation policy. What this involves is an enlargement of collective solidarity around issues of national consequence through a process of collective consensus formation involving widespread participation of organised groups at the base and at the intermediate level. In short, this chapter will argue that federation policy-making on critical domestic issues, that is, specific issues central to workers' everyday concerns, provides further evidence for a theory of participatory democracy that appreciates the importance of delegate decision-making in hierarchical organisations.

DEMANDING THE SPECIAL TRADES UNION CONGRESS

Continually rising prices coupled with the passage of the Conscription Bill in Parliament and its extension to married men in May 1916 produced a wholly new situation for labour, an ominous situation which compelled even some moderate sections of the workforce on the periphery of war production to demand the reestablishment of lost rights and standards. The labour movement seemed to wake up to the fact that the sacrifices it had made to the war effort now imperilled its very future. Fear that compulsion would enable employers to drive wages down even further and that compulsion would be used after the war to prevent the return of long-standing customs, rights, and, at least, the prewar standard of living agitated nearly every section of the movement. Indirect imposition of industrial conscription was a particularly deep-felt threat because the men believed that it would result in their virtual enslavement to capital. Thus, conscription was the straw that broke the camel's back. Beginning in February 1916, organised labour moved to regain what it had lost so easily and, indeed, to aspire to a new rung on the ladder in the social hierarchy of influence in British society. Discontent over inflation, industrial restrictions, and conscription provoked workplace organisations in the major unions to focus the attention of their official and unofficial representatives on the position of organized labour after the war. The result was a campaign by the leading sections of the labour movement to mould a program that would restore and then advance the rights and standards of organised workers. These pressures had their effect first on TUC policy and then on Labour Party policy. The latter's "Labour After the War" Program, the historical focus of this chapter, constituted its first collective commitment to the construction of a socialist society, thereby establishing the basis for the socialist commitment in Clause IV of the 1918 Constitution.

With the rising tide of concern over organised labour's future following passage of the Conscription Bill in late January 1916, the War Emergency Committee forced the hand of executive committees of other national organisations to come to grips with the prospect of increased exploitation. It did this initially by issuing a pamphlet auguring the likelihood of industrial conscription resulting from the introduction of military conscription in December 1915, and producing "A Memorandum on Labour After the War" in February 1916. By giving voice to the policy positions of the discontented rank and file, the War Emergency Committee contradicted official TUC and Labour Party policy and so endangered its own existence.

The War Emergency Workers National Committee (WEC or WNC) was an *ad hoc* committee formed at the outbreak of the war for the express purpose of defending the interests of the whole working class and, at the same time, defending labour unity. Its members and finances were supplied by the TUC Parliamentary Committee, the Labour Party National Executive Committee, and the management Committee of the General Federation of Trade and Unions,[1] which were more permanent and naturally jealous of any War Emergency Committee efforts to upstage them. J. S. Middleton, its Secretary, recognized that contradicting the official policies of its parent organisations put the future of the War Emergency Committee at risk. In a letter, Middleton argued that their policy papers were making waves.

Our line on the Munitions Act, more particularly certain references to its unpopularity in our Industrial pamphlet, as well as our confirmed opposition to the Military Service Acts, are the two chief instances where we have run counter to official policy. Our attempt to issue the *Memorandum on Labour Problems After the War* also upset some sections of the other committees largely because their representatives on the WNC had not reported back to their own bodies on the subject.[2]

The War Emergency Committee functioned as an informal channel for the voicing of active rank-and-file concerns as expressed through trade union policies. In so doing, the Committee was able to intimidate the three executive committees into action.

The War Emergency Committee's role of coordinating and voicing many workers' deeply felt grievances was not meant to usurp the role of the Labour Party or the Trades Union Congress as the major policy-making bodies of the labour movement. In response to a letter from one trade and labour council requesting War Emergency Committee sponsorship of lectures on disabled soldiers, paying for the war, women's employment during and after the war, and industrial reconstruction after the war, Middleton summarized the prospects for developing an after-the-war policy as somewhat uncertain,

> That day he [Middleton] is presenting to the [War Emergency Committee] full meeting a preliminary memo surveying the ground and setting forth certain immediate and palliative proposals. He believes that after consideration the [War Emergency] Worker's National Committee will sanction its issue throughout the movement.[3]

Middleton goes on to allude to the Joint Board's Subcommittee,[4] which had done nothing definite yet. Moreover, the Labour Party Executive Committee was scheduled to discuss the matter on February 14–15, 1916, and "nothing like an official view will emerge for some time as there must be a considerable period of general discussion" followed probably by district conferences throughout the country. But he hoped a wholly representative National Conference would crystallize the varying suggestions into a definite policy.[5]

Even though the War Emergency Committee's memorandum focused mainly on the problem of demobilization after the war, incorporated Sidney Webb's ideas on employment and relief, its implication that there was developing support for an agency to organise labour action on after-the-war problems inspired the Labour Party's National Executive Committee (NEC) to set up its own Subcommittee to deal with the subject. Webb, moving into the inner councils of the Labour Party and becoming its chief administrator of intellectual work, agreed to serve on the Labour Party Subcommittee in a move that broadened the political basis of support for his ideas.[6] Webb also joined the National Executive Committee in December 1915, when the Fabian Representative, Sanders, enlisted in the army. At the February 14, 1916, National Executive Committee meeting, Henderson, the Party's General Secretary, proposed joint NEC and Parliamentary Labour Party Subcommittees to consider peace terms, labour after the war, and electoral reform. These three issues were crucial to the making of the National Labour Party, although, as we shall see, it takes far more than committees to build a national party. At this meeting, the NEC resolved to set up its own Subcommittee to consider postwar labour policies and "that it should be instructed to undertake as its first duty the coordination of other official Labour Committees at present dealing with various aspects of this subject."[7] The NEC also appointed W. C. Anderson (Independent Labour Party), J. R. Clynes (General Workers), Hutchinson (Amalgamated Society of Engineers), Robinson (Textile Workers), and S. Webb (Fabians), along with the National Executive Committee Chairman G. J. Wardle (National Union of Railwaymen) and the Party Secretary A. Henderson, to the Subcommittee. Thus, the Labour Party moved to capture the growing support for a "Labour After the War" policy, which was quickly becoming the main concern of the trade union and labour movement.

The Labour Party's action on "Labour After the War" was largely in response to a growing concern among trade unionists with the conditions arising out of the war. For instance, on February 15, the NEC dealt with a letter from Ben Tillett of the Dockers' Union informing it of a series of resolutions carried at a meeting of their Executive in mid-January. These resolutions concerned the national economy, Munitions Act, restriction of wages by the Government, congestion of transport, and compulsory military service. Each of these resolutions protested the unfairness of the current Government policy and

call[ed] for a special Trades Union Congress to consider national resources, national economy, the State monopoly of food supplies, raw materials, wealth, banking, and all the material forms of industry and property for the purposes of general and national share in the cost and burdens of the war.[8]

The NEC discussed this letter and heard Wignall relate his recent experiences with the Bristol Dockers before the Committee on Production. The Committee then decided to make a representation to the Prime Minister and to make an attempt to enlist the cooperation of the TUC's Parliamentary Committee. When the Parliamentary Committee, however, received Tillett's letter containing these resolutions, it dismissed the request for a national Conference "as action had already been taken on these points."[9] Yet, the Dockers' resolutions represented only the beginning of a growing wave of trade union assertiveness, responding to an undercurrent of organised class consciousness and collective action aimed at redressing the unfairness of the wartime political economy toward wage labour.

Later that month, the Labour Party National Executive Committee decided to initiate common action on "Labour After the War" problems in an effort to take control of policy-making on postwar issues. Its Subcommittee met at the House of Commons on February 24 to discuss the work of the various subcommittees of the national organisations. Attention was given to the War Emergency Committee preliminary report which was being held up from publication while the responsibility for "Labour After the War" was resolved. A joint meeting of the Subcommittees appointed by the Labour Party NEC, the TUC Parliamentary Committee, the Management Committee of the General Federation of Trade Unions, the Joint Board, and the War Emergency Committee was called for March 1.[10] The TUC Parliamentary Committee and the Management Committee of the General Federation of Trade Unions were not taking any specific action, the former having no Subcommittee and the latter having disbanded its Subcommittee. Further, it was pointed out that the Joint Board representatives were attending in other capacities. Thus, after a full discussion of the possibilities for joint action, the NEC resolved by six to five to support the formation of a Joint Committee to consider and report on "After the War Problems." Despite efforts by Middleton to resist the formal loss of what had become the War Emergency Committee's role, thereafter Subcommittees of the TUC, Labour Party, and General Federation of Trade Unions Executives developed "Labour After the War" policies.[11] But on March 15, the Parliamentary Committee resolved "that continued increase of War Problems justifies a meeting of the three national executives to consider the whole situation."[12] On April 19, the three National Executive Committees met and considered at length the machinery for dealing with "After the War Problems." It was finally decided that the three National Committees and the Joint Board form a Joint Subcommittee to put forward definite recommendations on "Labour After the War."[13] On July 27, this last "Labour After the War" Committee subdivided its tasks into Committees on Trade Unionism, Taxation, Transport and Shipping, Land and Agriculture, Health and Insurance, Unemployment, Demobilization and Pensions, and Education. The Fabian Research Department was called in to assist. These were the beginnings of what later became the Labour Party Advisory Committees after the reconstitution in 1918.

Of a technical nature and limited to a few narrow issues, the work of these Committees cannot properly be considered as the source of the Party's "Labour After the War" Program. By January 1917, these Committees had produced a series of pamphlets, in spite of what Webb referred to as the real desire of trade union leaders to prevent anything from being published which would arouse expectations. The "Labour

After the War'' Committees responded in moderate fashion to the discontent among an increasingly militant rank and file in some unions, reluctant to assume responsibility for arousing or focusing pressure from below. The Committees, then, were an attempt to control or absorb strong pressures on the national leaders. Because the work of these Committees and the War Emergency Committee on "Labour After the War" was so sparse and distant from the attitudes of the organised rank and file and their trade union representatives, it seems unlikely that they provided the basis of the Labour Party's 1918 policy program "Labour and the New Social Order." Likewise, it is fallacious to argue that this program was based upon Webb's work on these Committees. He did not give the lead to what the Labour Party and the Trades Union Congress were focusing on substantively; rather his work followed what was happening among the militant rank-and-file organisations in the leading trade unions.

If the War Emergency Committee and the subsequent Joint Subcommittees did not provide the policy program underlying British socialism, the War Emergency Committee did play a crucial role in initiating a series of National Conferences that did in fact forge the postwar socialist program. In mid-March, the Dockers' Union submitted a second resolution to the Parliamentary Committee of the Trades Union Congress requesting a National Labour Conference to consider the national economy, Munitions Act, wages policy, and conscription. This request was supported by the Miners' Federation of Great Britain and the Paper Workers' Union.[14] There were also Press reports of a "strong body of opinion" in the labour movement anxious to have a special Labour Congress of all sections in order to consider war problems affecting labour, the position of labour after the war, and the necessary steps for reorganisation for that period. These reports suggested that the War Emergency Committee was the agency best suited to initiate convening of such a meeting.[15] Despite support for convening a National Conference, the Parliamentary Committee adhered to its February decision of no action. The Dockers, apparently desperate to get the Parliamentary Committee to act, sent in further specific complaints of unwarranted use of the Military Service Act involving the use of military personnel to displace civilian workmen on the docks. It was to no avail, however.[16]

Within a few weeks, the Government announced its intention to extend the Military Service Act to cover married men and to lower the recruiting age to eighteen, and pressure on the Trades Union Congress mounted further. Some organised rank and file and union representatives' fear of the repressive consequences of the Government's plans led to more calls for a National Conference. But the Trades Union Congress, the General Federation of Trade Unions, and the Labour Party balked, trying instead to overlook the growing unrest. In fact, federation executives were fearful that a National Conference might result in a decision to agitate for the repeal of the conscription legislation, setting off uncontrollable strikes and "down-tools" by militant sections. The national labour leaders were keen to assist the Government and were buffered from immediate rank-and-file agitation. The Parliamentary Labour Party expressed the view that "while it was anxious to cooperate in matters of military necessity," it would need more information before it could agree to an extension of the principle of compulsion.[17] A joint National Executive Committee–Parliamentary Labour Party meeting recommended that the Government hold a secret session of Parliament in order to inform the members of Parliament fully of the military situation.[18] Following a meeting on April 26 with leading members of the War Committee, including Prime Minister Asquith, Lord Kitchener, and Bonar Law, the Parliamentary Labour Party, NEC, TUC Parliamentary Committee, and Management Committee of the General Federation of Trade Unions met separately and resolved to assist wholeheartedly the Parliamentary Recruiting Committee in the new recruiting campaign for married men.[19] The Parliamentary Committee's decision was as follows:

That, as the Bristol Conference resolution dealing with conscription was based upon the absence of definite information, and as such information has now been submitted to the Committee by three responsible Ministers, the Parliamentary Committee decided to advise the trade unions to support the recruiting proposals put forth by the Government to obtain 200,000 unattested married men.[20]

The decision to support the Government in contradiction to a TUC resolution carried at the September 1915 Congress reveals the national executives' commitment to assisting the government. But they were also apprehensive of the growing distrust and uncontrollability of militant sections of Miners, Railwaymen, and Engineers, among others. As a result, a Joint Meeting of the Parliamentary Committee and the National Executive Committee agreed not to hold a Special Conference to decide to accept or reject the Government's proposals for fear that it might release anti-conscription sentiments.[21]

As a result of concern over the industrial conditions arising out of wartime legislation, a large number of both national and local trade union and labour organisations demanded a Special Trades Union Congress. The growing mood of militant opposition to conscription and the official Labour policy surfaced at two Conferences in May 1916. A Conference under the auspices of the Joint Committee Against Conscription, attended by over two hundred delegates representing ninety-four organisations, pledged itself to agitate for the repeal of the Act and against any extension of its principle or operation. Robert Smillie, President of the Miners' Federation of Great Britain and Chairman of the War Emergency Committee, spoke of the apprehension among the Parliamentary Committee and the National Executive Committee members over the prospect of calling upon the Labour Party to summons a National Conference to consider the extension of compulsion. Smillie reported TUC leadership response to rank-and-file pressure:

There was a widely established suspicion that the majority of those responsible for calling a conference had not done so because they were afraid of the result. It was their duty to call a conference, and he knew they had been inundated with resolutions from affiliated organisations demanding that a conference be convened.[22]

In addition, the Annual Delegate Conference of the Glasgow Labour Party carried the following resolution amid ''great enthusiasm'':

That this annual conference of the Glasgow Labour Party (not the Independent Labour Party) reaffirms its opposition to conscription, places on record its condemnation of the Labour Members of Parliament who supported conscription, and requests the National Executive to call a national conference to consider the situation created by the extension of conscription and the position of those members who supported the Bill; and, further, this conference repudiates the speeches and votes of George N. Barnes, MP, as being in direct opposition to the opinion of organised Labour in Glasgow.[23]

The intense opposition to conscription and the hostility shown toward prominent national leaders were indicative of not only the more militant rank-and-file attitudes, but a growing majority of more moderate trade unionists.

Despite resistance from the Labour Party, the Trades Union Congress and the General Federation of Trade Unions, the War Emergency Committee persisted in informally concentrating union pressure upon the TUC Parliamentary Committee to convene a Special Congress. On May 25, the War Emergency Committee resolved to organise a National Conference on conscription, its effects on trade union organisation and administration, industrial conscription, and the conscription of riches.[24] On the same day, the TUC Parliamentary Committee again refused to call a National Conference. Its action was precipitated by a London Trades Council deputation which pressed the issue of why the Trades Union Congress' consent to extending conscription had been given without having a National Conference. The deputation wanted a National Conference or, alternatively, a ballot. But the Parliamentary Committee, in response, decided to issue a circular "guardedly" stating its reasons for refusing to convene the National Conference so widely desired.[25]

The next day Middleton wrote to Bowerman, Chairman of the Parliamentary Committee, informing him of the pressing need for the convening of a National Conference. Middleton reported on the previous day's meeting of the War Emergency Committee and the opposition to a Conference by the General Federation of Trade Unions, the Trades Union Congress, and the Joint Board. However, the War Emergency Committee, according to Middleton,

share the opinion expressed by several larger Unions in the movement, that despite differences that may exist as to the principle of the conscription legislation it is urgently necessary that a Conference should be held to review the situation that it has created.[26]

Middleton then went on to enumerate the topics "felt very strongly" to "require careful and serious attention": trade union organisation and administration, the danger of industrial conscription, the conscription of riches, the position of young men of eighteen under the Act, the position of old-age pensioners, and food prices.[27] Moreover, he warned Bowerman

that failing the Conference being convened, several of the larger trade unions would consider taking action for themselves, with a view to focussing the opinions of the Movement as a whole on these various subjects.[28]

Yet, Middleton claimed that the War Emergency Committee had no intention of usurping the role of the Trades Union Congress.

The Committee, naturally enough, have no desire to take any action that would be instantly repudiated by its most important component organisations. At the same time, it does feel very strongly that action should be taken by one or other of the responsible National Committees on lines indicated.[29]

Middleton, then, urged the Parliamentary Committee of the Trades Union Congress on behalf of the Executive Committee of the War Emergency Committee to "reconsider their decision and to agree to convene a representative Conference on these subjects."[30] The War Emergency Committee was acting as a determined pressure group, giving voice to unleashed grievances against a recalcitrant Parliamentary Committee. No doubt, the Parliamentary Committee was angered by the presumptuousness of the War Emergency Committee, which had in their minds been effectively checked from influencing the "Labour After the War" policy proposals. If the War Emergency Committee's ability to initiate policy had been checked by the Subcommittees of the Joint Committee on "Labour After the War," its role in focusing trade union demands for a Conference to work out a national postwar policy to deal with the new industrial conditions created by the war had not.

On the defensive, Bowerman wrote condescendingly to Middleton in an attempt to ascertain the extent of the pressure. Bowerman asked for the names of the "several larger unions in our Movement (other than the Dock Workers' Union, as endorsed by the Miners' Federation) urging the convening of a National Conference." He indicated that the Parliamentary Committee had received a large number of resolutions from trade councils but very few from affiliated organisations.[31] Bowerman seemed out of touch with developments following upon the Government's announced intention to extend conscription, for the Dockers' and Miners' requests dated from mid-March.

Middleton's response to Bowerman's request singled out major unions pressing for the special Trades Union Congress and again stressed the possibilities of independent action in the event the Parliamentary Committee failed to act. The Postal Unions were "greatly concerned as to the national position occasioned by the Military Service Bill and that from a letter from a very representative official of the Textile Unions, that not a little uneasiness exists in their rank." Moreover, the Railwaymen were also seething with unrest. What was perhaps more convincing to the Parliamentary Committee's Chairman was the more emphatically repeated threat of independent action.

While there is no evidence of any organised movement, it is quite apparent that there is a great danger of certain sections acting independently unless the situation created by the Act, as apart from the merits of the Act itself, is very carefully considered by the national bodies.[32]

The mounting support for a Special Congress by significant bodies within the trade union movement and their apparent inclination to take action if the Trades Union Congress remained dormant were evidence which the Parliamentary Committee could not long ignore if it were to retain any claim to being the most representative forum on industrial matters.

The Parliamentary Committee of the Trades Union Congress did not act until its meeting of June 6, which was wholly concerned with the question of holding a Special Congress of the TUC. Bowerman reported on the last meeting of the War Emergency Committee which had uncharacteristically witnessed the full Trades Union Congress delegation in attendance.[33] J. S. Middleton's letter was read conveying the suggested agenda and other information supporting his demand for the Conference. Moreover, the Parliamentary Committee considered other requests to convene the Congress. Numerous letters from trades councils and trade union branches asking the Parliamentary Committee to take the initiative were considered. Requests for a Special Congress came from additional trade unions as well and carried much weight.[34] Furthermore, J. E. Williams of the National Union of Railwaymen and Herbert Smith of the Miners' Federation of Great Britain announced on behalf of their Executives that their organisations favoured holding a National Congress. After a long discussion, the Parliamentary Committee decided to convene the Special Congress. An amendment to the effect that holding a Congress would be no gain in time over the regular September Trades Union Congress lost by a vote of nine to five. The Parliamentary Committee's action convening a Special Trades Union Congress on June 30, 1916, in London was then made unanimous.[35]

To sum up, the great concern among workers over the unjust and repressive effects of wartime industrial developments generated a demand for action by the powerful industrial unions at the centre of war work as well as a large number of less-powerful organisations at the periphery of the war economy. It represented a decided shift away from the overwhelming earlier commitment to the war effort and a renewed assertion of working-class interests. The great welling-up of pressure from below that led to the threat of independent action by major trade union organisations forced the Parliamentary Committee of the Trades Union Congress to "climb down" from its strongly pro-war and pro-Government commitments and to come into line with its component organisations' more assertive position in defending trade union and working-class rights and standards. In short, these pressures enabled members to exercise control of the national federation's agenda.

THE SPECIAL TRADES UNION CONGRESS: LEADERS CAPITULATE

The Congress convened to consider the regulation of food and fuel prices, the increase of old-age pensions during the period of high prices, trade union organisation and administration, industrial conscription, conscription of riches, and the position of young men under eighteen years of age under the Military Service Act. This was precisely the agenda suggested by the War Emergency Committee in its correspondence to the Parliamentary Committee of the TUC and by the various trade unions and local labour organisations as being most urgent in the minds of their rank and file. By the time of the Congress, however, the Parliamentary Committee decided to put forward resolutions on these subjects in its own name. Its capitulation under the intense pressure of its affiliates was all too obvious. Yet, only by giving representation to these questions could it hope to check the militants' agitation for repeal of the Munitions and Conscription Acts. The resolutions it presented were in no way likely to inspire increased militancy, but were rather matter-of-fact expressions of grievances and remedies communicated to it. In the course of debate on the resolutions, militant pressures reasserted themselves. The most important resolutions from the delegates' point of view were the food and fuel prices question, the danger of industrial conscription, and the conscription of riches. In each case, the delegates strengthened the resolutions offered by the Parliamentary Committee.

The food and fuel prices resolution gathered the most enthusiasm and took up the greatest portion of the debate. F. Bramley (Furnishing Trades) moved the following composite resolution for the Parliamentary Committee:

That this Congress expresses its conviction that the government should at once take steps to regulate the prices of foodstuffs and fuel in order to prevent the exploitation of the working classes.[36]

In moving this resolution, Bramley emphasized how the workers were being exploited by their employers, often abetted by Acts of Parliament. The resolution contained specific proposals to stop profiteering, proposals which the Trades Union Congress, he hoped, would put to the Government. The war period had experienced an unprecedented increase in the cost of living, resulting in a "considerable reduction in the purchasing power of the sovereign." From July 25, 1914, to May 1, 1916, the cost of living rose 59 percent. This was no accident. Employers were taking advantage of the war to make huge profits. According to Bramley,

The shipowners had shown their appreciation of the services and sacrifices of the men of our Navy by acting in such a way as to increase substantially the cost of living to the dependents of those men left at home; the wives and widows, the mothers and the children of the men who were shedding their blood on the battlefields of Europe had to pay more for their bread on account of the greed and rapacity of the shipowners, the coalowners, and the food monopolists of Great Britain.[37]

This state of affairs was a "grave national scandal" and produced disunity in the nation.

To allow monopolists to grow rich at the expense of the poor was wrong at any time, to allow them in a period of great national crisis and anxiety to make profits undreamt of in times of peace was to allow the perpetuation of a crime against the community.[38]

In seconding the resolution, J. Cross (Textile Workers) asserted that the Government would have to be compelled to move to stop blatant profiteering. It was up to them to take action.

J. Wignall of the Dockers' Union then moved an amendment to strengthen the resolution. The Dockers wanted the resolution to call for the ownership as well as the control of shipping. Although he did not want to defeat the object of the resolution by suggesting something too drastic, he felt that it was important to let the Government know what the Congress meant by control. "They [the Trades Union Congress] ought to say that control meant ownership and thus have absolute and complete control." J. Stokes, in seconding the amendment on behalf of the London Glass Blowers, said that the "root of the disease was in the ownership and control by a capitalist class." Only ownership would give the control that could check unrepentant exploitation, and this applied not only to shipping but to "land, mines, railways, and all the things that went to make up the well-being of life." E. Cathery of the Seamen found Government Departments unreliable and untrustworthy and thought it was time for the Seamen to do their own work in improving their situation. The amendment was put and carried by 1,516,000 to 1,269,000 on a card vote. The Trades Union Congress delegates were determined to control prices and establish justice, and that meant industrial reorganisation in the interest of the workmen. The increasing assertion of class interests, while gaining only a narrow victory on this vote, underpinned and foreshadowed Clause IV and socialism in the Labour Party.

After the resolution was amended by two further provisions, one calling for penalties for holding up food stocks and one stipulating that children be given an adequate supply of milk, Robert Williams moved an amendment on behalf of the National Amalgamated Labourers' Union (an affiliate of the National Transport Workers Federation of which Williams was Secretary) aimed at putting some real force behind the original resolution. It added the following to Subsection 3:

If the Government offers objection to all or any of the foregoing recommendations, this Congress urges upon all Trade Unions, the members of which have not adequately protected themselves against increases in the cost of living, to take immediate steps to press forward prewar standards of life and physical efficiency.[39]

If the Government would not stabilize prices, then it was up to the workers themselves to restore a minimal standard of living, by whatever means they could find. He expected prices to continue to rise at an outrageous rate: they had already soared to 62 percent above the prewar level. He was convinced that "the overwhelming majority of the people were suffering from dire distress." Consequently, it was necessary for wages to follow prices. The amendment showed the only way in which they could protect themselves. Bellamy of the National Union of Railwaymen stated that the Congress needed some provisions for meeting the situation of no action by the Government. The National Union of Railwaymen leadership had at their recent Annual General Meeting persuaded their members to defer action on wage rises contingent upon the Government instituting a policy to regulate prices. He asserted that Government action would bring the "greatest good to the community," because everyone would benefit, not just those with the strongest industrial organisations. F. Bramley then spoke for the Parliamentary Committee, intimating that it wished the words to be dropped that gave the impression that the Congress thought the Government would oppose their proposals. But the feeling at the Congress, not sympathetic to that kind of argument, was more in line with the idea that, in the words of A. Gossip (Furnishing Trades), "[the delegates] would simply be making fools of themselves if they did not provide an alternative. They had found that the only way to make some people move was to put the fear of death into them."[40] The resolution as amended was put and carried unanimously. The resolution and debate clearly revealed that the rising cost of living forced organised labour to propose the "socialization" of industry for the collective interest of the working class.

The danger of industrial conscription was also the focus of the delegates' attention. As one of the delegates remarked in seconding a resolution on exempting trade union officials from the military, the absence of a direct vote on the conscription issue itself was a surprise. "He did think that when a Special Congress was going to be called one of the chief items would be a discussion on the question as to the repeal of the Conscription Acts altogether." But, if the Congress scrupulously avoided any confrontation on the Conscription Act itself, strong protest was registered against its administration. Again, delegates representing the more militant rank and file challenged the Parliamentary Committee's resolution. John Hill moved the following resolution:

That this Congress, finding that in actual practice the Military Service Acts and other measures passed by the Government, including the Munitions Acts, are being used for the purpose of industrial conscription, registers its protest and calls upon the Government to deal either by Orders in Council or immediate legislation with this grave menace to industrial labour.[41]

Hill stated that because the Parliamentary Committee believed that such restrictions were necessary in prosecuting the war, the resolution did not call for their repeal. The concessions agreed to by labour were temporary and guarantees were made that prewar arrangements would be restored. Yet, as the resolution stated, the Acts were being used for purposes for which they were not intended. Men in munitions industries who were desperately needed on the shopfloor found themselves in the colours. "What had to be done was not to repeal the Acts necessary for carrying on the war, but to see to it that they were not used for purposes for which they were not intended."[42] The Parliamentary Committee's position was a compromise. J. H. Thomas (National Union of Railwaymen), in seconding the resolution, stated his distrust of the Government's pledges regarding the abusive working of the Acts. In reference to specific features of the Conscription and Munitions Acts that gave employers the power of industrial conscription, Thomas said: "While they were willing and anxious to help their country in her hour of trial, they would be unworthy of their responsibility if they did not say that they were not going to stand by and allow their men to be victimized."[43] Militarism would not be ended by killing the trade union movement.

An attempt to get the Congress to repeal the Government's industrial and military Acts was then put forth by Ben Smith (Vehicle Workers). His amendment pledged the Congress "to use any and every means at its disposal to get the Acts repealed, and to remove a grave menace to industrial labour." The Acts were being used to force trade unionists into the army and this had to be stopped. Dawson (Spinners' Association) argued that rank-and-file militancy within the cotton unions was a product of industrial compulsion. He pleaded for the repeal of the Acts "on behalf of the thousands of men in the Trade Union movement who had been sacrificed to military service by the passing of the Military Service Acts." In his opinion, the real purpose of the Military Service Act was industrial conscription and only direct action would get it repealed. Tom Shaw (Textile Workers), a leading supporter of the Parliamentary Committee's pro-war policies, opposed the amendment. He was against political agitation for repeal of the Act, and asserted that the rank and file "would be the strongest opponents to the taking of such a step." It would, moreover, be a great mistake to reverse the decision of the Labour Party Conference. The amendment lost by 1,756,000 to 577,000. But the bloc votes of the Miners and the cotton unions clouded significant support for the amendment in their ranks. The support to repeal was far more popular than the defeat by over one million votes indicated.[44] Then, the original resolution as amended was carried. The feeling on this ran high, as the bitterness engendered by industrial conscription cut deeply into the class interests and traditions of the British trade unionist.

The last resolution taken up by the Congress that had significance for its determination to challenge its unequal sacrifice to the war effort dealt with the conscription of riches. Will Thorne moved the following resolution for the Parliamentary Committee:

> That this Congress expresses its opinion that the Government ought to have brought in a Bill for the conscription of riches as a natural corollary to the conscription of men, and calls upon the Government to take immediate steps in this direction.[45]

This was a reaffirmation of resolutions carried at the Bristol Trades Union Congress and the Bristol Labour Party Conference. Thorne believed that no one would oppose the principle expressed in the resolution. The conscription of wealth and profits was a bargaining counter to the conscription of men at the same time that it was a policy proposal designed to distribute the cost of the war. Workers firmly believed that they were unfairly burdened.

> Any employer who was making more money than he made in prewar days was absolutely immoral and it ought to be conscripted. All income over £1,000 should be conscripted in order that the idle rich should pay more.[46]

Stating that the general principle was not enough, T. E. Naylor (Compositors) moved an amendment that proposed "to (a) impose a war tax on personal wealth, and (b) increase the tax on earned and unearned incomes of over £500 per annum on a sliding scale rising to 20s. in the £." Naylor said the delegates were tired of "passing pious resolutions" and that they "were able to teach the Government how to get the money from persons who ought to pay instead of taxing the working classes of this and the next generation in order to pay for the war."[47] The amendment was agreed to and the amended resolution was then carried unanimously. As in the previous two resolutions, amendments from affiliated societies attempted to strengthen the Parliamentary Committee's lukewarm resolutions and made manifest the intensity of feeling that labour reassert its class interests, which the wartime conditions now threatened with extinction.

THE TRADES UNION CONGRESS: SUPPORT FOR A SOCIALIST REORGANISATION OF THE ECONOMY

Throughout the Spring and Summer months of 1916, there was a new spirit of working-class assertiveness within the trade union movement. This was aimed at both dealing with the day-to-day problems facing the workers and the development of proposals for the creation of a new social order after the war. Increasingly from March 1916 through January 1917, the attention of leaders and members alike turned to consideration of problems after the war. The Triple Alliance, for example, adopted resolutions on demobilization and the restoration of prewar conditions, which they presented to the Prime Minister. This new concern with after-the-war matters was reflected also in the writings of socialists. The guild socialist G. D. H. Cole and his co-author W. Mellor wrote weekly articles in the *Herald* on various aspects of how labour must deal with the eventual peace. The tremendous changes that had occurred in industry as well as within the trade union movement itself called for new ideas and interpretations. The Webbs, who had re-thought their ideas in the years 1912 to 1914 in response to the "great unrest" of the prewar period, had a leading role in formulating reconstruction proposals. Sidney Webb sat on the War Emergency Committee and the Labour Party Executive Committee, while Beatrice Webb worked on Government Reconstruction Committees. Many of his ideas were initially published in the *New Statesman*, but in the Summer of 1916 he felt compelled to appeal to a wider audience. In consequence, Webb ran a series of articles in late July and August in the popular, right-wing *Daily Mail* dealing with disbandment, the prevention of unemployment, industrial conflict, the "non-adult," and women in industry and scientific management. The socialist Independent Labour Party, however, gave less attention to "Labour After the War" problems, being more concerned with the war as an issue itself. Yet, the socialist thinkers and political parties fell behind the surging upthrust among the trade unions themselves for a new industrial and social structure, showing that it was the union rank and file that was exercising the greater influence.

Union activists imbued with the new spirit took the initiative again following the Special Trades Union Congress and inundated the Parliamentary Committee with resolutions for the September 1916 regular meeting of the TUC at Birmingham with what inadvertently amounted to a national program for reorganisation of industry after the war. *The Times* correspondent, in surveying the agenda, commented that the

general trend of the chief resolutions is in one direction. All point towards the re-organisation of industry and commerce, and seek to indicate, if not to define, a national programme to be prepared at once and worked for by labour in advance of the declaration of peace.[48]

At the Bristol Trades Union Congress, consideration of "Labour After the War" questions had been absent. A year later, the agenda was full of resolutions dealing with the "coming crisis." Yet, the question of war or peace was given little play, much to the chagrin of the militant Independent Labour Party and the editor of the *Herald*, George Lansbury. Rather, the attention of the trade union movement was firmly focused on industrial issues, and there was a determination to throw off the wartime restrictions and diminished standards as soon as possible. The resolutions of major importance dealt with various aspects of labour after the war, with military and industrial conscription, and with rising costs of necessities. All were put forth in response to deep feelings of rank-and file discontent. All were directed both at present problems as well as the future. And all demanded equality, justice, and liberty.

The high cost of living was the most pressing of all problems confronting the Labour movement, judged according to the prominent place it took on the agenda of the 1916 TUC Congress. The Boilermakers, who because of the absence of the Engineers were the most influential craft union belonging to the Congress, the Scottish Dock Labourers, and the Bookbinders introduced resolutions which demanded that the Government take action.[49] Moreover, a resolution from the National Amalgamated Labourers' Union criticized the way in which the members of the Parliamentary Committee had acted contrary to the interests of the men. It protested against those responsible for "Labour's participation in the Government's economy conference last year" which had prejudiced its claims for increased wages in the face of rising costs.[50] Next, there was "a large group" of resolutions dealing with conscription, many repetitious of those carried at previous conferences. The Vehicle Workers called for the repeal of "all Acts imposing economic, industrial, and military compulsion" and the "reestablishment of individual liberty, with the right voluntarily to refrain from organised destruction." Yet, the main body of resolutions expressed the general feeling that compulsory military service was a necessary evil to be immediately repealed "after the War," as the Northern Counties Weavers intimated in their amendment to the Vehicle Workers' resolution. If the bulk of trade unionists were not prepared to press repeal of the Acts during the war, they nonetheless felt that there should be immediate conscription of wealth.[51] The resolutions dealing with the position of labour after the war were legion and covered a great deal of ground. The most important were one by the Parliamentary Committee concerned with the restoration of trade union rights, one dealing with industrial adjustments after the war from the London Compositors, and one focusing on the problems of demobilization from the Liverpool Dockers. These resolutions made it clear that Labour was not going to leave events after the war in the hands of the capitalists or the Government. Various trade unions, under pressures from discontented members, had come to a common recognition: that greater justice for the workers required state planning and control of industry and employment. These resolutions revealed a general trend, involving the "pronounced movement in favour of nationalisation and organisation."[52]

The debate on the increased cost-of-living resolution stirred the Congress "more deeply" than any other topic. John Hill of the Boilermakers moved the resolution of the Scottish Dock Labourers, the Boilermakers and Bookbinders having, respectively, consented to withdraw their resolutions. The resolution expressed the widespread feeling that the intensified hardship of the war was without justification and that only Government regulation in the interests of the common people would end the malicious schemes of profiteers.

That this Congress . . . declares that the Government has failed to give proper attention to the serious grievances the masses of the people are suffering under by reason of the enormous and unjustifiable increase in the cost of living. It views with alarm the indifference of responsible statesmen to this subject, and, in view of the continued rise in the price of almost every necessary of life, remits to the Parliamentary Committee to place before the Government and the Labour Party the urgent necessity of immediate steps being taken to secure a revision of the prices of all such commodities, either by finding maximum prices or taking full control of supplies into their own hands in the interests of the people, and thus prevent them from being systematically robbed as they are at present.[53]

This was the most pressing grievance of the Trades Union Congress's constituents.[54] The central points in the debate on this resolution were the inequality of sacrifice and the threats of drastic action. I. Hill, the resolution's mover, pointed out that previous efforts to get the Government to act on this issue had been fruitless. Real wages had fallen and this resolution again asked that the Congress do "something immediately and urgently to mitigate this persistent evil." The workers deserved just treatment.

I think the sooner we get the Government to recognize that the workers of this country are not going to be the only people to be compelled to set aside the means for securing a proper return for their labour the better it will be for all concerned. War or no war, we must require that we shall be fairly treated, and I say we have not been fairly treated, so long as the Government allows our real wages to be depreciated, after we have given up all we can in the interests of the national cause.[55]

Hogan (Bookbinders), speaking in support of the resolution, also pointed to the inequality of sacrifice. Men had given up life-long principles, and others had refrained from industrial action that might have jeopardized the war effort. "Surely we have some claim to consideration at the hands of the Government under these circumstances." The delegates knew all too well the discontent among the membership resulting from a decline in real wages, despite increased work. What interested those who spoke on this resolution most was getting some action.

Delegates also threatened industrial action to wake up the Government, several indicating that the Parliamentary Committee could do nothing more. J. Houghton of the Scottish Dock Labourers saw the inevitability of strike action, in view of the failure of past efforts of the Parliamentary Committee and their deputations to the Prime Minister.

They [the Government] will not do anything, and there is no hope that they ever will do anything until we take the matter into our own hands and do what we do not want to do. I would not think of recommending a stoppage of work while the war is on. I am only one of the rank and file of the workers; but I mix among the men and women, and I know what they are saying. Whether the Government likes it or not, if they are not very careful, they will find that the men themselves will force this question to an issue in the only possible way, if they will not listen to the Parliamentary Committee when they try to get relief in a constitutional way. (Cheers)[56]

Bramley found Prime Minister Asquith's reply to the Trades Union Congress deputation following the Special Trades Union Congress insulting, and, in view of the continued rise in prices, felt that drastic action was necessary. He suggested that all trade unions and trade councils at all levels protest at the rising prices in the most strenuous way. Finally, J. Bromley of the Amalgamated Society of Locomotive Engineers and Firemen made light of Bramley's suggestion. Nothing had come from the protest at the Special Trades Union Congress nor the deputation to the Prime Minister. In response to the challenge of representing the desires of the members in this new and uncharted matter, he saw the need for something drastic, since "desperate diseases require desperate remedies, and we know that nothing has been gained by the Labour Party or by Trade Unionism in this country without really showing fight."[57] Moreover, it was the duty of the larger unions "to stand firm with the rest of the movement and tell the Government that there must be no more fooling upon this question." He proposed that the Congress adjourn and lobby the Government en masse. Needless to say, the resolution carried unanimously. As the *Manchester Guardian* reported,

It was clear from the general tone of the discussion that the increase in the cost of living and the suspicion that much of the gain is going into the pockets of private exploiters stirred the Congress more deeply than any other subject that has come before it during the week.[58]

The high-cost-of-living question was the leading factor in convincing the trade union movement of the need for State ownership and control of industry in the public interest. For the first time, a general statement proposing the ownership and control by the State of industry came before a main representative organisation. This was the resolution on the National Organisation of Industry, tabled for the Congress by the Parliamentary Committee as early as April 27.[59] On June 22, however, the Parliamentary Committee discussed the resolution, and differences of opinion resulted in its being withdrawn from the agenda under its auspices and submitted by the Boilermakers' Union. In the end, the resolution looks rather like a composite of the food and fuel resolution carried by the Special Trades Union Congress and a proposal for a Ministry of Labour. The distinguishing characteristic of the resolution is its general demand for the national ownership and control of industry in the national interest.[60] It touches upon the failure of the prewar Industrial system and the need for its reform.

Our vital industries should no longer be left in the hands of capitalists whose first object is profits, and workers whose first object is wages. Such industries should be regulated by the State in the national interest.

The resolution then goes on to propose a Minister of Labour and Industry whose function would be to control and organise the following:

1) Health of the Workers—The wage-earners, being the largest and most important asset of the nation, should have the first care of the nation; therefore all workshops, factories, and offices shall conform to a national standard of sanitation calculated to ensure, as far as possible, the safety and health of the workers employed.
2) Housing—The provision of adequate sanitary housing accommodation, where such is not already obtainable at reasonable rates.
3) Agriculture and Food Supply
   a) National control and direction of use of all land,
   b) Security of tenure for tenants,
   c) Shipping—State have first claim and rates at fixed national standard of profit,
   d) Nationally owned and controlled storehouses, with reserves of grain, frozen meat, dried fish, and other necessary food.
4) War Munitions, Ships, Railways, Mines, etc.
   a) Complete national ownership and production of all war material and ships of war, including the auxiliary ships necessary for national emergencies,
   b) National ownership and control of all railways, waterways, and mines.[61]

The Boilermakers' member of the Parliamentary Committee, J. Hill, moved the resolution, which was passed enthusiastically. The fact that the Government had to take over the railways and munitions factories and guarantee the business of banks showed that the present organisation of industry was a failure, Hill contended. The Furnishing Trades had asked that the Parliamentary Committee set out a "Charter of Trade Union Organisation," and here was the Parliamentary Committee's product. This represented "the first programme which that body [the Parliamentary Committee] has ever made itself responsible for in the matter of economic reconstruction," according to J. Jones of the National General Workers. The resolution, he asserted, was in the right direction, because it was about time the Parliamentary Committee stopped promoting policies that did injury to the working class. Other delegates offered their support and each seemed to want to participate in the bandwagon effect created by this resolution. B. Wild of the Amalgamated Society of Locomotive Engineers and Firemen wanted shipping and Parliament nationalized, whereas Ben Smith of the Vehicle Workers spoke up for the inclusion of all public services and transport.

On the conscription issue, the Birmingham Congress went beyond the Special Trades Union Congress resolution protesting the oppressive aspects of its administration. This resolution instructed the Parliamentary Committee to "lose no opportunity after the war to press for the repeal of all Acts of Parliament imposing economic, industrial, and military compulsion."[62] It was a composite resolution, consisting of the National Vehicle Workers' resolution demanding immediate repeal and the Weavers' amendment to repeal the Act after the war. W. Godfrey (Vehicle Workers), who moved the resolution, expressed fear of continued militarism and the destruction of trade unionism. But this danger was familiar to all delegates. The chief concern of J. H. Thomas (National Union of Railwaymen) and Will Thorne (National General Workers) was that the duration of the war was controlled by the same people who were responsible for the Conscription Act. Only a concerted and successful effort to have a majority of Labour Members of Parliament in the House of Commons would assure its repeal. By September 1916, the conscription issue was coming under the special province of the Labour Party, although some sections of the union movement readily would use industrial might if the political path proved impotent. The movement was unanimous in its opposition to conscription and more determined than ever to resist it in both principle and practice.

Two other important resolutions called for the transfer of wealth from the rich to pay for the war and outlined a policy to preserve the industrial future of the nation. The Cigar Makers, the Bleachers and Dyers, Agricultural Labourers, Pottery Workers, and the Dockers, the only one representing workers in central war industries, demanded the conscription of wealth. Ben Cooper (Cigar Makers) said that wealth should be used to pay off the National Debt and keep interest payments at a minimum. Increased taxation to cover interest on the debt meant higher prices that would only hurt the working class further, and ultimately all of industry.

So far as one can see at present, the borrowings in connection with this war, if unchecked, are calculated to bring about the ruin of the workers of the future; and that is why we should insist upon wealth being made to bear its proper share of the cost of this war. (Cheers)[63]

The resolution insisted that this demand was justified by the conscription of men "to resist foreign aggression, the maintenance of freedom, and the protection of capital." It also instructed the Parliamentary Committee to initiate a major campaign for the conscription of wealth. A resolution concerning industry after the war consisted of proposals from the Fawcett Association, the National Federation of Women Workers, and the London Compositors. Their intent was to organise industry to minimize the difficulty of economic reconstruction and social reform after the war. The resolution called for increased taxation on various kinds of wealth, a program of full employment, and the acquisition of the railways, mines, shipping, banking, and insurance by the State. Thus, in resolutions unanimously agreed to, state ownership and a proposal to transfer the nation's wealth into use for the public interest gained further support as key elements in the TUC's reconstruction program. Webb preferred the immediate conscription of wealth because he believed it likely to be more successful than the nationalization of industry and the concomitant transfer of administrative control. In the event, conscription of wealth was a firmly held policy proposal of the Trades Union Congress, nearly a year before the War Emergency Committee and Webb gave it more precise form in mid-1917.

Finally, there were numerous resolutions dealing with various aspects of easing dislocation after the war, such as demobilization and pensions to soldiers and sailors. But two important resolutions deserve mention because they typify the new spirit of the trade union movement in striving not only to correct the wartime grievances arising out of increased exploitation but also to improve upon the unions' prewar position. The first is a resolution on industrial adjustments after the war which was moved by T. E. Naylor on behalf of the London Compositors. Its purpose was to "preserve industrial peace" through increasing trade union unity and strength. It called for compulsory trade union membership, a forty-eight–hour week, a minimum wage of 30s. per week for all adult workers, and employers' complete recognition of all trade unions. Naylor claimed that these policies would enable the labour movement to negotiate with employers and the Government from a position of unity, "in order that when the boys come home they shall secure as some return for the sacrifices they have made during the war a fairer share of the wealth they are called upon to produce."[64] What the workers wanted and deserved was a better life and a new status in society. The workers would say to the employers:

We have done these things in the national interest, we have helped the Government when we might have stopped the progress of the war by withholding our labour, and we ask you now to recognize the position which we took up during the war. We ask you to admit that these demands of ours—more generous concessions and a greater share of the wealth produced, a higher standard of living, higher rates of pay for the lower-paid workers—are quite reasonable in character, representing concessions which we have a right to expect in return for what Labour has done in support of the nation in the greatest crisis of its history.[65]

These words evoked great enthusiasm from the delegates. This resolution carried with great support, even though some delegates were apprehensive about its closed-shop clause. The delegates recognized that there had to be a "big attempt to bring about the reconstruction of industrial conditions after the war."

The discussion of the other resolution, the restoration of trade union rights, revealed a sense of urgency as well as a recognition that it was up to the trade union movement itself to see a realization of the proposals and policies it demanded. The resolution, reflecting mainly the interests of craftsmen, demanded that the Government insist that employers fulfil their promises to labour to restore prewar conditions, and in the event that such promises were broken, it called upon the Parliamentary Committee to convene a Special Trades Union Congress with Government Ministers in attendance. It was moved by W. J. Davis, who put patriotism before working-class interests, on behalf of the Parliamentary Committee:

We have done everything possible to meet the exigencies of the national crisis, and we expect the Government of the day, whatever its complexion, to see that our rights and privileges are restored and that we are not betrayed.[66]

But the majority of delegates did not agree that Governments could be relied upon to protect workers' interests. Mary Macarthur (Women

Workers' Federation) expressed the feelings of most of the delegates when she warned that they should not be content with Ministers' promises. "Let us organise ourselves, and let the men and women determine to stand together in face of the common enemy we shall have to meet."[67] W. A. Robinson (Warehouse Workers) agreed that only greater reliance on their own organisation and action would advance workers' interests. He believed that their own leaders had failed them and that certainly no Minister or employer would act along lines of this "pious" resolution.[68] Again, he had found a point that was enthusiastically received by the delegates. The delegates would no longer trust "Government officials, Cabinet Ministers, and employers generally."

These "Labour After the War" policy proposals reflected a major change in the spirit of rank-and-file trade unionists. This was a constructive spirit of defence against inequality of sacrifice which had inspired the strongest and most influential as well as many of the weakest groups of workers to mount an offensive that, in common with those unskilled sections whose circumstances probably improved as a result of the war, would seek a fairer and more prosperous society after the war. And it was a spirit which reflected a shift in the relations of power within the unions. While the responses of rank-and-file activists to the conditions arising out of the war and the questions of labour after the war differed in relations to the specific problems faced by each section of organised workers, workgroup determination to rectify felt injustices compelled leaders to act on their behalf or be repudiated through independent rank-and-file action, at least in the most extreme cases. While it is difficult to draw conclusions about rank-and-file attitudes from the actions and statements of leaders, the special circumstances of war— the sense of injustice among the organised rank and file, the multiplicity of complaints, the demand for labour, and the widespread disaffection from authority—make it more likely than not that the actions of those delegates to the 1916 TUC Congress were genuinely representative of membership aspirations. No doubt, the efforts of delegates to strengthen several key resolutions put forward by the Parliamentary Committee reveal the pressure under which many union leaders operated.

THE "LABOUR AFTER THE WAR" PROGRAM AND THE LABOUR PARTY

Between September 1916 and January 1917, the labour movement's attention shifted to the Labour Party and its policy-making Conference.

The Asquith Coalition was replaced in December by a new Coalition Government headed by Lloyd George. The laissez-faire liberals like Asquith were to sit out the rest of the war. This political crisis yielded significant benefits for Labour. Lloyd George offered Labour more positions in the Coalition Government and hence greater influence in running the war, and agreed to several policies demanded by the recent TUC Congress, including the nationalization of shipping and mines and a Ministry of Labour. No doubt, while these policy sops by Lloyd George did not fulfil all the demands of Labour, they were in the right direction and, accordingly, held great appeal for organised labour. Moreover, the political question of whether or not Labour should participate in the new Coalition raised the issues of Labour's position toward the war, its success in promoting working-class concerns, and whether or not it had thrown away its independence.

While these issues emerged during the Labour Party Conference in late January 1917, during a long and heated debate on the National Executive Committee's and the Parliamentary Labour Party's decision to join the Coalition, the National Executive Committee, like the leaders of the TUC several months earlier, gave form to the assertiveness of the rank and file by getting at the head of the momentum for a comprehensive after-the-war policy. This well-formulated comprehensive policy constituted a turning point in the development of British socialism. For the first time, the Party adopted a comprehensive program that contained the general outlines of British socialism's planned economy and welfare state. This provided the basis for Clause IV in the 1918 Constitution and the Party's 1918 program "Labour and the New Social Order." Given a consensus among the trade unions that State ownership and control of the means of production were the only way in which justice could be established, these proposals aimed at a social reconstruction to guide the nation when seven or eight million war workers would return to the labour market. Their essential design was to use the State's powers to organise the economy for peacetime full employment and social services in order to give the workers a fairer share of the nation's wealth. The chief means to these ends was the nationalization of production, administered with the participation of the workers, and Government action to coordinate manpower with jobs and to maintain the aggregate demand for labour. The development of this socialist consensus within the industrial wing of organised labour was manifest at the June Special Trades Union Congress and the regular September

Congress of the TUC. There was a great deal of overlapping of personnel and constituents with the Labour Party. Even so, it is important to clarify just how the Labour Party's comprehensive "Labour After the War" Program came into being.

The Initiative

The first question to be answered is why the National Executive Committee decided to make "Labour After the War" questions the major policy issue of the Conference. At the same time that affiliates of the Trades Union Congress were inundating the Parliamentary Committee with demands for a Special Trades Union Congress, the Labour Party was being requested to convene a National Conference to consider the effects of the extension of the Conscription Act.[69] The Carpenters and Joiners, the Cumberland Ore Miners and the Halifax Trades Council called upon the Labour Party to hold a Special Conference.[70] Naturally, the Trades Union Congress action meant that the Labour Party need not act. But requests that the Labour Party hold a Conference on "Labour After the War" problems continued to pile up. And as rank-and-file bodies began to take action on their own to formulate postwar policies, pressure on the Labour Party to also focus on them mounted. On June 30, 1916, the National Executive Committee dealt with a letter from the Workers' Union, urging the Executive to hold a National Conference on "Labour Problems After the War." The Workers' Union was a large and very rapidly expanding union of unskilled labourers, whose position at the end of the war would be very much in jeopardy.[71] The Birmingham Trades and Labour Council sent a series of resolutions on "Problems of Labour and the War" adopted by the Council on July 1, 1916, to the War Emergency Committee.[72] And Newcastle sent resolutions passed at their meetings on "Labour After the War" to the Labour Party on September 28 and October 12.[73]

While it is difficult to assess the influence that resolutions from affiliates had on the Executive, in all likelihood the spontaneous action among local union organisations was less important to the national Party leadership than pressure from large unions. In addition to the Workers' Union, it is clear that at least the Amalgamated Society of Locomotive Engineers and Firemen called upon the Party to deal with "Labour After the War" matters. In a letter to the War Emergency Committee, Bromley indicated that his Executive at a recent meeting "considered the question of the Party nationally making some preparation to deal with" problems after the war. Branch resolutions had requested the Executive Committee to initiate a National Conference on these questions, and so the Executive Committee instructed him to approach the Labour Party to consider the advisability of such a Conference.[74] No doubt, too, the demand from the Scottish Advisory Council, a body of all Scottish Labour organisations affiliated to the Labour Party, for a Conference on postwar problems influenced the National Executive Committee.[75] Finally, a decisive factor was the character of the resolutions for the Annual Conference received by the Labour Party Executive from its affiliates. There was no coordination between the unions, the Trades Councils, or local Labour Parties. Yet, the resolutions submitted were overwhelmingly concerned with problems facing "Labour After the War." For example, in mid-September 1916, the National Union of Railwaymen's Executive Committee carried a resolution that was to be placed on the Labour Party agenda at the suggestion of two of its members most in touch with the rank and file, dealing with the problem of unemployment after the war and the necessity of reducing the hours of the normal work week.[76] By November 1, 1916, it was already clear from a printed version of the Labour Party Conference agenda that "Labour After the War" issues were the central concern of its affiliates.

Leaders Bow to Demand for a "New Social Order"

In October 1916, the National Executive Committee discussed the "advisability" of devoting the January 1917 Conference at Manchester wholly to the resolutions on "Labour After the War" problems. It also considered the possibility of having a full discussion at the Conference on the resolutions. In the event, it resolved to meet on November 3 to discuss the resolutions received from the affiliated societies and debate the possibilities of submitting Executive proposals on "Labour After the War" problems. It also instructed the Head Office to circulate as many of the resolutions already received as possible before that meeting.[77] It surveyed the work of the various After the War Committees and noted that only the Advisory Committee on the Restoration of Trade Union Conditions had a number of memoranda prepared. The other Committees had memoranda in preparation. At the November 3 National Executive Committee meeting, the resolutions which had been received for the Manchester Conference were discussed. The National Executive

Committee then decided to arrange to start the Conference one day earlier in order to permit fuller discussion of the various aspects of "Labour After the War" problems. It appointed a Committee to draft the Executive Committee's resolutions on (1) restoration of trade union conditions, (2) demobilization, (3) unemployment, and (4) the position of women.[78] In the end, the final list of NEC resolutions was more inclusive. In short, the Executive Committee's decision to make "Labour After the War" the main topic of the Conference represented an effort to get on top of the concerns of a wide variety of its affiliates and reflected the particular substance and number of actual resolutions submitted by those affiliates.

Despite what many recognized as the hand of Sidney Webb in the Executive Committee's resolutions, it would be a mistake to jump to the conclusion that Webb's Fabian socialism had finally overtaken the Labour Party. The Executive Committee's reconstruction proposals not only mirrored the contents of the resolutions spontaneously submitted by its affiliates but they also constituted a compilation of fragmentary and overlapping resolutions that touched upon all aspects of "Labour After the War." Webb apparently pressed his Executive Committee colleagues as early as October to use the affiliates' resolutions as the basis of a "Labour After the War" policy, because he thought they would yield "an impressive and consistent programme."[79] The evidence for this conclusion comes from the Chairman of the National Executive Committee. Wardle, writing in the *Railway Review*, asserted that the Executive Committee "prepared a series of resolutions dealing with these problems, based on resolutions already sent in by the various societies."[80] The Executive Committee made every effort to amend, extend, and improve upon the submitted resolutions in order to present a "considered and logical programme." The *New Statesman*, a Fabian organ, confirms this view.

Nor is this programme the product of any one personality, or the outcome of any particular school of thought. It is almost wholly compiled from the resolutions ... which have been spontaneously sent in by the four hundred organisations representing every imaginable industry in all parts of Great Britain.[81]

And the Independent Labour Party's *Labour Leader*, expressing surprise at "how many points the various sections" still agreed on, reported that the "somewhat fragmentary resolutions sent up by the affiliated societies on these after-war subjects do not differ materially from the Executive proposals.''[82] It was not an ideological *tour de force*, but a pragmatic guide to reconstruction, having a common thread of ''more deliberate Organisation'' and ''increased efficiency in all its social and industrial machinery.'' While the proposals did signify a call for more organisation and efficiency, they did not represent a capitulation to strictly Fabian tenets of reliance on greater bureaucratization. Trade unions were adamantly opposed to increased bureaucracy in Government, having had such bad experiences with it. It was pragmatic class concerns that undergirded these proposals, not realization of a commitment to principles like organisation and efficiency. The state had proven itself by concentrating control during the war, and it was necessary to continue the exercise of this concentrated state power on behalf of the workers if justice were to be achieved in times of peace. Thus, trade unions arrived at a ''Labour After the War'' Program that only superficially resembled Fabian Socialism; in fact, it was the necessity of a pragmatic response to the wartime industrial and political conditions that focused their varied concerns around the need to control the state.

But the Manchester Conference in January 1917 laid out a ''Labour After the War'' policy that was more than a manifestation of demands for increased organisation. It constituted an outline of the Labour Party's full-blown democratic socialism. The cornerstones were a planned economy, welfare services, and civil, political, and industrial liberties. Underpinning every aspect was a desire to establish justice and equality for the working class, a desire which the wartime experiences made imperative. In order to rectify deeply felt grievances, the political economy would have to be guided by deliberate effort.

The main elements of the state-regulated economy were nationalization, full employment, and taxation policies. The Executive's resolutions called for nationalization of railways, mines, banking, land, and foodstuffs. All of these were suggested in resolutions submitted by ten different affiliated organisations. The Amalgamated Society of Locomotive Engineers and Firemen submitted two resolutions calling for railway nationalization, a long-standing policy demand of all railway unions. What made it clearly distinct from Fabian ideology was its call for workers' participation in the management at local and national levels. The Miners and the North Monmouthshire Labour Party restated the policy demand for mines nationalization, and the Executive's resolution, like that on Railways, advocated a share in the control of the industry for the workman. It also called for nationalization of the distribution of coal, not just its production. In moving the resolution, Robert Smillie indicated an intellectual debt to Webb for his booklet on nationalization of coal. But he went on to say why the Miners themselves became convinced that nationalization was appropriate.

They did not think that the conditions of their class ought to be decided by capitalistic competition and bargaining on the market. They did not think that the public consumer should be left to the tender mercies of the exploiter.[83]

Nationalization of mines would provide higher and more stable wages. The rate of accidents, a matter of great concern to the Miners, would decline. These were reasons that had been continuously and seriously debated in conferences of the Miners' Federation of Great Britain. Further, the resolution on agriculture, mirroring resolutions received on the cost of living, proposed Government control of agricultural land, state farms for production, and organised distribution of food. National ownership of the land was the only solution to its unfair and inadequate utilization for the people of the nation. Finally, MacDonald moved for the Executive Committee a resolution on taxation, which was a reworked composite of resolutions submitted on taxation and nationalization of land. It called for the conscription of "accumulated wealth," increased taxes on unearned income and land, and the complete nationalization of banking "in order to free the community from private exploitation." C. T. Cramp pinpointed the delegates' sentiments when he asserted: "Many would have liked to have seen taxation during the War securing some equality of sacrifice and some system should be devised whereby all superfluous incomes should be diverted to the needs of the State."[84]

If national state ownership of production was the means to bring an end to exploitation of the workers, it was equally necessary to protect the value of labour when the demobilized flooded the labour market in excess. Another series of resolutions dealing with manpower policy after the war aimed at easing the transition to a peacetime economy and protecting workers against even greater exploitation of their labour.

Resolutions from the Executive dealing with the machinery for securing employment, demobilization, and the prevention of unemployment, although mirroring resolutions from affiliates, show the technical work of the After the War Committees and Webb in their elaboration. The resolution calling for Government machinery to ensure employment

for the "disbanded soldiers and discharged munitions workers" dealt
with improvement in the Employment Exchanges, which was the point
of a resolution submitted from the London Trades Council. The resolution dealing with demobilization plans asserted the need for "deliberate National Organisation." It wanted the Government to present its
own plan to assist the returning soldiers, as requested by Wolverhampton
Trades and Labour Council. It went on, however, to call for the demobilization to correspond to the demands for labour "required for the
revival of peace production" and to prevent any congestion. Moreover,
it proposed a series of Governmental provisions and benefits to assist
the workmen during the transition. Lastly, the prevention of unemployment resolution was based on a resolution submitted by the Fabian
Society, demanding that the Government arrange public works so as to
"maintain the aggregate demand for labour." It went on to specify
various areas wherein public works would be useful, such as rehousing
and new roads. Moreover, this resolution demanded that the Government institute a forty-eight–hour week in order to help meet the problem
of unemployment. The Executive Committee had in hand four resolutions making this demand, including that of the National Union of
Railwaymen. Nonetheless, it is this series of resolutions, policies requiring more technical competence, which reveal the greatest contribution from the Executive Committee's Subcommittee that drafted the
resolutions through the pen of Sidney Webb.

Other Executive resolutions focused on safeguarding the position of
groups of workers who had benefitted from wartime employment. This
objective was manifest in two resolutions demanding the maintenance
of standard rates of pay and a guaranteed minimum wage. These Executive resolutions followed the lead given in proposals on minimum
wages from the Chatham and District Trades and Labour Council and
the Manchester and Salford Labour Party as well as a resolution on the
position of women after the war. The minimum wage proposal of 30s.
per week that carried at the Birmingham Trades Union Congress was
reaffirmed. As one delegate emphasized, "the Government should see
to it that no worker worked and starved at the same time."[85] But the
transition to peace would require temporary assistance while men and
women were unemployed. The demobilization resolution spoke to this
issue, demanding unemployment benefits and gratuities. War pensions
were a deep-felt concern of the trade union movement and quite a few
resolutions demanded adequate pensions for soldiers and sailors as well

as their dependents.[86] The "Labour After the War" Program included welfare provisions, but the force of its main proposals was directed toward reorganisation of the means of production as the most suitable means to betterment of the working class.

Two resolutions dealt with the restoration of trade union conditions. This was one of the movement's main preoccupations, especially of the craft unions, and was the method of protecting wage-earners from possible reduction of wages and harsh discipline in the factory. The resolution in the name of the Executive was derived from an Amalgamated Society of Engineers' resolution, although it lacked the specificity of the ASE's proposal. The Executive Committee resolution called upon the Government to remember that it was "pledged unreservedly and unconditionally" to the restoration after the war of all "rules, conditions and customs that prevailed before the War." Moreover, all changes introduced in the factories for the purpose of diluting the workforce must be abrogated. Any resistance by employers would be met with the full force of the Government's authority. A second resolution proposed by the ASE and supported by five other organisations calling for the repeal of restrictive legislation dealt with machinery by which restoration would be accomplished. This demanded the return of the right to strike and the end of compulsory arbitration. It also demanded an end to all restrictive legislation "directed against workpeople" immediately after the war. The Conference agreed that the control over work rights and customs should not be allowed to fall into the hands of unscrupulous employers and that the best means of promoting the rights of workmen were the time-tested trade union methods.

The "Labour After the War" Program constituted a comprehensive democratic socialist policy. It advocated the reorganisation of industry under State ownership and control, shared in part by the workers and operated in the public interest. Full industrial and political liberties were also demanded. It was a program intended to protect the workers' interests after the war, but it was a policy framed in response to the intensified exploitation during the war and to the power of the State to determine labour's well-being. What is more, it was a program that emerged from the uncoordinated resolutions spontaneously sent in for the Manchester Conference. The Executive, in response to pressures from its affiliates, used them to develop a consistent and complete set of "Labour After the War" proposals. What identifies the influence of the members' pressure is not only the direct pressure in the form of resolutions but indirect threats that unions would turn elsewhere if the Labour Party leadership failed to respond to their interests. This surge of rank-and-file protest, given form by an active minority and then by trade union leaders, translated into an intense and widespread support for a radical industrial policy designed to countermand the wartime exploitation.

The War Issue Still Divides Labour

If the Labour Party united around a full-fledged socialist policy program by January 1917, the decision to join the Lloyd George Coalition led many of its members to fear that continued support for a pro-war foreign policy might threaten the new consensus and divide the Party. While the decision to participate in the Coalition of December 1916 indicated substantial support for continuing to prosecute the war until a decisive victory could be won, Labour was increasingly divided on this issue. This question was considered in a debate at the 1917 Conference on the Executive's Report, which detailed the facts of the meetings with Lloyd George, the majority vote of the Parliamentary Labour Party and the National Executive Committee to accept the Prime Minister's invitation and assignment of Labour representatives to various positions in the new Government. The Parliamentary Labour Party and National Executive Committee met Lloyd George on December 7, 1916, to hear him assert his aim of making everything "subservient" to the relentless prosecution of the war. Lloyd George indicated the offices he held open for the Labour representatives and announced his aim of taking control of the mines and shipping as well as taking charge of food distribution, the home production of food-stuffs, and mobilization of labour. The Labour officials accepted his invitations and received three Cabinet-level appointments, including Arthur Henderson, M.P., as member of the War Cabinet of five, and John Hodge, M.P., as the first Minister of Labour.[87]

At the 1917 Manchester Conference, Henderson moved the adoption of the report. Cleverly, he drew upon the delegates' loyalty to their country and to their Party, noting that the national crisis required that they should concern themselves with what they could give.[88] He was proud of the policy concessions offered by Lloyd George. Moreover, he invoked the fact that the earlier Bristol Conference had endorsed the action of the Party entering the Asquith Coalition.

Therefore, he hoped that in view of the fact that they had acted in what they thought were the best interests of the country and consistently with the decisions of the last Conference, the delegates were prepared to confirm that action.[89]

In the final analysis, the Conference needed to reassure the world that they were firmly committed to the prosecution of the war to a successful conclusion. He believed that at the conclusion of the debate the

message that would go forth would be that they were not weakening in their position, that they were as determined today as they were in August 1914, to carry the War to a successful termination, and that they believed they could best assist in doing that by allowing the Labour Members in the Government to carry on the work they had undertaken.[90]

Support for the resolution also came from staunch backers of the war effort, J. H. Thomas, Clynes, Sexton, Gilmour and Shaw. One leader, Thomas, reaffirmed his commitment to fight industrial conscription and to work for the State control of mines and shipping. But he was afraid that if Labour stayed outside the Government, it would weaken the war effort.

He thought it would be fatal to the best interests of the Movement to reject the Report. That would mean that their men must come out of the Government. There would be no alternative then but a General Election. He was afraid of anything that was going to weaken the country, that was going to dishearten those who had already sacrificed so much.[91]

The same argument had come up at the Bristol Conference and had weighed heavily with the bulk of the movement. Loyalty to the nation and to the Party's own past commitments was necessary in the time of crisis.

Opposition to the report came from the British Socialist Party and the Independent Labour Party, although there were large minority sections in each of the trade unions that were sympathetic to their cause. F. Bramley of the Furnishing Trades spoke under Independent Labour Party auspices. He asked what definite intentions Lloyd George had in mind when he referred to control of the mines. He feared that a vote for the report constituted a blank cheque of approval for the Government. C. G. Ammon of the Bermondsey Labour Party and an Independent Labour Party Spokesman suggested that Lloyd George had degraded political life and that the Labour members of the Government were hostages for the good behaviour of Labour.

Everything they had fought and striven for in the past was being taken away from them. They must take the matter in their own hands, dictate their own terms that they were not going to have some of their men held as hostages for their good behaviour.[92]

Philip Snowden, a socialist and the peace advocate, argued that Labour had given plenty and the result was legislation "inimical to Trade Union, Labour, and social interests." The usefulness of Labour representation in the Government had been tested and the results proved it to be a failure. The rise in the cost of living was greater after Labour went in than before. The Munitions Act, the National Registration Act, and the Military Service Act all proved the worthlessness of the Labour Ministers in defending labour's interests. Moreover, he felt there should be a general election if necessary, but he believed it would not deter Lloyd George and his friends from acting as they pleased. Snowden knew the vote would go against his cause, but he believed firmly that it was right.[93] A final speaker against the motion was Ernest Bevin of the Dockers, who found fault with Snowden for not supporting strikes and with Henderson and his colleagues for associating with the enemies of the workers who sat in the Cabinet.

The vote, in the end, was 1,849,000 for and 307,000 against, overwhelmingly in favour of sanctioning the Executive's and the M.P.'s policy choice. Yet, the vote clouded over an undercurrent of growing dissatisfaction with the war. The delegates gave a great cheer to Wardle's Presidential Address when he mentioned President Wilson's peace proposals, and they gave enthusiastic ovations to Snowden and J. R. MacDonald. Moreover, the "bloc voting" system concealed significant minority support. At least one-third of the Miners' 600,000 votes were on the minority side.[94] The situation was similar among the cotton operatives (350,000) and the Amalgamated Society of Engineers (136,000), where anti-war sentiment was growing strong.[95] The delegates were coming to fear that their support for the Government's war effort was sacrificing the Labour Party's independence and future.[96]

The attitude of loyal subordination to the declared national needs was being overstrained, and Henderson and his fellow Executive members were not unaware of the limited support on which they could draw in future. The delegates' anger flared up when Henderson, whose association with Lloyd George had clearly undermined the workers' confidence in him, defended the deportation of the members of the Clyde Workers' Committee as justified by the Government's dilution campaign. Labour representatives in the Government had too often offended the interests of large sections of the active rank and file. When the 110,000–strong Glasgow Trades Council sent Henderson a resolution demanding the release of the deported militants, he side-stepped their demand. At the Manchester Conference, the irate delegates heckled Henderson while he attempted to defend his actions. Henderson was so perturbed with the show of distrust that he appealed for a committee of inquiry to vindicate the good aims of labour organisation and officialdom.[97] But the Conference's passion rose "like the snarl of an angry beast" and overrode Henderson and the Executive in carrying a resolution demanding the immediate release of the deportees.[98] As this incident shows, Labour Ministers were increasingly under strain from militant workgroups and their representatives, as disaffection in the ranks mushroomed.

CONCLUSION

The Conference at Manchester witnessed a major step in the development of the Party. The "Labour After the War" proposals showed a new unity on industrial policy and an expanded and intensified class consciousness within the movement. The new consciousness was the worker's response to wartime conditions and experiences. It produced a greater belief in the necessity of political control over industrial affairs and a new aggressiveness that worked its way into Party policy. As the Party entered the new year, what divided the Party and kept it subordinate to the other parties were divisive attitudes toward the war. But, 1917 would see the pro-war commitments of the Party give way to the class interests of the organised membership, bringing a peace policy alongside and interdependent with Labour's bold reconstruction program.

The making of socialism clearly illustrates the episodic character of a political process by which the organisational members mobilize their intermediate-level delegates, the union officials, who, in turn, influence federation executives. The process of remoulding a collective consensus from the bottom up is slow and ponderous, requiring massive input of energy by a wide array of those at the base and at the intermediate level of the trade unions. Only severe environmental conditions could evoke the feelings of injustice that would provide incentives for numerous and diverse workplace organisations and trade unions to mount collective action on the scale required to influence policy-making at the top of these huge national organisations. Moreover, the politics of TUC and Labour Party policy-making in this period, a period of perhaps unprecedented pressure from below, reveal significant leadership functions. Top leaders are far more immune to the pressures of collective solidarity than the typical workshop representative or even the trade union executive. More important, top leaders exercise a large degree of discretion, balancing the representation of members' expressed desires with what are perceived as the members' real interests.[99] The inability of TUC Executives to resist calls for a Special Congress to deal with problems arising from the war and the Labour Party's National Executive Committee's decision to place the "Labour After the War" Program at the center of the Manchester Conference agenda demonstrate the power of the organised membership to influence leaders. The leaders' ability to go beyond the role of mere spokesmen of majority opinion by moulding a policy program consistent with members' moral ends shows the facilitating character of leadership in participatory democracy.

Recognition of the importance of collective action, social pluralism, and leadership initiative helps elaborate and enrich the theory of participatory democracy advanced in this study. Each factor contributes to explaining how leaders can be made responsive to members' interests through a process in which leaders are compelled to trade services on behalf of members' interests in return for the support required to maintain and develop leadership authority and organisational unity. This exchange depends upon an environment that provides incentives for the extensive participation of the diverse groups comprising the organised membership in the process of participatory control. While electoral mechanisms play an important role in determining conference policy and leadership choice, the evidence of this chapter supports the proposition that the dynamic relations of interest and support shape power relations in collective decision-making. This, in turn, depends on participation in shaping collective ends and solidarity. The genesis of socialism during 1916 and 1917 shows how collective solidarity can be built on a commitment to the moral goal of greater equality in social relations and can promote processes of widespread participation in collective consensus formation in workplace groups and their unions. The processes of creating collective solidarity give members autonomous control of interest and support and establish the value boundaries within which leaders take actions on behalf of their membership. The delegate councils in the national federations were responsive to specific substantive demands precisely because these were inspired and evaluated by the moral principles of liberty and equality in social relations. This conclusion confirms G. D. H. Cole's proposition that representation of one man by another cannot be general but must be specific to a particular interest.[100] Participatory democracy thus relies on the exertion of unusual energies by those at the base in compelling their leaders to pursue increased equality and justice, not on constitutional arrrangements, party competition or leadership composition.

CHAPTER 7

Delegate Democracy in the National Federations and Foreign Policy

As we have seen, the postwar domestic policy programs of the Trades Union Congress and the Labour Party were based on the aggregation and coordination of specific demands by various trade unions and socialist societies that reflected their peculiar responses to the wartime political economy. On the other hand, Labour's major foreign policy commitment, its loyal support to pursuit of total victory, resulted from an outpouring of patriotism that made its prewar internationalism irrelevant. Because patriotism provided diffuse or unspecific attitudes toward the war and heightened loyalty toward leaders, union and party officeholders could exercise considerable automony in supporting the war and taking other specific policy actions. In addition, the ability of leaders to invoke their privileged links to Government Ministers and their technical expertise in foreign affairs reinforced their authority. In short, the patriotic response of workers can be expected to enable leaders to take charge of wartime foreign policy issues which, as Michels argues, typically strengthen oligarchical tendencies in mass organisations.[1]

This chapter examines whether elitism or participatory democracy prevailed as the labour movement developed a peace policy during 1917. Because the war policy was broad in scope and unspecific in relation to particular material and political interests of union members, its lack of immediacy and concreteness might be thought to inhibit the processes of participatory democracy that we have seen on domestic issues. Foreign policy typically works to elites' advantage because they can use its diffuse character to claim expertise, on the one hand, and to justify their actions in the national (general) interest, on the other. Yet, these advantages do not inevitably preclude the formation of a foreign policy consensus through widespread discussion and pressure on the basis of equal status among diverse groups composing the larger community of organised labour or, in turn, the exercise of participatory control on foreign policy issues. As this case attempts to show, our analysis of participatory democratic policy processes can be extended to the critical issue-area of war and peace.

POLITICIZATION OF RANK-AND-FILE PROTEST

The class consciousness and assertiveness that produced the socialist "Labour After the War" Program, as discussed above, intensified during 1917. Hardship increased due to the rising cost of living and scarce food supplies. The loss of industrial and political liberties resulting from the Munitions Acts and the Conscription Acts became more pronounced as military manpower needs rose sharply. The larger unions demanded rationing when food became scarce. By the Summer of 1917, the Government moved into action as a result of industrial militancy and the exigencies of prosecuting the war. Moreover, the proposed extensions to the Munitions Act to include work in private firms and the extension of the Military Service Act to squeeze out every available man furthered the workers' sense of unnecessary injustices and consequently met with protest and hostility. As the material and mental condition of those workers most affected by the sacrifices and discipline of war production became more severe, class conflict became increasingly political.

Further, the Russian Revolution gave industrial conflict a distinctly political character. As the news from Russia spread throughout Britain, workers became more assertive and self-confident. As J. Ramsay MacDonald, in the wake of May Day rallies, noted, "The Russian Revolution has greatly changed the minds of many people and has made them breathe the atmosphere and feel the sentiments of Revolution. Our people are more cocky and believe they are winning."[2] Even without full knowledge of the events in Russia or their meaning, sections of the British working class were quick to find inspiration in the overthrow of the oppressive Czarist regime. More and more workers now felt that they too must throw off their oppressive Government and establish a People's Democracy.

The rising cost of living and the restrictive legislation fostered an unremitting unrest among the organised rank and file, especially those working in the war industries. Unrest ebbed and flowed, but labour leaders and Government officials were constantly fearful of the revolutionary potential that was building. To an increasing extent, labour leaders were convinced that only an immediate amelioration of the conditions fostering the unrest would restore their control over the rank and file and assure Britain's ability to make its contribution to the war effort.

The explosive industrial situation peaked during the May strikes throughout the engineering industry. In Lancashire, the introduction of dilution of private work fostered the rebellion in which unofficial shop stewards gave focus to rank-and-file aspirations. In other centres, the Government's intention to withdraw the Trade Card Scheme which protected Engineers from the draft was mainly responsible for the industrial militancy. The Government's policy toward conscription was constantly threatening the extension of *de facto* industrial conscription; during the early months of 1917, the Government let it be known that it was considering the introduction of full industrial conscription. The May strikes revealed the bitter sense of injustice that Engineers felt for the possible advent of overt industrial conscription and the introduction of unskilled labour to skilled work in firms not involved in munitions. Each time the government extended its control over manpower, class unity arose and became politicized even where economic and territorial ties did not exist.[3]

But the May strikes were only part of the seething discontent over conscription, prices and the war itself. There were wildcat strikes among the Miners as pithead organisations pressed their national officials to halt food profiteering and to force the Government to institute food rationing. The Railwaymen were pushing for increased wages. The London busmen were out and the textile trade was on the verge of a general stoppage in an effort to get a wage rise.[4] Industrial discontent frightened the Government and the governing class. But, while industrial activity diminished after May, a revolutionary potential continued to vex the minds of labour and Government officials.

Most trade union leaders and Executives of the Trades Union Congress and the Labour Party realized the dangers to their own activities as workplace discontent became politicized. John Hill (Boilermakers), in his Presidential Address to the Trades Union Congress in September, drew attention to the "growing discontent in the workshops" which had "assumed alarming proportions this year." He made reference to the findings of the eight Commissions on Industrial Unrest, which in response to the May strikes investigated the sources of the discontent, pointing out the deep and continuing grievances.

Perhaps the most important finding is that "Trade Union officials are distrusted." As leaders we were appointed to lay down the hammer or the trowel, and stand on the ramparts to warn our members of danger, and in their opinion we had either fallen asleep at our posts, or we have sold their birthright for a mess of pottage.[5]

The combination of compounded grievances and distrust of authority fostered more and more rebellious activity amongst the active rank and file in each of the key sectors of the wartime economy. In late August, Robert Smillie spoke of the potential for unrest and the danger it posed to the unity of the Miners' Federation.

I think the unrest being evinced in many mining districts, if not in all mining districts, points out to us that a serious state of matters may be anticipated at any time so far as labour is concerned in our country. That is one thing, I think, that every responsible person in the Labour movement is anxious to avoid. . . . We cannot ignore the fact that on account of an accumulation of circumstances, the continued increase in the price of the commodities of life, the continuance of the exploitation of the people of this nation by the exploiters and profiteers; these things side by side with the terrible suffering in the homes of our people caused by the loss, it may be, of dear ones at home, is bringing about a state of matters, a state of unrest which, at any moment, may break out.[6]

Union activists believed that true power to enhance the workers' fortune was within their grasp if they only took political issues into their own hands. If the working class of Russia could give themselves liberty, then so could the British workers. The Governments of the militarists could no longer be trusted; thus, the Russian Revolution, by its model, gave the British worker reinforcement in his ambition to improve his condition and shift the balance of power in society to his side. The deep-felt grievances and the disaffection that were the causes of the unrest had their origins in the heightened sense of economic and political exploitation that the British workers in the war industries in particular experienced. During 1917 these grievances came to focus on a demand for political, economic, and civil liberty. If a more just and equitable society were to be achieved, the common people, they felt, would have to have power. If peace were to be lasting, a People's Democracy would be necessary at home as well as abroad. These were the attitudes that increasingly pervaded the labour movement from the time of the Russian Revolution. These were attitudes pressed upon the leaders of powerful unions by mobilized members in constitutional and unconstitutional organisations. Claims to a higher status and greater power for the working class were worked out in a series of Conferences, which called for more liberty and changed the internal relationships within the labour movement.

The Labour Party's development of a peace policy took place against this background of rank-and-file discontent and disaffection. Leaders were hard pressed to propose solutions to the grievances of their members, at the same time that their members were less willing to put their fate into the leaders' hands. Needless to say, the prospect of an uncontrolled outbreak of revolutionary activity was feared by union and Labour Party leaders as much as it was feared by the Government. This potential for independent rank-and-file outbursts accompanied demands for a new, fairer social order and distrust of those Government and union officials who failed to promote such changes. Thus, the structural conditions for participatory democratic policy-processes on the war issue were beginning to emerge.

THE CAMPAIGN FOR PEACE, LIBERTY, AND EQUALITY

As the discontent over prices, industrial restrictions, and conscription became politicized, the view that an early conclusion to the war was the best way to end the ongoing injustices and exploitation spread among pace-setting sections of the organised rank and file. With the Labour Party resolutely committed to the Government's war effort, anti-war and pro-war leaders committed to defending working-class interests moved quickly to transform the new longing for peace into a united and powerful force. The mobilization of rank-and-file support to reestablish domestic liberties, to introduce economic and political equality, and to pursue a democratic peace took shape through a series of Con-

ferences nominally celebrating the Russian Revolution and created a
massive movement for an early peace to which Labour leaders would
soon be forced to give way.

The first important National Conference to celebrate the Russian
Revolution and the cause of liberty at home was held at the Albert Hall,
London, during the first week of April. It was a gathering of all the
more active elements in the socialist and radical movements as well as
militant trade union organisations like the Triple Alliance, the pact
between the Miners, Railwaymen, and Transport Workers promising
mutual support and coordination of industrial action. The sentiment was
one of a new "beginning" that "marked a turning-point in the mood,
the spirit, the activities of our country."[7] Enthusiasm ran very high
among the overflow audience. Those who attended congratulated Russia
upon its Revolution and sought to "initiate a revolution in the political,
social, and economic life of the British Commonwealth." They supported peace, personal liberty in speech and action, social democracy,
and unity among socialist parties in allied and belligerent countries.
Significantly, speakers exercised freedom of speech without fear of the
Defence of the Realm Acts, which had previously silenced them.

In congratulating the Russians, the speakers, who included middle-
class socialists, working-class and women's groups' representatives as
well as pro-war and anti-war spokesmen, emphasized that the fight for
liberty in Russia and Britain was one which united men and women of
all political views. Robert Smillie (Miners) emphasised the lack of
freedom at home: women were denied the right to vote and conscientious
objectors were imprisoned. He called upon the people to press the
Government to free political prisoners and to force the Government to
do as the "People" please. Robert Williams of the National Transport
Workers Federation suggested the Defence of the Realm Acts were
"calculated more to defend the rights and privileges of the profiteering
classes than the rights of the sovereign realm." He wanted a "dilution
of capital" to spread the burden of paying for the war, a burden that
would otherwise fall upon the shoulders of future generations of workers. Likewise, industrial compulsion had to be prevented by the force
of the "people's will." When he mentioned Government figures, like
Labour Representative Henderson or the Head of the National Service
Department, N. Chamberlain, hisses arose from the audience. Clearly,
a spirit of rebellion was expressed against the authority of the Government which was being compared to the oppressive Czarist regime in

Russia. Further, A. Bellamy of the National Union of Railwaymen equated Russian aims with those of the British workers and suggested that the meeting was a beginning to real freedom. "From now we are going to unwind the chains that have bound us—(applause) . . . from now we are going to try to do some of the controlling ourselves—(applause)—instead of allowing everything to be done for us." The purpose was to "secure for the people that which is their right."[8] In short, militant leaders and workers now asserted their right to control the Government in their own and the national interest.

A series of Regional Conferences enthusiastically backed the Russian achievement and the goals of liberty and peace.[9] In mid-May, a demonstration was held in Glasgow to congratulate the Russian people on overthrowing the Czar and undermining imperialism. As the *Herald* commented:

The demonstration was unique: it was the witness and the sponsor of new life in the International; it kindled a democratic flame which may light up Glasgow as the Petrograd of Britain. . . . For it was a demonstration of people who knew no barriers of race, speech, or colour, and welcomed all men as brothers. Moreover, it heralded the dawn of peace and resolved on the abolition of war, which it recognised as fratricide and therefore an outrage on humanity.[10]

The enthusiasm in Glasgow also produced two major rallies: One was an overflow crowd of some three thousand, who proceeded to hold an open-air celebration, and the other was the meeting in St. Andrews Hall of "over five thousand revolutionaries." Both gatherings agreed to promote a revolution at home and an early peace abroad. "Emulation, it was unanimously agreed, was the best way of congratulating Petrograd, whose people, having conquered Imperialism, expect us to follow their example."

A number of top labour leaders spoke at the meetings. Smillie repeated the same themes that evoked enthusiastic responses at Albert Hall—a revolution at home in order to halt the war and to stop the exploitation. As the *Herald* reported:

He expressed himself as opposed to a separate peace and thought we should join with Russia in demanding an end to Imperialistic aims so that the way might be prepared for a peace on the will of the people. As an alternative to bread riots he commended an immediate peace, and argued that the policy framed by MacDonald was more in accord with that of Russia than the policy

represented by Henderson and Thorne [Gasworkers]. There could be peace next
week were it not for the exploiters.[11]

Smillie captured the mood among a growing majority of rank-and-file
workers, even among those who preferred to fight the war to a finish,
that only a democratic and socialist reorganisation of society would
bring a successful peace.

These Conferences reveal the responsiveness of anti-war leaders to
the changing attitudes of workers typical of participatory democracy.
As a result of the unionists' view that an end to the war would bring
an end to injustice and repression, anti-war activists who had previously
been restrained in opposing the war were now able to act in this extra-
constitutional capacity. The Conferences, composed of the most progressive elements, did not represent a counter-elite whose intent was
to displace the leaders of the major labour organisations. Rather, they
reflected the developing anti-war attitudes among organised labour.
Anti-war socialists and radicals, many of whom were part of labour's
official leadership, could now mobilize, even if they did not create, the
new sentiment for liberty, justice, and peace. In so doing, these leaders
renewed their support among the rank and file and enlarged the influence
of the anti-war perspective.

THE LEEDS CONFERENCE: MOBILIZATION OF
THE DEMAND FOR PEACE

By June 1917, socialists, militant trade unionists, and an increasing
number of moderate trade unionists agreed that a solution to the war
had become imperative to reestablishing political, economic, and civil
liberties and obtaining the full fruits of workers' efforts. They also
believed that the burden of bringing about a peace rested with the
working-class movements in Britain and abroad. This, of course, meant
that the British labour movement was increasingly challenging the policy
of the Coalition Government and was setting itself on a collision course
with the Government. While the resignation of Henderson from the
Lloyd George Government, signalling the establishment of Labour as
the Party of peace in opposition to the Coalition Government, did not
come until August, the course for a Labour peace policy was set by the
Leeds Conference, which took place on June 3. The mismanagement
of the war, the "unbridled swindling and profiteering" which accom-

panied it, and the obvious incapacity of the Government to settle the conflagration led many in the labour movement to recognize the need to take the war issue into their own hands, as the people of Russia had done. The Leeds Conference was organised to decide how to achieve a workers' peace and socialist society in the name of the labour movement.[12]

The Conference was convened by the United Socialist Council, an amalgamation of the Independent Labour Party, British Socialist Party, and trade unionists. There were about 1,200 delegates present, including 209 from Trades Councils and local Labour Parties, 371 from the trade unions, 294 from the Independent Labour Party, 88 from the British Socialist Party, 16 from other socialist societies, 54 from women's organisations and 118 from miscellaneous bodies like the National Council for Civil Liberties and the Union of Democratic Control. The shop stewards' movement gave enthusiastic support, and delegates from several major trade unions presented their members' anti-war feelings. Even so, the Labour Party NEC did not sanction it and not all the delegates attended as official representatives of their organisations. Nonetheless, the enthusiasm for peace and for a Government by and for the working people marked the Conference as a decisive turning point at which anti-war and pro-war elements first joined hands and set the labour movement on a course challenging the Government's pro-war, fight-to-the-finish policy.

The Conference opened with letters from, among others, the Soviet Workers' and Soldiers' Council, which offered to meet with a delegation from Leeds and proposed an international conference on the war in Stockholm. Next, a speech by the Conference Chairman, Robert Smillie, set the direction and tone of the Conference:

We want to endeavour to concentrate the opinion and will of the people in this country on peace. (Loud Cheers) I think it is fairly well agreed now the Central Powers cannot knock out the Allies or the Allies knock the Central Powers out. When peace comes—even if it is forty, fifty, or sixty years hence—it will be peace by negotiation. (Cheers) Is there any use in murdering a few million more of the sons of the people?[13]

He suggested that a lasting peace could only be made by the "common people" and that if Britain and France joined with America and Russia in denouncing imperialism and annexation, the Germans would be forced to negotiate on their terms, or there would be revolution in Germany itself.

Smillie also noted that, after the Albert Hall Conference in April, there had been a series of meetings in different parts of the country welcoming the Russian Revolution. They had "seized the psychological moment." Now "it has been thought wise to concentrate the enthusiasm that has been evinced in every part of the country in this great central Conference, representative of the democracy and of organised Labour in this country."[14] He reiterated the call for liberty and equality in Britain, a theme upon which all participants were united. In short, peace was the efficient means to end the militarist domination and establish a new democracy more fair to the interests of the common people.[15]

To this end, a number of resolutions were introduced. J. R. MacDonald moved the first resolution hailing the Russians for a revolution which

has liberated the people of Russia for the great work of establishing their own political and economic freedom on a firm foundation, and of taking a foremost part in the international movement for working-class emancipation from all forms of political, economic, and imperialist oppression and exploitation.[16]

MacDonald emphasized that the true celebration of the Russian Revolution was the emulation of the seizure of liberty, a theme with which the delegates expressed full agreement.[17]

The second resolution declared the Conference in favour of a democratic peace, without annexations, and demanded that the British Government state its war aims. Philip Snowden, who moved it, indicated that the resolution accepted the declaration made three days prior by the congress of Russian soldiers demanding an end to the war at the earliest possible moment with annexation or indemnity.[18] Snowden was weary of asking the government to announce their peace terms. "The time has now come for us to tell the government what *our* peace terms are. (Cheers)" He was supported by E. C. Fairchild of the British Socialist Party, who asserted that "we must have a people's peace," and R. Buxton, who pointed to a "great democratic wave" that was passing through all the countries that were at war.

Despite the support for a negotiated peace amongst most delegates, opposition emerged on this anti-war resolution. Tupper of the Seamen's Union, in a staunchly pro-war statement, asked for indemnities for the six thousand sailors who had perished. Ernest Bevin of the National

Transport Workers Federation, in also criticizing the anti-war position, asked, "When we have arrived at this policy and have associated ourselves with our Russian friends, and there is no response from Germany, will they join in a vigorous prosecution of the war until Germany does respond?" He did not trust the Germans and wanted to be sure that in the future there would be peace. Finally, Tom Mann (National Transport Workers Federation) supported an expression of opinion on this issue. "I am quite sure from my knowledge that there has been a vast change in the opinion of organised Labour and what has hitherto been presented to the nation as its opinion. However true it might have been, it certainly is not true now."[19] The resolution, he felt, was consistent with long-standing principles of trade unionism and internationalism and was consistent with current rank-and-file attitudes. The resolution then carried with only two or three opposed.

The third resolution was a call for a charter of civil liberties in England. It demanded that the Government follow the lead given by Russia and to proclaim its determination to achieve "unrestricted freedom of the press, freedom of speech, a general amnesty for all political and religious prisoners, full rights of industrial and political associations and the release of Labour from all forms of compulsion and restraint." C. G. Ammon, in moving the resolution, noted how the Russian Revolution made workers realize what freedoms they had lost. The resolution carried unanimously after Bertrand Russell spoke on behalf of the thousands of men in prison. The support for immediately reestablishing civil, political, and economic liberty was in marked contrast to the resolution of the 1916 Trades Union Congress and 1917 Labour Party Conference which demanded restoration of civil rights after the war.

Finally, the fourth resolution challenged Britain's governing class as well as the Labour Party. It called for the establishment of Councils of Workmen and Soldiers' Delegates for the purpose of "initiating and coordinating working-class activity in support of the policy" set out in the foregoing resolutions. Such councils were to be the vanguard of labour, coordinating activity and resisting every unjust encroachment upon the common people. W. C. Anderson, the mover of the resolution, said that

we are asking for a means of taking the food profiteers by the throat. We are asking for an organisation that is going to strengthen Trade Unionism, that is going to have fewer Trade Unions and more combination among work-people, that is going to strengthen the power of organised Labour and help in every way to enlarge its power.[20]

He also noted:

If a revolution be the conquest of political power by an hitherto disinherited class, if revolution be that we are not going to put up in the future with what we have put up with in the past, we are not going to have the shame and poverty of the past, then the sooner we have revolution in this country the better. (Cheers)[21]

Robert Williams (National Transport Workers Federation) wanted "to accept the resolution in its very fullest implication . . . The *dictatorship of the proletariat*. (Cheers)" Williams argued that the governing classes, who were difficult to control, were capable and would do anything to defeat the working people. "They have taken your own leaders from your ranks and used them against you. . . . They will make every conceivable sacrifice and concession short of getting off your backs." But, he said, it was time to "break the influence" of the "gang who are in charge of our political destinies at this moment." The working class had the right and the desire to demand the ownership and control of the country. Organised workers had a greater right than anybody else to speak in the name of the common people, the soldiers and the workers. "We are competent to speak in the name of our own class, and damn the Constitution. (Loud cheers)"[22] Other speakers also called for practical suggestions for getting organised, although one delegate did not want to see any new organisation threaten the already "sufficient organisations." But the support shown among the delegates for this resolution reflected the hope and longing for a Labour Government, one constituted by the workers, exercising policies on their behalf. In the words of the suffragist Sylvia Pankhurst, "it [the resolution] is an attempt to make a straight cut for the Socialist Commonwealth that we all want to see."[23]

LEEDS AND THE DEVELOPMENT OF THE PEACE POLICY

The Leeds Conference, like those that preceded it around the country, reflected and contributed to a growing desire for liberty, equality, and peace. The Conference served to focus and mobilize support for these ends in a manner that the Labour Party was unable to do as a result of its past policy commitment to fully support the war effort. Although many of the speakers and delegates were leaders of the Labour Party, they acted in this extra-constitutional capacity as a result of their own ideological positions but, more importantly, as a result of the rank-and-file's demand for an end to exploitation and the war that coincided with a withdrawal of support from the movement's official leadership. As the rank and file took political affairs into their own hands, they undermined the effectiveness, representativeness, and solidarity of the Labour Party and the Trades Union Congress. As the *Socialist Review* commented, Leeds constituted an unequivocal "warning sign of the spreading feeling of labour revolt in the country."[24] Consequently, the widespread support for "revolution at home" and a peace by negotiation was making it likely that the split between pro-war and anti-war elements in the Labour Party would have to be reconciled in accord with the new attitudes of the majority of Miners, Railwaymen, Transport Workers, and Engineers.

As discontent over the rising cost of food, industrial restrictions, and military and industrial conscription became a political rather than simply an industrial issue, more organised workers demanded an early peace that would facilitate the "revolution at home" and establish equality of sacrifice based on a new "social contract" of liberty and a just reward for the working people. In May 1917, a mass meeting at Hull sponsored by the Triple Alliance of the Miners, Railwaymen, and Transport Workers called for a national campaign in favour of a "real measure of control by the workers of their respective industries, with a view of obtaining for the entire working class the full produce of their labour." These same sentiments were repeated at a National Union of Railwaymen rally preceding their Annual Conference in June. Delegates supported one resolution protesting further industrial conscription in view of the sacrifices already made and another resolution calling for peace. At the Railwaymen's Conference, President Bellamy said: "Labour has not yet taken its proper place. Let our claim for the present and for the future be 'audacious.' . . . We claim our full share of the fruits of our labour."[25] By September, many unions were pressing for an early peace, more wages, and more control of their lives by formulating their own industrial "After the War" programs.[26]

This attitudinal shift in union ranks was the key to labour's emerging peace policy, since it created pressure on most of the labour movement leadership to change their stance on the war. The National Union of Railwaymen Annual General Meeting in June carried one resolution calling for labour representation in peace negotiations and another congratulating the workers of Russia. In June and July, the union's Executive received numerous branch resolutions calling for peace. In mid-July, the rank-and-file–dominated Manchester District Council requested the Executive to summons the Labour Party NEC to call a Special Labour Party Conference to permit the workers to determine their policy in view of the Russian Revolution and the proposals for a negotiated peace.[27] The Miners also began to support an early peace by negotiation. In May, the Scottish Miners convinced the Scottish Trades Union Congress to adopt by a decisive majority a resolution favouring peace by negotiation.[28] In the Summer, twenty-five thousand South Wales Miners supported the Leeds resolutions. At a meeting of the Western District of the South Wales Miners' Federation, seven thousand miners passed the following resolution:

That this district meeting heartily approves the conduct of the Russian Workmen in calling an International Socialist and Labour Conference to devise ways and means to secure common action with the object of ending the war, and also urges the central Executive Council to call a special Conference to consider the advisability of South Wales Federation being directly represented at the Conference.[29]

The South Wales Miners also called for a referendum of the whole labour movement on the proposals for an international conference.[30] Further, the Amalgamated Society of Engineers, under pressure from the independent shop stewards' organisations, supported moves for an early peace. Delegates at the Dockers' Triennial Conference proclaimed themselves to be internationalists and urged the setting up of Allied conferences to abolish the military despotism of any class or nationality.[31] The Textile Workers supported an international conference and requested that the Labour Party rescind its resolution banning international conferences.

In addition to the mounting pressures for an early end to the war, those mining, engineering, and transport trade union officials coping with militant workgroups saw peace as a means of controlling the serious industrial unrest and regaining the lost confidence of many of their members that resulted from their own identification with Government policy. In his Presidential Address to the National Transport Workers Federation, Harry Gosling said:

Labour has been willing and anxious during the whole period of the war to render service to the State; but Labour is becoming increasingly distrustful because of the manner in which its confidences have been abused, its counsels rejected, and its loyalty exploited by those who place profit and . . . advantage above genuine patriotism. . . .

The Government . . . have carried the principle of selecting Trade Union and Labour representatives to serve on various committees and other Government posts to such an extent that it has led to a feeling of disaffection and suspicion. Moreover, the principle of selection without consultation is certainly mischievous. . . . I am afraid that many of us who have accepted various nominations and desire to render assistance wherever possible to the State have lent ourselves to this growing system, but it ought not to go on.[32]

Gosling implied that labour's class interests not only differed from those of the Government but were being systematically abused. As a result, top union and Labour Party officials ought to disassociate themselves from the Government or its policy.

Because of insistent rank-and-file calls for peace and liberty, in late August, the politically moderate TUC Parliamentary Committee lagged behind this growing charge of enthusiasm. The Parliamentary Committee's moderation can be seen in its support for the Council of Workmen and Soldiers' Delegates in Petrograd:

[The Parliamentary Committee] congratulate the workers of Russia on the overthrow of the old regime and assure them of our willingness to cooperate with them in the direction of strengthening the powers of democracy and Trade Unionism for the purpose of securing the economic and political emancipation of the people.[33]

The Parliamentary Committee wanted to see the Russians develop a trade union movement similar to that in Britain and was quick to offer help in that direction. But it was blind to the symbolism of the Russian Revolution as a beacon for more working-class power in Great Britain. It came under fire in June, when the small Paper Workers' Union demanded that the Trades Union Congress take a plebiscite of the affiliated membership as to whether it was in favour of "bringing the war to a victorious conclusion or of opening up Peace negotiations on the lines formulated at Leeds.''[34] The Paper Workers' Union, concerned about the representativeness of the Leeds Conference, noted that many delegates of other organisations had failed to consult their members. The union wanted to get a more authoritative decision on the peace issue, but the Parliamentary Committee, aware of the growing demand for an early peace yet fearful of its consequences for the war effort and the labour movement, deflected the challenge by suggesting an amendment for the Trades Union Congress in September. The Parliamentary Committee was sticking to its decision of June 6, refusing to participate in any international conference on peace aims.

The immediate effect of the Leeds Conference was a great, if ineffectual, campaign for realizing the principles and aspirations expressed there. The proposed Soldiers' and Workers' Council, consisting of thirteen district councils and the central council, never took institutional form. Partly because of harassment from the Government and opposition from the pro-war Press, the proposal for the Soldiers' and Workers' Councils won support only from militant socialist and shop stewards' movements. In late June, the *Herald* responded to the buoyant mood by proposing "Plans for the People's Party," which proclaimed the need for (1) the conscription of wealth and the equality of income, (2) the economic independence of all men and women, (3) a complete democracy, (4) the opportunity to enjoy life through education and higher standards of amenities, and (5) peace by international agreement.[35] The reception of this initiative for a new party was greater than the *Herald* had expected.[36] The program was an amalgamation of the politically advanced ideas among the unions, expressing labour's militant mood.

If these immediate results of the Leeds Convention and its precursors were minor, the larger and lasting legacy was the uniting of pro-war with anti-war groups in the Labour Party and its subsequent reorganisation into a national party.[37] The growing demand by a majority of workers in the largest and most militant unions for liberty, peace, and control threatened to cripple the Labour Party's ability to act as the political voice of the labour movement. Anti-war leaders from the movement joined with those who had been identified with the pro-war policy to mobilize the anti-war sentiments of these crucial groups of workers into a united and powerful force. The war issue, linked to liberty and to an end to inequality of sacrifice, further focused this active rank and file's bitter sense of unfair sacrifice into the quest for control over the State—a goal that cut across divisive sectional concerns. By early July it was clear that the Labour Party would have to take up the issue of the search for peace and in the process become the major Party of opposition, or face impotence and fragmentation as a result of a loss of legitimacy through its inability to focus the policy preferences of militant workgroups in the most powerful industrial and craft-based unions. Taking up consideration of the Russian and International Socialist Bureau's initiative for an international conference at Stockholm to discuss peace terms was precisely the policy by which the Labour Party Executive could attempt to move closer to the rank and file and regain the credibility required for leadership.

THE LABOUR PARTY SPECIAL CONFERENCES: MEMBERSHIP PRESSURE AND LEADERS' ORGANISATIONAL INTERESTS

In August 1917, the Labour Party summoned a Special Labour Party Conference to decide whether or not to send delegates to the Stockholm Conference. The Committee's decision to let the Conference decide on Henderson's pro-Stockholm report on the situation in Russia was a radical about-face from its previous decisions along the lines of the Manchester resolution rejecting participation in any international conference. The decision to hold the Labour Party Conference was taken in late July on Henderson's recommendation, just after he had returned to Britain from nearly two months in Russia as the Government's Representative. Henderson returned firmly convinced that British Labour should participate in the Stockholm Conference. On July 25, he urged the Labour Party Executive Committee to accept the Russian invitation on the condition that it was "consultative" and not mandatory. He was supported by a delegation from the Russian Council of Soldiers and Workers. Henderson's advice carried much weight with the Labour Party Executive, no doubt; but it is a mistake to attribute to Henderson's influence alone the Executive's decision, taken by a three-to-one majority, to recommend that the Special Conference accept the invitation. The National Executive Committee had letters from two sections of the Party urging a Special Conference to discuss Party policy toward the war in light of the Russian Revolution.[38] In addition, Henderson and the Executive were well aware of Leeds and the developing peace movement among union affiliates and were intimidated by the revolutionary potential revealed by the May strikes and the frequent threats of industrial militancy.[39] Henderson's conversion to internationalism during his trip to Russia dovetailed with the new options for the British Labour Party afforded by the invitation to Stockholm. By pursuing the Stockholm option, the Labour Party could fill the leadership vacuum created by the workers' pressure for a negotiated peace.

Resolutions for the Nottingham Labour Party Conference to be held in January 1918 reflected the mood of the constituents during the Summer months of 1917 and influenced the National Executive Committee. Of fifteen resolutions and amendments on the war, all but one called on the Labour Party to pursue a peace-by-negotiation policy. These resolutions can be illustrated by that submitted by the York Labour Party:

This Conference of the Labour Party declares that the war has demonstrated the inability of Capitalism to preserve Peace among the nations; the prolongation of the war only seems to complicate the issues involved and render more remote the possibilities of Peace; and this Conference therefore declares that the best interests of the working class will be secured by a speedy termination of hostilities and demands of the Government that it declares its readiness to enter into immediate negotiations for Peace.[40]

Not ideologically inspired, the resolution represents a reaction to the hardships and injustice precipitated by the war. Another set of resolutions indicated that many Labour Party affiliates were determined that Labour leave the Government Coalition and assert the Party's independence in order to facilitate the realization of Labour's most important domestic demands. The resolution from one Party affiliate captured the character of these resolutions:

That this Conference is of opinion that the continued inclusion of representatives of the Labour Party in the Coalition Government is a violation of the Constitution of the Party and is seriously detrimental to the best interest of Labour, and declares that in order to regain for Labour the freedom of complete independence when dealing with the grave economic, industrial and social problems which must inevitably be dealt with in the near future, the Parliamentary Labour Party should at once take the necessary steps to withdraw from the Coalition Government, and that all offices held by Labour Party Members in the same be relinquished.[41]

In the meantime, the stance taken by Henderson and the Labour Party Executive Committee on the peace issue led to a Cabinet crisis. Henderson's position had been presented to the Prime Minister and his Cabinet colleagues before he, Wardle, and J. R. MacDonald had left for Paris to prepare for the Stockholm Conference with the French socialists. Henderson even announced that he would gladly resign, since the other four members of the War Cabinet were lined up against him. Upon his return on August 1, Henderson was kept waiting on the "doormat" for an hour while Lloyd George and other members of the full Cabinet debated whether or not they would allow him to continue as a Labour Minister while he was Secretary of the Party. Apparently, the Cabinet decided Henderson should stay on at least momentarily. During the next ten days prior to the Special Labour Party Conference, the Cabinet made subtle but unsuccessful attempts to influence Henderson to reject his support for the Stockholm Conference, in the belief that he could determine the Party's decision. In the end, Henderson resigned or was finally permitted to resign from the cabinet after the Party Conference on August 10, 1917, had voted to send delegates to Stockholm. Henderson thought the Stockholm option would be defeated, but Labour had decided to follow an independent course.[42] Lloyd George's machinations, intended to weaken the threat of the anti-war left to his war policy, were not decisive in Labour's vote.[43] Rather, it was the need to resolve internal contradictions between working-class grievances and political commitments that were daily encouraging deeper discontent. In the end, Henderson's loyalty to Labour proved stronger than his loyalty to the Government.[44]

Labour's decision-making process on the war illustrates the responsiveness of Party Executives and delegates to organised labour, especially the attitudes of the Miners, Railwaymen, and Engineers, rather than the view of one man. In his introductory remarks to the Special Labour Party Conference, Chairman W. R. Purdy cautioned the delegates that the decision they were about to make was "probably the most important in the history of the Party." He said:

For that reason they should calmly and fully discuss the situation, without bitterness, exercising full toleration for each other's views, always keeping in mind that those whom they represent expected, and indeed had a right to demand, a clear and settled policy, so that Labour may take its rightful and proper position in the counsels of the nation, now and when Peace once more returns to a harassed and distressed world.[45]

Then Henderson appealed to the delegates on two grounds to support the invitation to Stockholm for a consultative conference. First, it was a means of assisting the development of freedom in Russia. He had found "the most confused ideas" there, and it would be inadvisable for the Russians to meet representatives from enemy and neutral countries alone. "The conference on limited conditions would be of great good," and it could not do any harm to get war aims on all sides clearly stated. Second, Henderson appealed to the delegates to use political methods to supplement military ones. He intimated that he had not changed his attitude on the war nor his attitude on the need for a final settlement,

but I want to say that in a War in which losses, of such terrible magnitude, are being imposed on all the Nations it appears to me not only wise but imperative that every country should use its political weapon to supplement all its military organisation, if by so doing it can defeat the enemy. That is why I continue in favour of a consultative Conference with proper safeguards and conditions.[46]

The Conference then adjourned to give delegates an opportunity to decide how to vote on the Executive Committee's resolution favouring Stockholm.

The Miners' Federation of Great Britain, which controlled a quarter of the total Party Conference votes, met in full caucus. The Party Executive's resolution was opposed by pro-war advocates from four districts. Walsh, speaking for Lancashire, made it clear that his District Council was firmly in favour of prosecuting the war and he thought the Stockholm meeting would not be representative enough in any case. Further, he objected to the Labour Party Executive Committee taking charge of this issue, overruling a decision of the Manchester Conference. But all the others favoured the Stockholm meeting. They made it clear that, while their areas would not support a mandatory conference, it was necessary to do what was possible by consultation to get an early peace. J. Winstone of militant South Wales supported the resolution because it "fairly represented" the views of the South Wales Miners' Federation. He argued that there can be no sound argment [sic] against our meeting face to face as a democratic organisation all the other representatives of democracy in the world, and having a clear and well defined interchange of opinion and giving a report back in order that we may have from the democracies of the world who are in this war a real and true statement of what their position means.[47]

W. Carter from Nottinghamshire favoured the resolution of the Labour Party Executive of which he was a member. He indicated his support both for fighting the war to the end and for this resolution. Everyone was agreed on ending the war and "if we can devise any means which will bring this world struggle to a close on a satisfactory basis, then it is up to us to do so." Durham, the second largest area, was represented by W. P. Richardson, who said that his district would not agree to a mandatory conference, yet believed that democracy was capable of solving the war. It was imperative, he argued, to have the meeting: "If it will save one single human life it is worth the effort of the Miners' Federation of Great Britain."[48] The two largest counties in Scotland favoured the Labour Party resolution and so Smillie, the Chairman, recorded their vote in favour of the resolution as well. The final vote at the Miners' caucus was 547 to 184 in favour of the proposed Stockholm Meeting.

Next, the Miners confronted the issue of the method of representation at Stockholm. W. Adamson, M. P., moved a resolution to limit representation at Stockholm to one voice—that of the Labour Party, whose constituents would be bound by its decision. While such a proposal in other instances had been seen as an act of hostility against the Independent Labour Party, it represented a concern by the Miners that their own representation be given the due accorded by their large membership. Caucus Chairman Smillie pointed out that under the rules of the International, the Independent Labour Party and the British Socialist Party were entitled to separate representation, but the Miners' representatives disagreed. T. Richards summed up:

It is unthinkable, it is unfair, because these men are connected with the Labour Party in some form or other or should be; if not, they have no business to be discussing this question. I say that the delegation should be limited. I think that the whole of the delegates elected by this Conference should be representative of the British Labour forces, and this Federation ought to make it perfectly clear if the other bodies select representatives, then this Federation claims the right to select representatives commensurate with its great numbers. . . . I hope the Federation will take a strong stand. We want people who go to talk in the name of the British democracy representing the democracy and answerable to the democracy.[49]

Almost unwittingly, the Miners had sprung an issue which would undermine the original proposal for Stockholm they had just so overwhelmingly sanctioned. But the Miners were determined that the unions would have predominant representation at Stockholm.

When the Party Conference reconvened in the afternoon, it found itself reproducing the events of the Miners' Federation caucus, only on a larger scale. W. C. Robinson (United Textile Factory Workers) moved the resolution for the Party's Executive Committee, stating that the invitation be accepted on condition of its being consultative. Complete independence for the small nations was necessary to peace. His appeal was simple: if the workers could save lives and end the misery and oppression of war, it was worth the effort. "Without a Conference how was it possible to convince them [German workers] that our quarrel was not with them but with their autocratic rulers?"[50] W. Carter (Miners) and J. H. Thomas (Railwaymen) declared their patriotism but argued that changed international circumstances demanded a conference that would also express its views of liberty to the German workers. On the other hand, opposition to attending Stockholm came from pro-war leaders associated with Government policy. Sexton (Dockers) proposed an amendment prohibiting attendance at any international conference. The Amalgamated Society of Engineers' G. N. Barnes, who admitted that he was a minority of one among the Engineers, and G. H. Roberts, both of whom were Government Ministers, feared that an international conference would hurt the Allies' ability to fight the war and bring Germany to its knees. On the other hand, J. Ramsay MacDonald (Independent Labour Party), speaking in favour of Stockholm, called upon the Party delegates to assist Russia.[51]

The trade union delegates, responding to the shift in rank-and-file attitudes toward the war, now favoured efforts to achieve peace. Hutchinson (Amalgamated Society of Engineers) declared "that no responsible Trade Union leader could now say with any confidence that his members were for continuing the war."[52] Unlike the Independent Labour Party which on ideological grounds had been against the war from its inception, the union representatives to the Conference wanted Britain to win the war but now perceived that peace would diminish the bitter class discontent that threatened the very existence and power of trade unionism. Peace was imperative and the political route appeared to offer a ray of hope. Trade union leaders, representing the Miners, the Dockers, the Amalgamated Society of Engineers, the Steel Smelters, and the Boilermakers, no longer supported the Government's war policy as grievances intensified and as distrust and suspicion undermined their authority. The final vote on attending the Stockholm Conference carried by 1,846,000 to 550,000.[53]

When W. Adamson, M.P., then moved the Miners' amendment restricting representation to the Labour Party alone, he precipitated a conflict that necessitated another Labour Party Conference in eleven days' time. The Miners' amendment was carried without discussion after E. Bevin of the Dockers emphasized that control over who was going was a serious concern of many unions. Snowden for the Independent Labour Party stated that the Labour Party had no power to prevent it from attending. Henderson, recognizing the hiatus that had arisen between the unions and the socialist societies, suggested that the Conference reconvene on August 21 to discuss the matter of representation and a war aims document.[54]

Before the adjourned Conference met on August 21, the Miners' Federation of Great Britain held another caucus at which it reversed by a slim majority (376 to 360) its previous decision to support Labour Party delegates attending Stockholm. The issue of representation and the fear that the Independent Labour Party and British Socialist Party would be present at Stockholm resulted in several officials reversing their votes after consulting with the rank and file in their districts. According to one member, the socialist parties were part of the larger Labour Party and in actual numbers represented only a small fragment of the labour movement. The Miners wanted Labour to be represented by a delegation agreeing unanimously on its position.[55] Thus, the Miners were forcing the issue of who controlled and implemented Labour Party policy, raising the possibility that the Labour Party's commitment to Stockholm would be overturned because of disunity over who would represent the Labour Party.

When the adjourned Labour Party Conference reassembled on August 21, conflict over who was going to be represented at Stockholm continued. But the commitment to a negotiated peace remained strong, as revealed in the enthusiasm for Labour's break with the pro-war Coalition Government. Henderson's resignation immediately after the August 10 decision to support Stockholm signalled Labour's independence as a political party. Its anti-war policy now constituted a real alternative that was incompatible with support for the Lloyd George Coalition. According to the *Herald*,

[Henderson] realised the gravity of the existing position because it would make the Government's position more difficult in dealing with Labour questions. The organised working class would have less and less respect for and confidence in a Government which had behaved as it had.[56]

While he advocated that Labour remain in the Government, the position of the other Labour Ministers vis-à-vis the Party deteriorated rapidly. By continuing to support the Government's war policy as the Party took steps to implement its industrial and international policy, they increasingly lost touch with the bulk of the movement.

At the Conference, disagreement over the mode of representation threatened to cut short the leadership's effort to regain the support of the delegates. A large majority (1,536,000 to 789,000) voted against the Executive Committee's proposal to allow the Independent Labour Party, the British Socialist Party, and the Fabians to have ten delegates in addition to a Labour Party delegation of twenty-four with eight selected from the TUC Parliamentary Committee, eight from the Party's NEC, and eight from the Conference. Hamstrung, the Labour Party Conference again adjourned until after the Inter-Allied Conference met in London at the end of August. But it never reconvened because a compromise solution between pro-war and peace-seeking sections of the unions was reached at the Trades Union Congress during the first week of September.

To sum up, while militant trade union minorities and pacifist socialists had advocated a peace policy for some time, the two Labour Party Conferences in August made peace the policy of the labour movement and revealed the determination of many union representatives to take charge of Labour Party foreign policy-making. The national officials were compelled to respond by a heightened class consciousness among workgroups in the mining, transport, and engineering unions among others that enabled them to exercise participatory control. They now demanded more equality, an early peace, and a greater political influence in shaping the nation's policies and linked their support only to officeholders who were willing to serve these ends. That a majority of organised workers wanted peace in order to expedite the end of exploitation and to increase the power of the unions and the Labour Party made it impossible for national leaders to continue their earlier support for the war effort. Participatory democracy occurred during the Summer of 1917 when union members exercised control over their Party Conference delegates, many of whom were leaders of district or local unions. The latter felt the necessity to maintain the backing of the membership in order to hold their unions and the Labour Party together and, if possible, to enlarge their collective power.

THE TRADES UNION CONGRESS: LEADERS ACCOMMODATE TO THE MEMBERSHIP'S DEMANDS FOR PEACE AND REPRESENTATION

When the Trades Union Congress met, the Parliamentary Committee presented a report and recommendations with respect to Stockholm. The Parliamentary Committee had been taking steps to share control over international policy with the Labour Party since July 25, when the Party decided to hold a Special Conference to decide its policy about Stockholm. The Parliamentary Committee decided to inform the Party Secretary that in the future it wished to be consulted and made party to any joint body responsible for the convening of an international labour conference arising out of the war.[57] The Parliamentary Committee insisted that any such conference should be called, so far as British labour representation was concerned, only on the joint responsibility of itself and the Party Executive committee.[58]

Robert Smillie, the Miners' President and member of the Parliamentary Committee, presented the report to the Congress. That Smillie, one of Labour's most trusted representatives and militant leaders, spoke for the Parliamentary Committee symbolized the power of the militant rank and file to shape the policy of the TUC. Because the Parliamentary Committee's purpose, Smillie stated, was to restore unity to the labour movement, the report and proposals were compromises.[59] He noted that only a united movement could consolidate the industrial and political power that was required to realize the aspirations for greater justice now demanded by rank-and-file unionists. Smillie asserted:

I believe we shall have closer relationship in the Labour movement in our own country before long. Events are moving now in our own country which will force us to unite, whether we like it or not. You who are spending your working lives as Trade Union officials in the great industrial centres must know that an enormous change of opinion has taken place there, and that there is a great longing and desire on the part of our people that something should be done in order to secure an early peace.[60]

The Parliamentary Committee's initiatives were therefore necessary, given the general feeling among the people it claimed to represent.[61] According to Smillie,

The Trades Union Congress in this country hitherto has done too little work in connection with international matters. The Congress, in fact, has been brushed aside by bodies less able to present the view of the Trade Union movement of this country.[62]

Smillie called upon the delegates to support the resolution in an effort to get on with finding common aims among the democracies and "settling a lasting and satisfactory peace."[63]

The Parliamentary Committee's proposals attempted to reconcile the conflicts that divided the British labour movement as well as the various Allied parties. In view of the "divergence of opinion" among the Allies that they found at the recent Conference of Allied Socialists, the Parliamentary Committee believed that given the current conditions a Stockholm conference would not be successful. Consequently, it offered three recommendations, which it hoped would produce peace and foster unity of purpose among the working classes. First, it recommended that an attempt be made in "every possible way to secure general agreement of aim among the working classes of the allied nations," since it posited that common agreement was a fundamental condition of a successful international conference. Second, it believed that because an international labour and socialist conference would contribute and be necessary to peace, it wanted to assist in arranging and taking part in such a conference. Third, it supported the voting pattern for the Stockholm conference recommended by the Miners at the Labour Party Conferences. Given common agreement among the movements, voting should be by nationalities, "sectional bodies within nationalities to be governed by majority of that nationality, or alternatively . . . each section should be given voting powers according to the number of persons actually represented."[64] In conclusion, it declared against Stockholm and for a later international conference.[65]

The Committee's proposals drew support from pro-war groups represented by Will Thorne and Ben Tillett. Thorne emphasized the seriousness of the Parliamentary Committee's effort to achieve unity in the labour movement while at the same time pursuing a peace initiative. He asserted his agreement with the consensus on the desirability of unity and declared his loyalty to working-class concerns.[66] He conceded that a division in the trade union movement and in its Parliamentary Committee over the war had developed and implied that the pro-war advocates were forced to give way to those wanting a peace initiative. Rank-and-file pressure on the peace issue and the imminent prospect of industrial disorder required that the movement adopt a position of unity in order to defend the workmen's interests. Thorne told the delegates that there were two groups in the Parliamentary Committee.

When you have a very large minority either upon the executive committee of a union or upon the Parliamentary Committee, you are bound to recognise each other's point of view. It is impossible to have all your own way, whatever view you may hold; and if there had been no give-and-take between those who take my view of things and those who support Mr. Smillie, there would have been no resolution before the Congress to-day of an agreed character from the Parliamentary Committee. As a consequence of that failure to agree amongst ourselves, the Congress would have been thrown into confusion; and, in my humble judgment, it might have meant the wrecking of the whole Trade Union movement, which is what we all want to avoid.[67]

If there were to be an international conference, it was necessary that the union membership be adequately represented, and that would entail representation governed by the majority.[68] Thorne's views represented the moderate pro-war wing and signalled the new strength born of a united labour movement.

The hard-core, pro-war element was isolated and drastically reduced in the face of the various pressures that shaped the Parliamentary Committee's proposals for peace. Sexton, J. H. Wilson and others from the Sailors and Firemen Union expressed their bitterness for the murder of their brethren, demanding that the war go on until the Germans were humiliated and repentant. But most delegates responded to the mood for peace and pressure for organisational unity. Tillett, the pro-war stalwart from the Dockers, appealed warmly to his colleague, Wilson, to make his pride subordinate to the interests of the movement and the working class. He suggested that the exigencies of settling the war and dealing with the reconstruction after it made unity in the movement imperative. Collective justice and power necessitate support for the Parliamentary Committee's peace recommendations. In the end, the delegates supported overwhelmingly, on a card vote of 2,849,000 to 91,000, the Parliamentary Committee's report. Immediately the Parliamentary Committee and Party Executive Committee resolved to take joint action on the Parliamentary Committee's report and to attempt to promote unity on war aims.[69]

The September Trades Union Congress was the consummation of the move toward a peace policy begun at Leeds. The mounting discontent over the war provided the driving force behind the union shift toward peace initiatives. The Russian Revolution had given the British labour movement a model for taking charge of its own lives. It also helped to put the struggle against inflating prices and political-industrial restrictions on a political level. Throughout 1917 the intensified class struggle converged with international events to open channels for the expression of pent-up and repressed grievances and aspirations. From the Spring of 1917 until Leeds in early June, the more militant political elements in the labour movement focused the rising demand among the rank and file for regaining lost liberties and achieving a negotiated peace. But from July on, the Labour Party and the Trades Union Congress accommodated to these pressures and recaptured their lost position.

By taking on the responsibility involved in pursuing a negotiated peace, the 1917 Trades Union Congress yielded to the peace policy initiatives of the organised rank and file located largely in the industrial and craft unions, and, at the same time, assured the predominance of the organised industrial workers over socialist societies in the labour movement's more assertive role in international affairs. The ability of these workplace organisations and trade unions to absorb their members' increased participation, to respond to their changing attitudes, and to focus and mobilize their support for an anti-war policy shows participatory democratic policy processes at work in determining Party and TUC leadership responsiveness. In so doing, the Trades Union Congress provided the impetus for the reshaping of the Party into a national institution based upon union numerical strength, finance, and policy.

CONCLUSION

The development of Labour's peace policy, then, offers further confirmation of the theory of participatory democracy in large-scale delegate councils. Some leaders articulated the views of their members as they shifted toward support for a negotiated peace while others resisted. A political activist minority mobilized the demand up to the Leeds Conference, after which peace became the main policy concern of Party and TUC Executives. Leaders sympathetic to anti-war attitudes also gave the members' diffuse anti-war sentiment greater clarity and put forward policy proposals consistent with members' attitudes toward the war. The Leeds resolutions, the Special Labour Party Conference proposals, the TUC program merging the pro-war views into an anti-war compromise show leaders, even pro-war stalwarts, responding to imperatives from below. Federation leaders, then, creatively responded to rank-and-file pressures in developing greater power for their members. In spite of significant leadership initiative, however, executives and delegates did conform to the change in the community consensus. They did so in order to retain their support and stay within the bounds of the community's collective solidarity. Further, the organisational diversity at all levels again reveals how social pluralism facilitated the expression and aggregation of rank-and-file attitudes in a fashion that effectively transformed the class community's consensus on the war. Social pluralism permitted freedom of expression and, at the same time, contributed to the determination and strengthening of the collective consensus. This is evident in the way in which organisations responded to members' growing consensus for a negotiated peace and effectively turned their national unions around. Unions, in turn, joined with parties and groups supporting an early peace to put the war issue on the agenda of the national labour federations. Ultimately, the rank and file's rejection of continued injustices, arising from the wartime political economy, led to a demand for peace and inspired a dramatic reversal of Labour's foreign policy. In short, what was essential to participatory democracy in the national federations was the shift in attitudes toward the war among the organised rank and file, a shift that though general and diffuse contained a precise ultimate objective—greater justice for wage labour—and put union and federation leaders in a position of conforming to the new consensus or being deprived of their leadership capacity.

CHAPTER 8

Why Participatory Democracy?

PARTICIPATORY DEMOCRACY AND THE BRITISH LABOUR MOVEMENT: A SUMMARY

These cases of British labour politics during the First World War provide a valuable crucible for investigating participatory democracy. The war strengthened leadership and constantly limited workers' willingness and ability to push their struggles for justice as far as they might have wished. According to Michels, his "general conclusions as to the inevitability of oligarchy in party life, and as to the difficulties which the growth of this oligarchy imposes upon the realization of democracy, have been strikingly confirmed in the political life of all the leading belligerent nations immediately before the outbreak of the war and during the progress of the struggle."[1] Yet, as we have seen, the representative structures of the British labour movement constituted a conduit through which rank-and-file workers could mobilize for the defence of their liberties and living standards. Not only did mass participation in British trade unionism and the British Labour Party during this period establish the modern contours of the movement, but the popularity and experimentation with participation were carried to unprecedented lengths. Given the circumstances of the war, thus, our cases of increased participation in policy-making in modern trade unions and party organisations provide the basis for theorizing about manifestations of participatory democracy in other, less-hostile conditions.

Our studies of policy-making in labour organisations during World War I, then, give evidence for a theory of participatory democracy that is designed to answer Michels' challenge to democratic theory. Under exceptional wartime conditions, class-conscious workgroups, major trade unions, and the TUC and Labour Party national federations all deviated from Michels' theory of oligarchy in two ways. First, evidence shows members, not leaders, shaping the agenda on critical issues. Members' concerns were not ideological but pragmatic responses to inequalities experienced in daily work and family life. Second, in each case the pressure of the organised members, even when mediated by representatives at higher levels, also shaped the substance of policy decisions and established the criterion for their implementation. While office-holders and delegates clearly exercised their own initiatives and prerogatives, in the final analysis they were compelled to follow the guidelines of members' collective interests. The organised workgroups' active involvement, by having made the grant of their support contingent on leaders' service, formed the structural imperative for leadership responsiveness.

The conclusions derived from the theoretical analysis of participatory democracy and the cases of direct and delegate democracy in the British labour movement during the First World War suggest that participatory democracy involves very different political processes from those characterized by the concepts of rational–bureaucratic organisation. Conditions of membership participation included a high level of membership involvement, an emphasis on moral concerns of equality, and a constant scrutiny of leaders' policy actions by participating organisational members. Consequently, our analysis of participatory democracy in labour organisations is more optimistic than previous efforts to construct a theory of democracy which would meet the challenge of Michels by those who follow the less-stringent criterion of democracy as organised competition.[2] It is more optimistic because it raises a realistic prospect for participatory democracy in modern society. This study suggests not only that an answer to Michels' theory must be more fundamental than the analyses of these proponents of the theory of democratic elitism; it also provides a theory of democracy that is a radical alternative to democratic elitism. At the same time, it argues that the conditions that foster participatory democracy are recurrent, if not permanent, in liberal democracies.

Before discussing why this concept of participatory democracy contributes to democratic theory and why a wider practice of participatory democracy is both necessary and likely, it will be useful to summarize the general propositions and hypotheses that help explain participatory democracy during the First World War.

I. *Membership Interest and Participation.* Workers' participation depends on group or class consciousness—the recognition of inequality and aspiration for justice—that is supported by a strong bargaining position. Class consciousness motivates a moral revolt against injustice and gives rise to substantive and ultimate (value-rational or moral) ends. It depends on labour processes that permit workers to interact as an informal and solidaristic grouping and on experiences of inequality which encourage comparisons with capital and identification with other workers. Contributing factors include (1) repressive state intervention that politicizes industrial conflict, providing a common target for diverse grievances; (2) rigid and arbitrary management that, relying on direct control of the less-skilled workers and responsible autonomy for the skilled, engenders class consciousness; (3) a decline in living standards that coincides with an advance in profits, encouraging workers to make comparisons with capitalists, thus heightening their sense of relative deprivation that fosters class consciousness; and (4) a high demand for labour that provides workers with the power to assert their subjective interests. Common interests in ultimate objectives like liberty and greater equality foster collective solidarity and community bonds, complementing sociability. Significantly, collective consensus, involving the "will of a victorious element" and a more general will which "unites those who win and those who lose,"[3] leads to autonomous interests and decision-making. This is the principle of community autonomy. Collective decision-making in workplace organisations entails the participation of all group-members, although the more extensive and complex the organisation, the more the workers' politicization of broad or inclusive issues is needed to enlarge collective solidarity and participation and to promote collective action.

II. *Participatory Control.* Ultimate and substantive (moral) interests in equality and liberty enable members to possess a criterion by which to evaluate leaders' policy actions. Consequently, by linking their support to their own autonomously created moral ends rather than to authority in general, members can influence leaders to act on their collective ends in order to maintain and develop their authority and external power. This is the principle of participatory control. Members exercise control of policy substance, if not detail, by participating in a process of trading their support in return for leaders' action on the substance of their ultimate and substantive ends. The exchange of support for leadership service is contingent on (1) members' bargaining power which can be heightened by the frequency and diversity of demands; (2) the delegitimation of authority which gives members control of the object (for example, policy, nation, officeholders, or organisational role) and determines the degree of their support; and (3) class consciousness which enables workers to autonomously formulate specific moral demands. Further, organisational and collective needs for stability and order constrain leaders' options in avoiding or overriding members' interests. Ultimate and substantive egalitarian ends provide guidelines within which leaders have autonomy in selecting the means to attain the collective goals. Unfortunately, when the imperatives of a collective consensus based on the moral ends of liberty and equality in decision-making processes and results are eroded, rational–bureaucratic policy processes favouring leadership domination are likely to reassert themselves and to prevail, leading to autocratic control or to shared control by competing leadership factions.

THE DISTINCTIVENESS OF PARTICIPATORY DEMOCRACY

The historical cases of policy-making in British workgroups, trade unions, and national federations, then, provide evidence for a concept of democracy in which participation is both extensive in scope and effective in shaping organisational issue-agendas and policies.[4] Participation refers to group and individual actions in negotiating the exchange of support and information concerning members' subjective interests. Moreover, participation involves face-to-face relations through direct decision-making processes among workgroups at the base and indirect processes of delegate assemblies. Yet, at every level in the hierarchy, representative mechanisms provide the necessary basis for the realization of the collective consensus essential to participatory democracy. This analysis of organisational complexity satisfies C. B. Macpherson's dictum that participatory democracy in modern industrial societies must consist in "direct democracy at the base and delegate democracy at higher levels."[5]

Michels, drawing upon his experiences with the German Social Democratic Party before the war, constructed a powerful argument against the possibility of either direct democracy or representative democracy ever giving adequate representation to workers' interests. His arguments countered, first, the Marxist visions of revolutionary organisation and action and, secondly, the utilitarians' arguments that the mass could compel leaders to act in their general interest through electoral mechanisms. More recently, democratic elitists revitalized the concept of democracy by emphasizing process as its essence while attributing it value only for its regularity. Schumpeter, Lipset, and Dahl stand out among those who divorced democracy from its participatory and substantive elements and focused primarily on electoral and competitive mechanisms as sources of stability.[6] Yet, as Macpherson has suggested, even though the democratic elitist and pluralist visions have been the reigning concepts of democracy, the theorists did not really advance democratic theory; rather they reverted to its Benthamite roots.[7] By focusing on elections, democratic elitists not only exclude the possibility of extensive popular control of decision-making and implementation, but fail to confront Michels' argument that electoral processes were no guarantee for leadership responsiveness to members' interests. Since elections cannot prevent leaders from manipulating issues or the choice of candidates, limiting potential opposition, aggregating resources, and exercising final authority by virtue of their administration of everyday decisions, in order to check organisational tendencies toward oligarchy and conservatism, representative procedures must be supplemented by the process in which members' grant support to officeholders only in return for service in pursuit of their interests. This notion of participatory democracy, then, centres on a problem—that organisation itself fosters leadership domination of followers—that has long been neglected by democratic elite theorists. They have side-stepped the issue by focusing on electoral competition among leadership teams and by accepting as inevitable that the masses cannot effectively participate in decision-making.

The theory of elitist democracy, thus, is neither an adequate response to the elitist challenge to democratic theory nor a complete account of democracy. By emphasizing electoral competition and leadership initiative as the mechanism of accountability, democratic elitism conceptualizes democracy in terms of a rule-bound competition whose outcome depends on differentially distributed resources.[8] Insofar as an opposition prevents officeholders from obtaining a monopoly in control of organisational authority, democracy is said to exist. Such a model rests on an instrumental value-orientation in which organisational norms and actors' objectives rely on legal, cocrcive, material, and psychological instruments of leadership control. Just as consumers or workers can never become owners of the means of production no matter how equitable their income distribution, individual citizens cannot assume the role of leaders whose privilege it is to make authoritative decisions. As a result, democratic elitism cannot provide an alternative answer to Michels' contention that the aggregation of the organisational means of power confers elite domination; it can only account for limits on the concentration of that power. Nor can it provide for the possibility of participatory democracy, since, according to democratic elite theorists, members are largely passive actors, who respond to initiatives from above by passing a judgment of approval or rejection.

Yet, a theory of participatory democracy cannot reject all elements of the democratic elitist's conception. The theory argues that the formal mechanisms of electoral competition—elections to delegate councils or executive committees—are necessary, if not sufficient, to participatory democracy itself. The formal procedures of representative democracy constitute channels of communication that can be utilized through collective action driven from below. Similarly, a highly developed social pluralism is necessary, though not sufficient, to ensure participatory democracy. Social pluralism provides multiple sources for the autonomous articulation of interests and support which enable groups at the base to exercise control over leaders at higher levels. In other words, social pluralism guarantees liberty from centralized power but, even more, constitutes a necessary condition for the exercise of control from below. Finally, the theory of participatory democracy does not deny the importance of leadership. In workplace organisations operating along lines of direct democracy, leadership is still crucial to the translation of the group consensus into policy and for its implementation whether through bargaining with employers or coordination with other workgroups in pursuit of a common end. At higher levels, in delegate assemblies and in executive committees, leadership is crucial to the distillation of the group interests, the proposing of plans that make members' interests more realizable, and strategies for the effective pursuit of group ends. More specifically, in the context of reciprocal relations between leaders and members created by common ends, the leaders who are influenced more than influencing are judged competent to the extent that they can effectively promote the moral ends that foster greater participation. In short, if the processes of liberal democracy do not constitute the heart of our concept of participatory democracy, the formal mechanisms of competition and adversarial decision-making do provide arteries through which the substance of participatory democracy—interests and support—can be moved.

Our concept of participatory democracy identifies the exchange of interests and support as the key control mechanism through which followers can control organisational policy. It also argues that the requisite motivational force underlying membership participation in power relations lies not in a competitive process but in the way that the environment fosters members' consciousness of injustice and thus the stimulus for collective action. While a diversity of groups at the base and the formal mechanisms of representative democracy are essential to participatory democracy, the ultimate and substantive commitments to liberty and equality that spring from subordinates' claims to reciprocity in social relations constitute a collective solidarity that binds individuals into groups governed by direct democracy and then these groups into larger collectivities governed by delegate democracy. The ends of greater social justice, moreover, foster a reciprocity in internal power relations that makes the exchange of leadership service on behalf of members' interest in return for support possible. Unless members demand substantive and ultimate ends involving equality and liberty and then make leadership action in pursuit of those ends the condition of their support, they will not be able to overcome the oligarchical tendencies by which leaders aggregate and manipulate material and legal resources. By giving leaders support in general or even as a reward for material benefits, members lose control of the exchange of support for service, enabling leaders to increasingly usurp decision-making prerogatives. Only by making support conditional on service toward objectives that entail clear criteria for assessment can members be in a position to know whether their support can be exchanged for responsiveness. Participatory democracy, in other words, is a form of collective action in which leaders are guided by the imperatives of collective consensus and solidarity and motivated by the exchange of support for service.

Contrary to Michels, we can now argue that participatory democracy is possible in large-scale organisations insofar as they operate according to egalitarian value-rational policy-making processes. Scholars have recently argued that community is essential to successful protest move-

ments.[9] Similarly, consciously developed substantive or ultimate objectives oriented toward greater social reciprocity and equality can create
a collective community that can provide an alternative mode of social
organisation to the rational-bureaucratic model presupposed by Michels'
theory of oligarchy. Community can provide an alternative to legal-
rational and coercive bases of social control and order, typical of bureaucratic organisation and the state.[10] What is important for participatory democracy is that the principles of moral control be intentional,
orient action toward equality among group members and other corporate
groups, and provide incentives for collective solidarity. Such principles
can be found in class-conscious workgroups as well as "intentional
communities" like cooperatives and communes. The moral imperative
of equality, when activated by environmental conditions, can provide
incentive for the growth of groups that are internally controlled by
popular participation and that can pyramid that involvement into participation in the control of larger organisational expressions of the collective community. Michels' challenge to democratic theory can be
answered by the argument that the development of value-rational–oriented collective consciousness and action depends on a community that
entails collective consensus on ultimate ends, face-to-face intimacy at
the base and bonds of collective solidarity at higher levels, and a commitment to reciprocity in all social relations. Insofar as our theory of
participatory democracy reveals why particular episodes of policy-making described in earlier chapters occurred, it offers an explanation of
policy processes in which community decision-making processes extend
beyond direct democracy to delegate democracies. Collective action
depends on a community of shared interests and solidarity among numerous and diverse groups and individuals who are brought together,
motivated, and ordered by the moral imperatives of equality. This community-based collective action, emerging in response to injustice, provides the independent bases for interest formulation and participatory
control presupposed by participatory democracy.

To argue that the notion of an egalitarian community is essential to
a theory of participatory democracy provides a response to those rational-choice theorists who argue that widespread participation in organisational decision-making is impossible. Rational-choice analysis is
valuable because it reminds us that in certain circumstances the pursuit
of the collective interest cannot be explained in terms of individual
calculations of self-interest and that the "group consciousness" required

could not be sustained indefinitely.[11] Over time, organisation must rely on leaders and reward them with such benefits as power, money, or status. A rational-choice argument confirms Michels' maxim: "Who says organization says oligarchy."[12] The elements of a rational-choice argument reduce to three inter-related propositions: (1) that it is not rational for anyone to incur a cost where the increased amount of a public good he will receive is negligible;[13] (2) that, as a result, organisation relies on selective incentives to hold leaders and followers; and (3) that over time, leaders become dominant, taking the lion's share of the organisational benefits, while the majority of members, gaining little, have no incentive to participate in decision-making.[14] As a result, Olson argues that members do not join trade unions because they benefit all workers in, say, a particular industry or firm, but because unions provide them with selective incentives, such as health benefits or higher wages.

As the cases make obvious, value-rational–based collective action guided by the principles of equality and liberty involves interests, circumstances, and a type of organisation incompatible with the rational-action approach to political participation. Value-rational ends can motivate participation without benefit of or in addition to selective incentives. For instance, a belief that an early end to the war would end the misery of exploitation at home generated collective action involving large numbers of British workers. In the cases discussed, members joined and participated in workplace organisations and trade unions during the war, not because they sought to realize private gain, but because they sought to resist political and economic injustices and to advance a more equitable industrial order. Moreover, the unique or abnormal circumstances of the wartime environment do not fit well with Olson's theory. War workers' expectations of the results of their action may well have been heightened by the unprecedented bargaining power they experienced, by the recognition of the fact that only collective action could enable them to defend their rights and standards—given union promises not to strike and leadership support for Government policies—and by political and economic conditions that galvanized class consciousness. Finally, union growth and the increase in informal work-group organisation contributed to increased participation in union policy-making. The upsurge in informal collective organisation responded to and stimulated informal discussion about industrial and political issues among those in similar social circumstances, factors that typically increase political participation.[15] In short, intentional value-rational responses to injustice motivate the collective action essential to participatory democracy, whereas rational-action explanations of participation seem most appropriate to large, instrumentally oriented organisations.

Moreover, this study reinforces and adds to previous arguments justifying participatory democracy. The theory developed in this book argues that participatory democracy depends on a value-rational response to exploitation and inequality. The policy processes outlined constitute a means to greater justice as well as a manifestation of heightened commitment to ideals of equality and fraternity. Consequently, the theory advanced here is consistent with the so-called protective argument in favour of participatory democracy. John Stuart Mill argued that participation was the only means by which the individual could safeguard his rights and interests.[16] Rousseau, more broadly, argued that the general will defends the community against the destructive impulses and influences of particular wills.[17] Still, my argument that the active involvement of workers is essential to the pursuit of greater equality and justice adds the element of progressive change to the protective argument. Participation means not just better decisions in the sense of reflecting a wider array of members' interests; rather, participatory democracy is the means by which decisions aimed at changing the balance of power and status between the privileged and the underprivileged in industrial society as well as within political institutions are both formulated and pursued.

A frequent objection to the argument that participatory democracy promotes the common interest is that participation in fact serves narrow, sectional goals. Because workers' participation involves objectives like higher wages or more control of work, it enables unions, according to some, to promote their particular interests at the expense of others, such as consumers, thereby injuring the larger societal (general) interest.[18] Yet, while the link between particular interests and the general interest cannot be taken for granted, the case studies do show clearly that workers can and do combine particular objectives with a general interest in a more humane and cooperative social order. Workers have both subjective and objective bases in a capitalist system for sentiments of injustice, since capitalism presupposes the subordination and exploitation of wage-earners. As a result, workers' particular interests (grievances) and struggles can contribute simultaneously to the general interest in a more equitable system of social relations.[19]

That participation can prepare workers for a higher status and more power confirms what Mill considered a more important, second argument in support of participatory democracy: that participation promotes individual self-development and public-spiritedness.[20] The policy-making processes in the British labour movement that resulted in a program calling for socialism at home and an early, negotiated peace abroad grew out of increased participation of workers at all levels of union organisation and on issues of both intra-class and national importance. The war did more than make the nation's rulers aware of the importance and power of workers. It involved organised labour in decision-making that affected the future of the nation; rank-and-file participation in the shaping of those policies raised their consciousness of issues, improved their competency, and enlarged their self-respect as full-fledged members of the political community. Participatory democracy, in other words, elevated active members morally and intellectually by enabling them to shape labour's vision of a more just world and to participate in achieving it, in however a limited fashion. Thus, participation in collective decision-making and action was more than simply a protest or rebellion against oppression; it was ultimately a constructive action. For, despite the failure to realize the higher ideals contained in numerous union and federation programs, like the Labour Party's "Labour After the War" Program, the pursuit of policies forged during the war did, in fact, effect basic changes in the status and power of labour in British society. Because this study has illuminated cases in which collective solidarity and action make use of representative mechanisms to foster policy processes appropriately characterized as participatory democracy, it can be posited that similar policy-making processes can occur in large political systems. In the end, the participatory and democratic struggle for justice and equality may well be the best means to a more humane and peaceful world.

THE NEED FOR PARTICIPATORY DEMOCRACY

What, then, are the prospects for participatory democracy? The answer to this question lies in applying our presupposition that the environment shapes issue conflict and power relations to contemporary conditions. The environment of the World War I British political economy was in many ways unique. The overt repression of working-class living standards and rights coincided with an overt collusion between

Government and business that brought the latter many privileges. Yet, the absence of unemployment, the unprecedented expansion of state intervention in the economy, and labour processes favourable to class consciousness all helped foster an acceleration of the trends that were pushing toward an enlarged class community before the war. What is most notable about the wartime environment is that it mobilized a response to injustice on an unparalleled scale, despite the fact that the war strengthened leadership. The level of workers' involvement in workplace and national politics went far beyond that of usual peacetime politics. Total war mobilized society, transforming the condition of democratic processes. War, on the one hand, centralized unprecedented power in the state executive, the Prime Minister and his War Cabinet, and, on the other hand, by causing hardship and injustice in the context of full employment evoked widespread participation at the base. Such participation is consistent with Marx's view of democratic practice during the Paris Commune, in which democracy is portrayed as the popular control of elected officers under constant scrutiny by a politically mobilized public.[21]

What is crucial to participatory democracy is that the concern for injustice and liberty become central to individuals. Some evidence from Sweden points to the ability of union and party leaders to raise class consciousness and so heighten the sense of relative deprivation.[22] But few socialist and labour movements are as ideologically motivated as the Swedish movement. Even more important, to place great hope in an effective campaign of consciousness-raising is to invest too much faith in a strategy that can only affect the periphery of most citizens' lives. In contrast, Rousseau's notion of a proper education in preparation for citizenship was much more involved with and fundamental to individuals' lives, while J. S. Mill believed that participation in public life would promote the self-development necessary for further participation.[23] Yet, because class societies contain inequalities of wealth, status, and power, the potential for feelings of injustice being central in people's lives is enormous. As hypothesized above, injustice can become the focus and basis of protest and participation when workers or others objectively and subjectively undergo relative deprivation, unfair sacrifice, and/or a loss of rights.

The post-World War II welfare state consensus initially held little prospect for the advance of participatory democracy. Prosperity and anti-communism helped to relegate consciousness of inequality and injustice to the periphery of most people's lives. Material, familial, and other private concerns typically predominated. Yet, out of the prosperity in the 1960s emerged the civil rights movement in the United States, a worldwide protest movement aimed at stopping American involvement in Vietnam, and a countercultural movement among the young. These movements gave a new life to popular democracy, in ideology if not always in practice. The *Port Huron Statement* of the Students for a Democratic Society, the Berkeley Free Speech Movement, and May 1968 in Paris exemplify this mood of liberation. By the 1970s, a reaction set in as fears of too much democracy and economic deterioration fueled new efforts to find governing strategies that would restore public authority and economic stability in industrialized states. The most important of these strategies are corporatism and neoliberalism.

Corporatism refers to a relationship between the state and interests groups. Some scholars use it to refer to a mode of policy formation, others to identify the state's role in organising the way associations represent their members and simultaneously act as agents controlling members' interests. This social control aspect is what distinguishes corporatism from interest group pluralism and is important to the prospects of participatory democracy. Because corporatism, as manifest in incomes policies, involves arrangements between the state and unions, it involves the government directly in limiting members' rights and living standards. As Cawson argues and as the evidence from the first World War confirms, when "the state is itself the producer . . . or the regulator of non-individually-based interests—of trade unions, economic sectors and the like in incomes policy and economic planning— the intervention has to be purpose-rational, that is, justified in terms of effective results rather than legitimate procedures."[24] Though Cawson may be thinking of material results, his argument applies even more to moral ends. Consequently, corporatism contains the potential for politicizing questions of liberty and equity in social relations, thus encouraging episodes of participatory democracy in unions. The British Miners' strikes in 1972 and 1974 and the multitude of unofficial strikes against Callaghan's pay policy in the Winter of 1979 testify to this.

Ultimately, the theory of participatory democracy challenges the theory and the practicality of corporatism. By showing that members' moral ends can become the basis of controlling organisational policy, it poses a problem for an analysis which focuses solely on the relationship between groups and the state. Corporatist theory consequently has to rely on the mistaken assumption that leaders can always control their ranks. Instead, the theory of participatory democracy suggests the need for a revised analysis, one that examines the ebb and flow of inter-organisational relations. Such an alternative would start from the perspective of the dynamics of groups' internal power relations and thereby examine the bases of inter-organisational relations.

Recent disillusionment with corporatism has brightened the hopes of proponents of neoliberalism with its faith in the market and in limited but strong government. The very alienation and narcissism that neoliberalism encourages would seem to inhibit the development of community-based responses to injustice. Marcuse argues that modern capitalist society has created a one-dimensional mentality unable to imagine alternatives to mass consumerism.[25] Similarly, Lasch portrays the modern individual as dependent on others for his sense of worth, a consequence of state and corporate manipulation and paternalism.[26] And there is much evidence that the British union movement under the Thatcher regime is itself very much divided and lacking in a sense of collective solidarity.[27]

But the apparent triumph of capital over labour associated with the declining power of the labour movement need not thwart the potential for participatory democracy. The hardship and injustices of poverty and repression are broadening and will in all likelihood provoke popular concern for securing basic human needs, peace, ecological survival, and human rights. Already, the rise of groups pursuing absolute ends, such as pro-life, peace, and environmental organisations, has undermined the authority of officeholders, making them responsive to the groups' specific normative ends. These groups can further complicate leaders' ability to generate authority because they can place officeholders in the untenable position of trying to reconcile incompatible ends. As a result, officeholders are being forced increasingly to justify in moral terms their policies in order to gain legitimacy and so to govern effectively.

In short, recent trends are creating conditions that can facilitate the advance of participatory democracy. A growing concern among the young for a more participatory, egalitarian society has already motivated them to take a leading role in the emerging social movements. The enthusiasm for participatory democracy is in part evidenced in the growth of communes and workers' cooperatives.[28] Even more, increasing demands for greater democracy in voluntary groups, the workplace, corporate enterprises, and politics reflect a recognition that greater participation and popular control are required to resolve the severe threat of impending nuclear war, ecological disaster, poverty, and alienation that are so overwhelming today. While revolutionary changes can be ruled out, a growing minority is pressing for greater participatory democracy in many advanced industrial societies. Just as British workers responded to and effectively fought injustice during the First World War, the ideal of participatory democracy can similarly inspire citizens of the late twentieth century to mitigate, if not resolve, contemporary crises of injustice and inequality.

Notes

INTRODUCTION

1. Tony Benn, *Arguments for Socialism* (Harmondsworth, England: Penguin, 1980), p. 140.

2. Ibid.

3. Martin Carnoy and Derek Shearer, *Economic Democracy* (Armonk, NY:M. E. Sharpe, 1980). Also see Paul Blumberg, *Industrial Democracy: The Sociology of Participation* (New York: Shocken, 1969); Paul Bernstein, *Workplace Democratization: Its Internal Dynamics* (New Brunswick, NJ: Transaction Books, 1980); John F. Witte, *Democracy, Authority, and Alienation in Work: Workers' Participation in an American Corporation* (Chicago: University of Chicago Press, 1980).

4. Arguments for and against participatory democracy are contained in the following works: C. George Benello and Dimitrios Roussopoulis, eds., *The Case for Participatory Democracy* (New York: Grossman, 1971); Terrance Cook and Patrick Morgan, *Participatory Democracy* (San Francisco: Canfield Press, 1971); Ronald M. Mason, *Participatory and Workplace Democracy: A Theoretical Development in Critique of Liberalism* (Carbondale: Southern Illinois University Press, 1982); Benjamin R. Barber, *Strong Democracy: Participatory Politics for a New Age* (Berkeley and Los Angeles: University of California Press, 1984).

5. Carole Pateman, *Participation and Democratic Theory* (Cambridge: Cambridge University Press, 1970), pp. 42–43.

6. Ibid.

7. Peter Bachrach, *The Theory of Democratic Elitism: A Critique* (Boston: Little, Brown, 1967); Jack L. Walker, ''A Critique of the Elitist Theory of

Democracy," *American Political Science Review*, Vol. 60, No. 2, 1966, pp. 285–95; G. Duncan and S. Lukes, "The New Democracy," *Political Studies*, Vol. 11, No. 2, 1963, pp. 156–77.

8. Moise Ostrogorski, *Democracy and the Organization of Political Parties* (London: Macmillan, 1902); Robert Michels, *Political Parties: A Sociological Study of the Oligarchical Tendencies of Modern Democracy*, translated by Eden and Cedar Paul, introduction by S. M. Lipset (New York: Free Press, 1962); Max Weber, *Economy and Society*, 2 vol., edited by G. Roth and Claus Wittich (Berkeley and Los Angeles: University of California Press, 1978), chs. 10–11.

9. Michels, *Political Parties*, p. 355.

10. J. David Edelstein and Malcolm Warner, *Comparative Union Democracy: Organisation and Opposition in British and American Unions* (New Brunswick, NJ: Transaction Books, 1979), p. 3.

11. C. B. Macpherson, *The Life and Times of Liberal Democracy* (Oxford: Oxford University Press, 1977), p. 108.

12. See, for example, G. D. H. Cole, *Self-Government in Industry* (London: G. Bell and Son, 1917); Antonio Gramsci, "Soviets in Italy," *New Left Review*, No. 51, September–October 1968, pp. 28–58.

13. Discussions of these developments include G. D. H. Cole, *Workshop Organisation* (Oxford: Clarendon Press, 1923); Carter Goodrich, *The Frontiers of Control: A Study in British Workshop Politics* (London: Pluto Press, 1975; originally published in 1920); James Hinton, *The First Shop Stewards' Movement* (London: Allen and Unwin, 1973); Bob Holton, *British Syndicalism, 1900–1914* (London: Pluto Press, 1976).

14. Michels, *Political Parties*, p. 358.

15. Throughout I will refer to these theories as democratic elitism. They are identified and explained in Chapter 1.

CHAPTER 1: ELITISM AND DEMOCRACY

1. Robert Michels, *Political Parties: A Sociological Study of the Oligarchical Tendencies of Modern Democracy*, translated by Eden and Cedar Paul, introduction by S. M. Lipset (New York: Free Press, 1962). Restatements and assessments of Michels' theory include S. M. Lipset's introduction in *Political Parties*, pp. 15–39; J. Linz, "Robert Michels," in the *International Encyclopedia of Social Sciences* (New York: Macmillan, 1968), Vol. 10, pp. 265–72; C. W. Cassinelli, "The Law of Oligarchy," *American Political Science Review*, Vol. 47, 1953, pp. 773–84; G. Hand, "Roberto Michels and the Study of Political Parties," *British Journal of Political Science*, Vol. 1, April 1971, pp. 155–72; J. D. May, "Democracy, Organization, Michels," *American Political Science Review*, Vol. 59, 1965, pp. 417–84; R. T. McKenzie, *British Political Parties* (New York: Praeger, 1963); Peter Y. Medding, "A Framework of Power in Political Parties," *Political Studies*, Vol. 18, No. 1, 1970, pp. 1–

17; Philip J. Cook, "Robert Michels's Political Parties in Perspective," *Journal of Politics*, Vol. 33, No. 3, August 1971, pp. 773–96; and David Beetham, "Michels and His Critics," *Archives Europeenes de Sociologie*, Tome 23, No. 1, 1981, pp. 81–99.

2. For a discussion of the development of Michels' thought, see David Beetham, "From Socialism to Fascism: The Relation Between Theory and Practice in the Work of Robert Michels: I. From Marxist Revolutionary to Political Sociologist," *Political Studies*, Vol. 25, No. 1, March 1977, p. 14.

3. Max Weber, *The Theory of Social and Economic Organization*, edited by Talcott Parsons (New York: The Free Press, 1964), p. 337.

4. Michels, *Political Parties*, p. 70.

5. Ibid., p. 353.

6. Ibid., pp. 172–73.

7. Max Weber, *Economy and Society*, 2 vol., edited by G. Roth and Claus Wittich (Berkeley and Los Angeles: University of California Press, 1978), p. 948.

8. Ibid., p. 985.

9. Ibid.

10. Joseph Schumpeter, *Capitalism, Socialism, and Democracy*, 3rd ed. (New York: Harper and Row, 1950), Part 4. Major restatements of Schumpeter can be found in S. M. Lipset, "The Political Process in Trade Unions," in his *Political Man* (Garden City, NY: Doubleday, 1960), ch. 12, and Giovanni Sartori, "Anti-Elitism Revisited," *Government and Opposition*, Vol. 13, No. 1, Winter 1978, pp. 58–80.

11. Schumpeter, *Capitalism, Socialism, and Democracy*, p. 282.

12. Ibid., p. 283.

13. S. M. Lipset, M. Trow, and J. S. Coleman, *Union Democracy: The Internal Politics of the International Typographical Union* (New York: Free Press, 1956).

14. Ibid., p. 459.

15. J. David Edelstein, "An Organizational Theory of Union Democracy," *American Sociological Review*, Vol. 32, 1967, pp. 19–39; J. David Edelstein and M. Warner, *Comparative Union Democracy* (New Brunswick, NJ: Transaction Books, 1979).

16. Roderick Martin, "Union Democracy: An Explanatory Framework," *Sociology*, Vol. 2, 1968, pp. 205–20.

17. Roderick Martin, "The Effects of Recent Changes in Industrial Conflict on the Internal Politics of Trade Unions: Britain and Germany," in C. Crouch and A. Pizzorno, eds., *The Resurgence of Class Conflict in Western Europe Since 1968*, Vol. 2 (London: Macmillan, 1978), pp. 110–22.

18. John Hemingway, *Conflict and Democracy: Studies in Trade Union Government* (Oxford: Clarendon Press, 1978), p. 11.

19. S. M. Lipset, "Introduction," pp. 33–34.

20. Other important mechanisms that purportedly give citizens access to policy-making influence are the referendum, the initiative, and the recall.

21. Michael Margolis, *Viable Democracy* (Harmondsworth, England: Penguin Books, 1979), p. 120.

22. Peter Bachrach and Morton S. Baratz, "Two Faces of Power," *American Political Science Review*, Vo. 56, 1962, pp. 947–52.

23. See, for example, Samuel H. Beer, *British Politics in the Collectivist Age* (New York: Vintage, 1969), ch. 6.

24. Ralf Dahrendorf, *Class and Class Conflict in Industrial Society* (Stanford: Stanford University Press, 1959).

25. Steven Lukes, *Power: A Radical View* (London: Macmillan, 1974), p. 34.

26. Dennis H. Wrong, *Power: Its Forms, Bases and Uses* (New York: Harper and Row, 1979), p. 196.

27. William E. Connolly, "On 'Interests' in Politics," *Politics and Society*, Vol. 2, 1972, pp. 459–77.

28. Gaventa's application of Lukes' analysis illustrates this point. See John Gaventa, *Power and Powerlessness: Quiescence and Rebellion in an Appalachian Valley* (Urbana: University of Illinois Press, 1980), ch. 7.

29. G. Duncan and S. Lukes, "The New Democracy," *Political Studies*, Vol. 11, June 1965, pp. 156–77; Peter Bachrach, *The Theory of Democratic Elitism: A Critique* (Boston: Little, Brown, 1967).

CHAPTER 2: A THEORY OF PARTICIPATORY DEMOCRACY

1. C. B. Macpherson, *The Life and Times of Liberal Democracy* (Oxford: Oxford University Press, 1977), p. 108.

2. Anthony Giddens, *The Class Structure of Advanced Societies* (London: Hutchinson, 1973), p. 122.

3. Jurgen Habermas, *Legitimation Crisis* (Boston: Beacon Press, 1975), pp. 8–12.

4. Vincent Geoghegan, "Marcuse and Autonomy," in Graeme Duncan, ed., *Democratic Theory and Practice* (Cambridge: Cambridge University Press, 1983), p. 161. Also see Herbert Marcuse, *One-Dimensional Man* (London: Sphere Books, 1972).

5. Habermas, *Legitimation Crisis,* pp. 68–75.

6. Karl Marx, *Capital*, Vol. 1 (London: Lawrence and Wishart, 1974).

7. Injustice defined in terms of non-reciprocal social relations may lead to protest under certain conditions and to quiescence in others. This is discussed in Barrington Moore, Jr., *Injustice: The Social Bases of Obedience and Revolt* (Armonk, NY: M. E. Sharpe, 1978). Also see Alvin W. Gouldner, "The Norm

of Reciprocity," in his *For Sociology: Renewal and Critique in Sociology Today* (New York: Basic Books, 1973), pp. 226–59.

8. Adam Przeworski, "Proletariat into Class: The Process of Class Formation from Karl Kautsky's *The Class Struggle* to Recent Controversies," *Politics and Society*, Vol. 7, No. 4, 1977, p. 372–73.

9. Substantive and ultimate values denote what Weber called substantive rationality, as against formal rationality. This involves the "application of certain criteria of ultimate ends" to the evaluation of the outcome of economic activity. Max Weber, *Economy and Society*, 2 vols., edited by G. Roth and C. Wittich (Berkeley and Los Angeles: University of California Press, 1978), p. 85. Also see Joyce Rothschild-Whitt, "The Collectivist Organization: An Alternative to Rational-Bureaucratic Models," *American Sociological Review*, Vol. 44, No. 4, 1979, p. 512.

10. Mancur Olson, *The Logic of Collective Action* (New York: Shocken Books, 1968); Russell Hardin, *Collective Action* (Baltimore: Johns Hopkins University Press, 1983).

11. T. Nichols and P. Armstrong, *Workers Divided: A Study in Shopfloor Politics* (London: Fontana, 1976); T. Nichols and Huw Beynon, *Living with Capitalism: Class Relations and the Modern Factory* (London: Routledge and Kegan Paul, 1977).

12. Nichols and Armstrong, *Workers Divided*, pp. 69–73.

13. Michael Burawoy, *Manufacturing Consent: Changes in the Labor Process Under Monopoly Capitalism* (Chicago: University of Chicago Press, 1979), ch. 4.

14. David Gordon, "The Best Defense Is a Good Defense: Toward a Marxian Theory of Labor Union Structure and Behavior," in M. J. Carter and W. H. Leahy, eds., *New Directions in Labor Economics and Industrial Relations* (Notre Dame, IN: University of Notre Dame Press, 1981), pp. 188.

15. See L. Sayles, *Behavior in Industrial Work Groups* (New York: John Wiley, 1958), ch. 3; T. Lupton, *On the Shop Floor* (Oxford: Pergamon, 1963), ch. 13; Richard Edwards, *Contested Terrain: The Transformation of the Workplace in the Twentieth Century* (New York: Basic Books, 1979); Burawoy, *Manufacturing Consent*.

16. On the sources of bargaining power, see M. Kalecki, "Political Aspects of Full Employment," in E. K. Hunt and J. G. Schwartz, eds., *A Critique of Economic Theory* (Harmondsworth, England: Penguin, 1972), pp. 420–30; William Brown and Keith Sisson, "The Use of Comparisons in Workplace Wage Determination," *British Journal of Industrial Relations*, Vol. 13, No. 1, March 1975, pp. 23–53; P. Dunleavy, "The Urban Basis of Political Alignment: Social Class, Domestic Property Ownership, and State Intervention in Consumption Processes," *British Journal of Political Science*, Vol. 9, 1979, pp. 409–43; Eric Hobsbawm, "The Forward March of Labour Halted?" in M. Jacques and F. Mulhern, eds., *The Forward March of Labour Halted* (London: Verso, 1981), p. 14.

17. On incorporation, see Leo Panitch, "Trade Unions and the Capitalist State," *New Left Review*, No. 125, January–February 1981, pp. 21–43.

18. H. A. Clegg, *Trade Unionism Under Collective Bargaining: A Theory Based on Comparisons of Six Countries* (Oxford: Basil Blackwell, 1976); W. G. Runciman, *Relative Deprivation and Social Justice: A Study of Attitudes to Social Equality in Twentieth Century England* (London: Routledge, 1966); J. H. Goldthorpe, *The Affluent Worker in the Class Structure* (Cambridge: Cambridge University Press, 1969).

19. Ira Katznelson, *City Trenches: Urban Politics and the Patterning of Class in the United States* (New York: Pantheon Books, 1981).

20. W. Brown, ed., *The Changing Contours of British Industrial Relations* (Oxford: Basil Blackwell, 1981), ch. 5; M. Mann, "Industrial Relations in Advanced Capitalism and the Explosion of Consciousness," in T. Clarke and L. Clements, eds., *Trade Unions Under Capitalism* (London: Fontana, 1977), p. 298.

21. S. Hill, "Norms, Groups, and Power: The Sociology of Workplace Industrial Relations," *British Journal of Industrial Relations*, Vol. 12, No. 2, 1974, pp. 218–22.

22. Sayles, *Behavior in Industrial Work Groups*, pp. 70–93.

23. Lupton, *On the Shop Floor*, ch. 13.

24. Allan Flanders, *Management and Unions: The Theory and Reform of Industrial Relations* (London: Faber and Faber, 1970).

25. Clegg, *Trade Unionism Under Collective Bargaining*, chs. 4, 5.

26. Jane J. Mansbridge, *Beyond Adversary Democracy* (New York: Basic Books, 1980), chs. 17–21.

27. Joyce Rothschild-Whitt, "The Collectivist Organization: An Alternative to Rational-Bureaucratic Models," *American Sociological Review*, Vol. 44, No. 4, 1979, p. 512.

28. W. E. J. McCarthy and S. R. Parker, *Shop Stewards and Workshop Relations*. Research Paper No. 10. Royal Commission on Trades Unions and Employers Associations (London: HMSO, 1968), pp. 57–58. Other studies confirm the Commission's conclusions. See William Brown, *Piecework Bargaining* (London: Heinemann Educational Books, 1973), ch. 5; M. Pedler, "Shop Stewards as Leaders," *Industrial Relations Journal*, Vol. 4, No. 4, Winter 1973, p. 48.

29. Tony Lane, *The Union Makes Us Strong* (London: Arrow Books, 1974), pp. 199–200; Pedler, "Shop Stewards as Leaders," pp. 48–53; Alexandra Warren, "The Challenge from Below: An Analysis of the Role of the Shop Steward in Industrial Relations," *Industrial Relations Journal*, Vol. 2, No. 2, 1975, p. 57. On the idea that shop stewards are leaders of work groups rather than a single workgroup and that its constituency varies with issues, see Brown, *Piecework Bargaining*, pp. 132–33.

30. Lane, *The Union Makes Us Strong*, p. 203.

31. A. J. M. Sykes, "The Cohesion of a Trade Union Workshop Organization," *Sociology*, Vol. 1, No. 2, May 1967, pp. 160–61.

32. Brown, *Piecework Bargaining*, pp. 133–36.

33. Huw Beynon, *Working for Ford* (London: Allen Lane, 1973), pp. 178, 216, 233, 289.

34. Mansbridge, *Beyond Adversary Democracy*, chs. 1, 2.

35. Katznelson, *City Trenches*, pp. 18, 19, 206.

36. Runciman, *Relative Deprivation and Social Justice*, p. 389; John Goldthorpe, et al., *The Affluent Workers in the Social Structure* (Cambridge: Cambridge University Press, 1969).

37. S. M. Lipset, "Radicalism and Reformism: The Sources of Working-Class Politics," *American Political Science Review*, Vol. 77, No. 1, March 1983, pp. 1–18.

38. David Easton, *A Systems Analysis of Political Life* (New York: Wiley, 1965), p. 350. The emphasis is mine.

39. Robert Michels, *Political Parties: A Sociological Study of the Oligarchical Tendencies of Modern Democracy*, translated by Eden and Cedar Paul, introduction by S. M. Lipset (New York: Free Press, 1962), p. 339.

40. Weber, *Economy and Society*, p. 85.

41. Max Weber, *The Theory of Social and Economic Organization*, translated by A. M. Henderson and Talcott Parsons, edited with an introduction by Talcott Parsons (New York: Free Press, 1968), p. 236.

42. Ibid., pp. 214–15.

43. J. Roland Pennock, *Democratic Political Theory* (Princeton, NJ: Princeton University Press, 1979), pp. 484–91.

44. J. S. Mill, *Considerations on Representative Government* (London: J. M. Dent and Son, 1972), ch. 6; Jean-Jacques Rousseau, *The Social Contract* (London: J. M. Dent and Son, 1973), bk. 3, ch. 15.

45. Pennock, *Democratic Political Theory*, pp. 478–84.

46. Benjamin Barber, *Strong Democracy: Participatory Politics for a New Age* (Berkeley and Los Angeles: University of California Press, 1984), pp. 237–42.

47. Robet A. Dahl, *After the Revolution?* (New Haven: Yale University Press, 1970), pp. 8–56.

48. Dennis F. Thompson, *John Stuart Mill and Representative Government* (Princeton, NJ: Princeton University Press, 1976), p. 198–99.

49. G. D. H. Cole, *Social Theory* (New York: Frederick A. Stokes, 1920), p. 106.

50. See Rousseau, *The Social Contract*, passim.

51. R. Bendix, *Max Weber: An Intellectual Portrait* (Garden City, NY: Anchor Books, 1960), pp. 418–20, 432.

52. William Brown, "A Consideration of 'Custom and Practice'," *British Journal of Industrial Relations*, Vol. 10, No. 1, March 1972, 42–61.

53. Easton defines support engendered by benefits and performance as "specific support." See his "A Re-Assessment of the Concept of Political Support," *British Journal of Political Science*, Vol. 5, October 1975, pp. 435–57.

54. Habermas, *Legitimation Crisis*, especially pp. 68–75.

55. Robert A. Dahl, *Modern Political Analysis* (Englewood Cliffs, NJ: Prentice-Hall, 1963), ch. 5; Steven Lukes, *Power: A Radical View* (London: Macmillan, 1974), chs. 6, 7; Dennis H. Wrong, *Power: Its Forms, Bases, and Uses* (New York: Harper Colophon Books, 1980).

56. William E. Connolly, *The Terms of Political Discourse*, 2nd ed. (Princeton, NJ: Princeton University Press, 1983), ch. 3.

57. Andrew S. McFarland uses the terms "critical" and "routine" to distinguish issue scope. See his *Power and Leadership in Pluralist Systems* (Stanford: Stanford University Press, 1969), ch. 5.

CHAPTER 3: THE ENVIRONMENT OF DEMOCRACY

1. David Lockwood, "Sources of Variation in Working-Class Images of Society," in M. Bulmer, ed., *Working-Class Images of Society* (London: Routledge and Kegan Paul, 1975), p. 17.

2. S. Hill, "Norms, Groups, and Power: The Sociology of Workplace Industrial Relations," *British Journal of Industrial Relations*, Vol. 12, No. 2, 1974, pp. 213–35; L. Sayles, *Behavior in Industrial Work Groups* (New York: John Wiley, 1958); T. Lupton, *On the Shop Floor* (Oxford: Pergamon, 1963).

3. Harry Braverman, *Labor and Monopoly Capital: The Degradation of Work in the Twentieth Century* (New York: Monthly Review Press, 1974); Andrew Friedman, *Industry and Labour: Class Struggle at Work and Monopoly Capitalism* (London: Macmillan, 1977), ch. 6.

4. Friedman, *Industry and Labour*, ch. 6.

5. David Gordon, Richard Edwards, and Michael Reich, *Segmented Work, Divided Workers: The Historical Transformation of Labor in the United States* (Cambridge: Cambridge University Press, 1982), ch. 4.

6. W. R. Garside and H. F. Gospel, "Employers and Managers: The Organizational Structure and Changing Industrial Strategies," in C. Wrigley, ed., *A History of British Industrial Relations, 1975–1914* (Amherst: University of Massachusetts Press, 1982), especially pp. 104, 105, 108, 111.

7. James E. Cronin, "Labour Insurgency and Class Formation: Comparative Perspectives on the Crisis of 1917–1920 in Europe," *Social Science History*, Vol. 4, No. 1, February 1980, p. 138.

8. James Hinton, *The First Shop Stewards' Movement* (London: Allen and Unwin, 1973), p. 63; Eric Hobsbawm, *Labouring Men: Studies in the History of Labour* (London: Weidenfeld and Nicholson, 1964), p. 301. Also see G. D. H. Cole, *Trade Unionism and Munitions* (Oxford: Clarendon Press, 1923), p. 35;

Samuel J. Hurwitz, *State Intervention in Great Britain: A Study of Economic Control and Social Response, 1914–1919* (New York: Columbia Univeristy Press, 1949), p. 90.

9. Hinton, *The First Shop Stewards' Movement*, p. 97.

10. I. McLean, "Red Clydeside 1915–19," in R. Quinault and J. Stevenson, eds., *Popular Protest and Public Order. Six Studies in British History, 1790–1920* (London: Allen and Unwin, 1974), p. 222.

11. Hinton, *The First Shop Stewards' Movement*, p. 95.

12. The Government's dilution campaign is discussed in J. Hinton, *The First Shop Stewards' Movement*, chs. 3, 4; Also see I. McLean, "The Ministry of Munitions, the Clyde Workers' Committee, and the Suppression of *Forward:* An Alternative View," *Journal of the Scottish Labour History Society*, Vol. 6, December 1972, pp. 3–29; Roger Davidson, "Wartime Labour Policy, 1914–1916: A Reappraisal," *Journal of the Scottish Labour History Society*, Vol. 8, June 1974, pp. 3–20; Jose Harris, *William Beveridge: A Biography* (Oxford: Clarendon Press, 1977), pp. 216–26.

13. K. Middlemas, *Politics in Industrial Society: The Experience of the British System Since 1911* (London: Andre Deutsch, 1979), p. 80; Cole, *Trade Unionism and Munitions*, pp. 128, 130, 135–36. The role of women in munitions work is discussed in R. J. Q. Adams, *Arms and the Wizard: Lloyd George and the Ministry of Munitions, 1915–1916* (London: Cassell, 1978), ch. 8.

14. B. A. Waites, "The Effect of the First World War on Class and Status in England," *Journal of Contemporary History*, Vol. 11, No. 1, 1976, pp. 31–32, 43; Keith Burgess, *The Challenge of Labour: Shaping British Society, 1850–1930* (London: Croom Helm, 1980), p. 165.

15. M. Kalecki, "Political Aspects of Full Employment," in E. K. Hunt and J. G. Schwartz, eds., *A Critique of Economic Theory* (Harmondsworth, England: Penguin, 1972), pp. 420–30; M. Stewart, *Keynes and After* (Harmondsworth, England: Penguin, 1972).

16. Charles F. Sabel, *Work and Politics: The Division of Labor in Industry* (New York: Cambridge University Press, 1982), ch. 2.

17. William Brown and Keith Sisson, "The Use of Comparisons in Workplace Wage Determination," *British Journal of Industrial Relations*, Vol. 13, No. 1, 1975, pp. 23–53.

18. Brian M. Barry, *Sociologists, Economists and Democracy* (London: Collier-Macmillan, 1970), pp. 29–30.

19. Burgess, *The Challenge of Labour*, p. 157. Also see Humbert Wolfe, *Labour Supply and Regulation* (Oxford: Clarendon Press, 1923), pp. 14, 20–21.

20. *History of the Ministry of Munitions* (hereafter *HMM*) (London: HMSO, 1920–24), Vol. 1, Pt. 2, ch. 4, p. 98.

21. Ibid., ch. 1, pp. 15–18.

22. Ibid., p. 98.

23. Ibid., p. 29.

24. Ibid., Vol. 2, ch. 2, p. 3.

25. Ibid., Vol. 1, Pt. 4, p. 1.

26. Cole, *Trade Unionism and Munitions*, p. 115; Wolfe, *Labour Supply and Regulation*, p. 221.

27. Middlemas, *Politics in Industrial Society*, pp. 83, 86–87.

28. The system of occupational classification used to determine exemptions from military service for men indispensable to war work. It superseded the Trade Card Agreement in which union leaders awarded exemptions and helped members find munitions work.

29. Chris Wrigley, *David Lloyd George and the British Labour Movement: Peace and War* (Hassocks, England: The Harvester Press; and New York: Barnes and Noble, 1976), p. 182.

30. Parliamentary Papers, *Commission of Enquiry into Industrial Unrest*, Scotland, 1917 (Cmnd. 8669), p. 9.

31. Hinton, *The First Shop Stewards' Movement*, p. 24.

32. Ibid., pp. 62–63.

33. P. S. Bagwell, *The Railwaymen: A History of the National Union of Railwaymen* (London: Allen and Unwin, 1963), p. 345.

34. Seymour Martin Lipset, "Radicalism or Reformism: The Sources of Working-Class Politics," *American Political Science Review*, Vol. 77, No. 1, March 1983, pp. 2, 6–12.

35. Ibid.

36. R. H. Tawney, "The Abolition of Economic Controls, 1918–1921," *Economic History Review*, Vol. 13, 1943, p. 2.

37. Hurwitz, *State Intervention in Great Britain*, p. 151.

38. Ibid., p. 153.

39. Harris, *William Beveridge*, p. 205.

40. Ibid., p. 201.

41. *HMM*, Vol. 2, ch. 2, pp. 17–18; Hinton, *The First Shop Stewards' Movement*, p. 90.

42. Middlemas, *Politics in Industrial Society*, p. 114.

43. *HMM*, Vol. 2, ch. 2, p. 19.

44. Tawney, "The Abolition of Economic Controls, 1918–1921," p. 2.

45. Hurwitz, *State Intervention in Great Britain*, p. 157.

46. Chris Wrigley, "The Ministry of Munitions: An Innovatory Department," in Kathleen Burk, ed., *War and the State: The Transformation of British Government, 1914–1919* (London: George Allen and Unwin, 1982), pp. 40, 47.

47. Burgess, *The Challenge of Labour*, p. 157.

48. Ibid.

49. *HMM*, Vol. 3, Pt. 2, ch. 1, p. 2.

50. Hurwitz, *State Intervention in Great Britain*, pp. 109, 111, 117; also Noelle Whiteside, "Industrial Welfare and Labour Regulation in Britain at the Time of the First World War," *International Review of Social History*, Vol. 25, 1980, Pt. 3, especially pp. 309, 312–15.

51. *HMM*, Vol. 4, ch. 6, p. 128; ibid., Vol. 5, Pt. 1, ch. 2, p. 37.

52. Ibid., Vol. 5, Pt. 2, ch. 6, p. 77.

53. Middlemas, *Politics in Industrial Society*, p. 111.

54. Cole, *Trade Unionism and Munitions*, pp. 158, 163; Hurwitz, *State Intervention in Great Britain*, p. 126.

55. Middlemas, *Politics in Industrial Society*, p. 103.

56. George R. (Baron) Askwith, *Industrial Problems and Disputes* (London: John Murray, 1920), p. 380.

57. *HMM*, Vol. 1, p. 96.

58. Wolfe, *Labour Supply and Regulation*, p. 44.

59. Ibid., p. 49.

60. Wrigley, *David Lloyd George and the British Labour Movement*, p. 233; Middlemas, *Politics in Industrial Society*, p. 89.

61. Hurwitz, *State Intervention in Great Britain*, p. 61.

62. Sidney Pollard, *The Development of the British Economy, 1914–1967*, 2nd edition (London: Edward Arnold, 1969), p. 64.

63. Burgess, *The Challenge of Labour*, p. 156.

64. Wrigley, *David Lloyd George and the British Labour Movement*, pp. 86–87.

65. Middlemas, *Politics in Industrial Society*, p. 112.

66. My argument questions the notion that the working-class standard of living improved as a result of the war, increasing expectations and stimulating social reform. See Arthur Marwick, "Impact of the First World War on British Society," *Journal of Contemporary History*, Vol. 3, No. 1, January 1968, p. 62; J. M. Winter, "A Note on the Reconstruction of the Labour Party," *Scottish Labour History Society Journal*, No. 12, February 1978, p. 66; Wolfgang J. Mommsen, "Society and War: Two New Analyses of the First World War," *Journal of Modern History*, Vol. 3, 1975, pp. 530–38. On the effect of the war, also see Waites, "The Effect of the First World War on Class and Status in England", pp. 27–48; A. S. Milward, *The Economic Effects of the Two World Wars on Britain* (London: Macmillan, 1970).

67. Parliamentary Papers, *Commission of Enquiry into Industrial Unrest*, London and South-Eastern Area, 1917 (Cmnd. 8666), p. 2.

68. W. G. Runciman, *Relative Deprivation and Social Justice: A Study of Attitudes to Social Inequality in Twentieth-Century England* (Harmondsworth, England: Penguin Books, 1972; first published in 1966), p. 389. Also see Ted Robert Gurr, *Why Men Rebel* (Princeton, NJ: Princeton University Press, 1970).

69. Runciman, *Relative Deprivation and Social Justice*, p. 13.

70. Parliamentary Papers, *Commission of Enquiry into Industrial Unrest*,

Summary of the Reports of the Commission, by the Right Honourable G. N. Barnes, M.P., 1917 (Cmnd. 8696), p 6.

71. A. L. Bowley, *Prices and Wages in the United Kingdom, 1914–1920* (Oxford: Clarendon Press, 1921), p. 106.

72. Wages & Price Memorandum by the Minister of Labour 29/10/17, cited in B. A. Waites, "The Effects of the First World War on the Economic and Social Structure of the English Working Class," *Journal of Scottish Labour History Society*, Vol. 12, February 1978, p. 13.

73. Wolfe, *Labour Supply and Regulation*, p. 179.

74. Board of Trade, *Report of Departmental Committee on Prices*; Parliamentary Papers 1916 (Cmnd. 8358), cited in Arthur Marwick, *The Deluge* (London: Penguin, 1965), p. 126.

75. Parliamentary Papers, *Working Classes Cost of Living Committee*, 1918 (Cmnd. 8980), p. 7.

76. Bowley, *Prices and Wages in the United Kingdom 1914–1920*, p. 67.

77. Parliamentary papers, *Working Classes Cost of Living Committee*, 1918 (Cmnd. 8980), p. 6.

78. Compare J. M. Winter, "The Impact of the First World War on Civilian Health in Britain," *The Economic History Review*, 2nd Series, Vol. 30, No. 3, August 1977, p. 500. An indication of the extent of deprivation and its impact on physical health can be found in Winter's "Military Fitness and Civilian Health in Britain During the First World War," *Journal of Contemporary History*, Vol. 15, No. 2, April 1980, pp. 211–44.

79. Gerd Hardach, *The First World War* (London: Allen Lane, 1977), p. 130.

80. On improvements in health, see Winter, "The Impact of the First World War on Civilian Health in Britain," p. 502; on increased awareness, see Waites, "The Effects of the First World War on the Economic and Social Structure of the English Working Class," p. 39.

CHAPTER 4: DEMOCRACY AT THE BASE

1. G. D. H. Cole, *Workshop Organisation* (Oxford: Clarendon Press, 1923), p. 7.

2. Ibid., p. 9.

3. Ibid., p. 18.

4. J. T. Murphy, *Preparing for Power: A Critical Study of the History of the British Working-Class Movement*, foreword by Sir Stafford Cripps (London: Cape, 1934), p. 111.

5. Cole, *Workshop Organisation*, p. 42.

6. Ibid., p. 54.

7. Ibid., p. 43.

8. Robert Michels, *Political Parties: A Sociological Study of the Oligarchical Tendencies of Modern Democracy*, translated by Eden and Cedar Paul,

introduction by S. M. Lipset (New York: Free Press, 1962), Pt. 2, chs. 5, 6; S. M. Lipset, M. Trow, and J. S. Coleman, *Union Democracy: The Internal Politics of the International Typographical Union* (New York: Free Press, 1956), pp. 54–59.

9. J. Hinton, *The First Shop Stewards' Movement* (London: Allen and Unwin, 1973), p. 126. Also see John McHugh, "The Clyde Rent Strike, 1915," *Journal of Scottish Labour History Society*, Vol. 12, February 1978, pp. 56–62.

10. William Gallacher, *Revolt on the Clyde: An Autobiography* (London: Lawrence and Wishart, 1936), p. 38.

11. Noah Ablett, et al., "The Miners Next Step" in Ken Coates, ed., *Democracy in the Mines* (Nottingham, England: Spokesman Books, 1974; originally published in 1912), pp. 16–30.

12. J. T. Murphy, *New Horizons* (London: Lane, 1941), p. 44.

13. Murphy, *Preparing for Power*, p. 126.

14. Ibid.

15. Ibid., p. 127.

16. W. Moore, *Verbatim Report of a Discussion Between Veteran Engineers in Sheffield* (1953), p. 2, cited in Hinton, *The First Shop Stewards' Movement*, p. 169.

17. Murphy, *New Horizons*, p. 45.

18. Murphy, *Preparing for Power*, p. 128.

19. Ibid.

20. Murphy, *New Horizons*, p. 51.

21. Hinton, *The First Shop Stewards' Movement*, p. 175.

22. Murphy, *New Horizons*, p. 52.

23. Ibid., p. 53.

24. Hinton, *The First Shop Stewards' Movement*, p. 176.

25. Murphy, *Preparing for Power*, p. 132.

26. Murphy, *New Horizons*, p. 53.

27. Michels, *Political Parties*, p. 159.

28. Hinton, *The First Shop Stewards' Movement*, p. 156.

29. See also I. McLean, "The Ministry of Munitions, the Clyde Workers' Committee, and the Suppression of *Forward*: An Alternative View," *Journal of Scottish Labour History Society*, Vol. 6, December 1972, pp. 3–29; Jose Harris, *William Beveridge: A Biography* (Oxford: Clarendon Press, 1977), pp. 216–26.

30. William R. Scott and James Cunnison, *The Clyde Valley During the War* (Oxford: Clarendon Press, 1924), p. 139.

31. J. H. Jones, "Labour Unrest and the War," *Political Quarterly*, No. 6, August 1915, pp. 91–92.

32. Ibid., p. 93.

33. *Herald*, March 6, 1915.

34. Cole, *Workshop Organisation*, p. 32.

35. William Gallacher and J. M. Messer, on behalf of the Clyde Workers' Committee, July 1915, cited in Cole, *Workshop Organisation*, p. 146.

36. Labour Party Special Report on the Clyde Deportations, 1917, cited in Cole, *Workshop Organisation*, p. 145.

37. Ibid.

38. B. Pribicevic, *The Shop Stewards' Movement and Workers' Control, 1910–1922* (Oxford: Blackwell, 1959), p. 99.

CHAPTER 5: TRADE UNION POLITICS

1. The effect of size on forms of democracy is much discussed. See Robert A. Dahl, *After the Revolution?* (New Haven: Yale University Press, 1970); Jane J. Mansbridge, *Beyond Adversary Democracy* (New York: Basic Books, 1980), ch. 20; R. A. Dahl and E. R. Tufte, *Size and Democracy* (Stanford: Stanford University Press, 1973).

2. Robert Michels, *Political Parties: A Sociological Study of the Oligarchical Tendencies of Modern Democracy,* translated by Eden and Cedar Paul, introduction by S. M. Lipset (New York: Free Press, 1962).

3. Jack Lively, *Democracy* (New York: G. Putnam's Sons, 1977), Pt. 2, especially p. 51.

4. N. Mackenzie, ed., *The Letters of Sidney and Beatrice Webb*, Vol. 3 (Cambridge: Cambridge University Press, 1978), p. 72.

5. G. S. Bain, R. Bacon, and J. Pimlott, "The Labour Force," in A. H. Halsey, ed., *Trends in British Society Since 1900* (London: Macmillan, 1972), pp. 123, 125.

6. Calculated from the *Labour Party Conference Reports*, 1914–1918.

7. Giles Radice and Lisanne Radice, *Will Thorne: Constructive Militant* (London: George Allen and Unwin, 1974), pp. 81–82.

8. Hugh A. Clegg, *General Union in a Changing Society* (Oxford: Basil Blackwell, 1964), p. 63.

9. Richard Hyman, *The Workers' Union* (Oxford: Clarendon Press, 1971), p. 81.

10. Alan Fox, *History of the National Union of Boot and Shoe Operatives, 1874–1957* (Oxford: Basil Blackwell, 1958), pp. 384, 395.

11. Jonathan Schneer, "The War, the State and the Workplace: British Dockers During 1914–1918," in J. E. Cronin and J. Schneer, eds., *Social Conflict and the Political Order in Modern Britain* (New Brunswick, NJ: Rutgers University Press, 1982), ch. 5.

12. P. S. Bagwell, *The Railwaymen: A History of the NUR* (London: Allen and Unwin, 1963), p. 345.

13. Ibid., p. 349.

14. *Railway Review*, January 22, 1915.

15. Ibid., January 19, 1915.
16. Ibid., February 5, 1915.
17. Ibid., January 15, 1915.
18. Ibid., January 22, 1915.
19. Ibid., January 29, 1915.
20. Ibid., February 12, 1915.
21. Ibid., February 19, 1915.
22. Ibid., March 5, 1915.
23. Ibid.
24. Ibid., April 2, 1915.
25. Ibid., April 30, 1915.
26. Ibid.
27. Ibid., May 7, 1915.
28. Ibid.
29. Ibid., May 14, 1915.
30. Ibid., May 21, 1915.
31. Ibid., July 23, 1915.
32. Ibid.
33. Ibid.
34. Ibid., September 5, 1915.
35. Ibid.
36. Ibid., August 20 and September 10, 1915.
37. Ibid., September 24, 1915.
38. Ibid.
39. Ibid., October 1, 1915.
40. Ibid., September 17, 1915.
41. Ibid., October 29, 1915.
42. Ibid.
43. Ibid., November 5, 1915.
44. Ibid., April 21, 1916.
45. Ibid., May 19, 1916.
46. Ibid., July 14, 1916. These included the Bristol and South West England and the Newcastle District Councils.
47. Ibid.
48. Ibid., August 4, 1916.
49. Ibid., September 22, 1916.
50. Ibid., September 15, 1916.
51. Ibid., August 25, 1916.
52. Bagwell, *The Railwaymen*, p. 350; *Railway Review*, September 22, 1916.
53. Bagwell, *The Railwaymen*, pp. 352–53.
54. *Railway Review*, July 20, 1917.
55. Ibid., July 27, 1917.

56. Ibid., August 28, 1917.
57. Ibid., October 26, 1917,
58. Bagwell, *The Railwaymen*, pp. 353–54.
59. Ibid., p. 354.
60. Special General Meeting Decisions, November 28, 29, 1917.
61. Ibid.
62. *Amalgamated Society of Engineers Monthly Journal and Report*, October 1915.
63. Ibid.
64. Ibid., November 1915.
65. Ibid., January 1916.
66. Ibid., November 1915.
67. Ibid., October 1915.
68. Ibid., December 1915.
69. Ibid., Organizing District Delegate's Report Div. 9, December 1915.
70. Ibid., December 1915, p. 24.
71. Ibid., January 1916.
72. Ibid., Report of Conference on Full-Time Officials and Representatives from District Councils in the United Kingdom, p. 32.
73. Ibid.
74. Ibid., p. 33.
75. Ibid., p. 35. My emphasis.
76. Ibid., Organizing District Delegates' Report, Division 5.
77. James Hinton, "The Clyde Workers' Committee and the Dilution Struggle," in Asa Briggs and John Saville, eds., *Essays in Labour History 1886–1923* (London: Macmillan, 1971), pp. 152–84.
78. Miners' Federation of Great Britain (hereafter MFGB), *Annual Conference Report*, October 5, 1915, p. 10.
79. Ibid., p. 11.
80. Ibid.
81. MFGB, *Special Conference*, January 13, 1916, p. 5.
82. Executive Committee Minutes, January 5, 6, 1916.
83. R. Page Arnot, *The South Wales Miners—(Clowvr de Cymru): A History of the South Wales Miners' Federation* (Cardiff: Cymric Federation Press, 1975), p. 109.
84. Ibid.
85. Ibid.
86. Ibid.
87. MFGB, *Special Conference,* January 13, 1916, p. 10.
88. Ibid., p. 11.
89. Ibid.
90. Ibid., p. 14.
91. Ibid., p. 12.

92. Ibid.
93. Ibid., p. 12, 16, passim.
94. Ibid., February 8-9, 1916, p. 20.
95. Ibid., p. 30.
96. Ibid.
97. Ibid., p. 31.
98. Ibid.
99. Ibid., p. 16.
100. Ibid., p. 17.
101. Ibid., p. 33.
102. Ibid., p. 34.
103. Ibid.
104. Ibid., p. 40.
105. Ibid.
106. Ibid.
107. Ibid., p. 42.
108. After losing on the first and second ballots, militant South Wales (135,000) and Yorkshire (100,000) put their support behind Northumberland (38,000), and along with medium-sized Derbyshire (35,000), the Midland Federation (54,000), and the small districts of Bristol and Somersetshire determined the winning vote. While the Northumberland resolution got a total of 365,000 votes, the Durham resolution received 349,000. Durham (120,000), Scotland (90,000), Lancashire (70,000), and Nottinghamshire (30,000) were the largest districts which favoured no opposition to the Military Service Act.
109. Arnot, *The South Wales Miners*, p. 111.
110. G. D. H. Cole, *Labour in the Coal-Mining Industry, 1914-1921* (Oxford: Clarendon Press, 1923), p. 56; MFGB, *Special Conference Report*, September 7, 1917.

CHAPTER 6: DELEGATE DEMOCRACY AND DOMESTIC POLICY

1. Founded in 1899, the General Federation of Trade Unions was an offshoot of the Trades Union Congress, formed for the purpose of unions' mutual financial support. It became little more than a committee controlling a fund that represented only a quarter of the total TUC membership.

2. Letter from J. S. Middleton to H. M. Hyndman, July 6, 1916, cited in Royden Harrison, "The War Emergency Workers' National Committee, 1914-1920," in Asa Briggs and John Saville, eds., *Essays in Labour History, 1886-1923* (London: Macmillan, 1971), pp. 211-59.

3. War Emergency: Workers' National Committee, February 1916.

4. The Joint Board, established in 1905, was a committee of the TUC, the Labour Party, and the General Federation of Trade Unions with the purpose

of coordinating functions among them. It met infrequently, had limited authority, and no administrative staff.

5. Ibid.

6. J. M. Winter, *Socialism and the Challenge of War* (London: Routledge and Kegan Paul, 1974), p. 216.

7. National Executive Committee Minutes, February 14, 1916.

8. *Dockers' Record*, February 1916, p. 3.

9. Parliamentary Committee Minutes, February 16–18, 1916.

10. National Executive Committee Minutes, February 24, 1916. The Sub-committees met on March 9 rather than March 1 for the convenience of the War Emergency Committee.

11. National Executive Committee Minutes, letter from J. S. Middleton, March 29, 1916. Middleton suggested that the WEC's role in formulating postwar policy should be strengthened by the national organisations. The indifference of Robert Smillie, the WEC Chairman, and the ease with which Webb shifted his allegiances to the official Labour Party revealed the lack of institutional commitment for the WEC.

12. Parliamentary Committee Minutes, March 15, 1916.

13. National Executive Committee Minutes, April 19, 20, 26, 1916.

14. Parliamentary Committee Minutes, March 19, 1916; Miners' Federation of Great Britain Executive Committee Minutes, March 1916.

15. War Emergency Committee press cuttings from the *Daily Mail*, the *Sunday Times*, and *The People*, March 12, 1916.

16. Parliamentary Committee Minutes, March 19, 1916.

17. National Executive Committee Minutes, April 19, 1916.

18. Ibid.

19. Ibid., April 26, 1916; Parliamentary Committee Minutes, April 26, 1916.

20. Parliamentary Committee Minutes, April 27, 1916.

21. Ibid.

22. *Herald*, May 27, 1916.

23. Ibid.

24. Winter, *Socialism and the Challenge of War*, p. 211. The urgent need for such a Conference had been stated at the Executive Meeting of the WEC on April 27, and the resolution for the National Conference on conscription carried on the motion of Ben Turner and was seconded by Sidney Webb.

25. Parliamentary Committee Minutes, May 25, 1916.

26. J. S. Middleton to Bowerman, May 26, 1916, War Emergency Committee file.

27. Ibid.

28. Ibid.

29. Ibid.

30. Ibid.

31. Bowerman to J. S. Middleton, May 26, 1916.

32. Ibid.

33. Harrison, "War Emergency Workers' National Committee, 1914–20," p. 246.

34. Additional unions included the Amalgamated Society of Carpenters and Joiners, Furnishing Trades, Bleachers and Dyers, Polishers, the National Committee of Post Office Associations, Bookbinders, Vehicle Workers, and the Masons of Scotland.

35. Parliamentary Committee Minutes, June 6, 1916; Bowerman to J. S. Middleton, June 8, 1915.

36. *Trades Union Congress Report*, 1916, p. 95. The resolution continued:

It further expresses the conviction that such regulation can only be properly enforced by a Government Department which will have power to commandeer food supplies and fuel and distribute them through municipalities or other elected bodies; and by (1) the effective control (and ownership) of all shipping to secure the fixing of freight rates sufficient to meet increased costs without providing enormously increased profits for shipping companies; (2) steps to be taken to commandeer our home-grown crops, paying a fair price to farmers, but excluding speculation and exploitation. Further, steps to be taken to secure control of foreign and colonial supplies as may be necessary for the needs of the country; (3) the amendment of the Coal Prices Limitation Act fixing standard prices in various areas, by this means protecting the consumer against excessive prices imposed by coal-owners and merchants attempting to evade the intention of the Act.

37. Ibid.

38. Ibid., p. 96.

39. Ibid., p. 99.

40. Ibid.

41. Ibid., p. 103.

42. Ibid., p. 104.

43. Ibid.

44. *Labour Leader*, July 6, 1916. Another amendment calling upon the Government to enforce the provisions of its advisory Circulars L2, L3, and L6 in regard to the operation of the Munitions Act was passed.

45. *Trades Union Congress Report*, 1916, p. 105.

46. Ibid., pp. 105–6.

47. Ibid., p. 106.

48. *Times*, September 4, 1916.

49. *Herald*, September 2, 1916.

50. Ibid.

51. *Times*, September 2, 1916.

52. Ibid., September 4, 1916.

53. *Trades Union Congress Report*, 1916, p. 346.

54. *Manchester Guardian*, September 9, 1916; *Times*, September 4, 1916.

55. *Trades Union Congress Report*, 1916, pp. 346–47.

56. Ibid., p. 348.

57. Ibid., p. 350.

58. *Manchester Guardian*, September 9, 1916.

59. Parliamentary Committee Minutes, April 27, 1916. The Parliamentary Committee also decided to place on the agenda resolutions dealing with electoral reforms and the relaxation of trade union rights and their restoration.

60. *Trades Union Congress Report*, 1916, pp. 250–51.

61. Ibid.

62. Ibid., p. 266.

63. Ibid., p. 379.

64. Ibid., p. 255.

65. Ibid., p. 256–57

66. Ibid., p. 245.

67. Ibid., p. 247.

68. Ibid., p. 248.

69. National Executive Committee Minutes, June 29, 1916.

70. Ibid.; War Emergency Committee letter file, June 26, 1916; *Carpenters and Joiners' Journal*, July 1916.

71. Richard Hyman, *The Worker's Union* (London: Clarendon Press, 1971).

72. War Emergency Committee letter file, 1916. Middleton requested more copies so that the resolutions could go to all members of the newly formed Joint Committee of "Labour Problems After the War."

73. Ibid.

74. Amalgamated Society of Locomotive Engineers and Firemen letter, August 16, 1916.

75. Report of the National Union of Railwaymen, National Union of Railwaymen Decisions of the Executive, December 4–9, 1916.

76. Ibid., September 1916. The delegates were Cramp and Marchbank.

77. National Executive Committee Minutes, October 11, 1916.

78. The Committee included Chairman Wardle, J. R. MacDonald, J. R. Clynes, S. Webb, and A. Henderson.

79. N. MacKenzie, ed., *The Letters of Sidney and Beatrice Webb*, Vol. 3 (Cambridge: Cambridge University Press, 1978), p. 71.

80. *Railway Review*, January 19, 1917.

81. *New Statesman*, January 27, 1917.

82. *Labour Leader*, January 18, 1917.

83. *Labour Party Conference Report*, 1917, pp. 117–18.

84. Ibid., p. 121.

85. Ibid., p. 115.

86. Labour Party Conference Agenda, January 1917.

87. *Labour Party Conference Report*, 1917, p. 4.

88. Ibid., p. 87.

89. Ibid., p. 88.

90. Ibid.
91. Ibid., p. 91.
92. Ibid., p. 90.
93. *Herald*, January 27, 1917.
94. Ibid., February 3, 1917.
95. *Labour Leader*, February 1, 1917.
96. *New Statesman*, January 27, 1917.
97. *Labour Party Conference Report*, 1917, p. 110.
98. *Herald*, February 3, 1917.
99. J. Roland Pennock, *Democratic Political Theory* (Princeton, NJ: Princeton University Press, 1979), pp. 324–25.
100. G. D. H. Cole, *Social Theory* (New York: Frederick A. Stokes, 1920), ch. 6; A. W. Wright, *G. D. H. Cole and Socialist Democracy* (Oxford: Clarendon Press, 1979), ch. 4; Pennock, *Democratic Political Theory*, pp. 352–53.

CHAPTER 7: DELEGATE DEMOCRACY AND FOREIGN POLICY

1. Robert Michels, *Political Parties: A Sociological Study of the Oligarchical Tendencies of Modern Democracy*, translated by Eden and Cedar Paul, introduction by S. M. Lipset (New York: Free Press, 1962), Pt. 6, ch. 3.
2. David Marquand, *Ramsay MacDonald* (London: Jonathan Cape, 1977), p. 208.
3. Chris Wrigley, *David Lloyd George and the British Labour Movement: Peace and War* (Hassocks, England: Harvester Press; and New York: Barnes and Noble, 1976), p. 182.
4. *Herald*, May 19, 1917.
5. *Trades Union Congress Report*, 1917, p. 55.
6. Miners' Federation of Great Britain (hereafter MFGB), *Special Conference Report*, London, August 10, 1917. See also *Times*, August 21, 1917.
7. *Herald*, April 7, 1917; Stephen White, "Soviets in Britain: The Leeds Convention of 1917," *International Review of Social History*, Vol. 19, 1974, pp. 168–70.
8. *Herald*, April 7, 1917.
9. White identifies meetings in Brighton, Liverpool, and Merthyr Tydfil in "Soviets in Britain," p. 179, fn. 2.
10. *Herald*, May 19, 1917.
11. Ibid. Besides Smillie, speakers included W. C. Anderson of the Independent Labour Party and Labour Party NEC, George Lansbury, Editor of the *Herald*, and Clyde militants James Maxton, William Gallacher, and E. Shinwell.
12. *Labour Leader*, May 31, 1917.
13. *Herald*, June 9, 1917, p. 9.

14. Ibid.

15. White correctly argues that Leeds represented opposition to the war, but neglects its significance as an expression of the organised rank and file's demand for greater control of Government policy, in his "Soviets in Britain."

16. *Herald*, June 9, 1917, p. 9.

17. Ibid.

18. Ibid., p. 10.

19. Ibid., p. 11.

20. Ibid., pp. 11–12.

21. Ibid., p. 11.

22. Ibid., p. 12.

23. Ibid.

24. *Socialist Review*, Vol. 14, 1917, p. 199, cited in White, "Soviets in Britain," pp. 192–93.

25. *Railway Review*, June 5, 1917.

26. *Herald*, September 1, 1917. These included the Boilermakers, Transport Workers, Engineers, Miners, Railwaymen, and Shipwrights.

27. National Union of Railwaymen Executive Committee, Decisions of Quarterly Meeting, September 10, 1917.

28. *Herald*, May 5, 1917.

29. Ibid., July 7, 1917.

30. Ibid., August 4, 1917; August 11, 1917.

31. *Dockers' Record*, May 1917, p. 8.

32. Report of the National Transport Workers' Federation Annual Council, June 1916, p. 13; *Herald*, June 23, 1917.

33. Parliamentary Committee Minutes, April 24, 1917.

34. Ibid., June 28, 1917.

35. *Herald*, June 23, 1917.

36. Ibid., June 30, 1917.

37. James Hinton argues that Leeds was not an attempt to reconstruct the Labour movement on a revolutionary basis but was "in fact, the preface to the reconstruction of the Labour Party on a non-revolutionary basis." See his *The First Shop Stewards' Movement* (London: Allen and Unwin, 1973), p. 241.

38. National Executive Committee Minutes, July 18, 1917.

39. Wrigley, *David Lloyd George and the British Labour Movement*, pp. 194, 210. Henderson also knew that pacifism had been growing in France.

40. Labour Party Conference Agenda, 1918.

41. Ibid. This resolution was from the Lambeth Trades Council and Labour Representation Committee.

42. B. Webb, *Diary*, August 12, 1917, unpublished manuscript at the British Library of Political and Economic Science, London.

43. Wrigley, *David Lloyd George and the British Labour Movement*, pp. 212, 215.

44. R. I. McKibbin, "Arthur Henderson as Labour Leader," *International Review of Social History*, Vol. 1, 1978, p. 97.

45. *Special Labour Party Conference Report*, August 10, 1917.

46. Ibid., p. 13.

47. MFGB, *Special Conference Report*, August 9–10, 1917, p. 13.

48. Ibid., p. 17.

49. Ibid.

50. *Special Labour Party Conference Report*, August 10, 1917.

51. *Herald*, August 18, 1917.

52. N. Mackenzie, ed., *The Letters of Sidney and Beatrice Webb*, Vol. 3 (Cambridge: Cambridge University Press), p. 92. Sidney's letter is dated 13 August 1917.

53. *Special Labour Party Conference Report*, August 9–10, 1917.

54. Ibid.

55. MFGB, *Special Conference Report*, London, August 10, 1917.

56. *Herald*, August 25, 1917.

57. Parliamentary Committee Minutes, July 25, 1917.

58. Ibid.

59. *Trades Union Congress Report*, 1917, p. 71.

60. Ibid., p. 72.

61. Ibid., p. 71.

62. Ibid., p. 72.

63. Ibid., p. 74.

64. Ibid., p. 70.

65. *Manchester Guardian*, September 15, 1917.

66. *Trades Union Congress Report*, 1917, p. 74.

67. Ibid.

68. Ibid., p. 75.

69. *Manchester Guardian*, September 7, 1917; Labour Party Executive Committee Minutes, September 6, 1917.

CHAPTER 8: WHY PARTICIPATORY DEMOCRACY?

1. Robert Michels, *Political Parties: A Sociological Study of the Oligarchical Tendencies of Modern Democracy*, translated by Eden and Cedar Paul, introduction by S. M. Lipset (New York: Free Press, 1962), p. 7. Michels wrote these words in 1915.

2. S. M. Lipset, M. Trow, and J. S. Coleman, *Union Democracy: The Internal Politics of the International Typographical Union* (New York: Free Press, 1956); J. D. Edelstein and M. Warner, *Comparative Union Democracy* (New Brunswick, NJ: Transaction Books, 1979).

3. Collective consensus in participatory democracy involves various levels

of agreement and disagreement. See R. M. MacIver, *The Modern State* (London: Oxford University Press, 1926), chs. 6, 16; ibid., p. 200.

4. For a discussion of types of participatory democracy, see Donald W. Kiem, "Participation in Contemporary Democratic Theories," in J. Roland Pennock and John W. Chapman, eds., *Participation in Politics* NOMOS 16 (New York: Lieber-Atherton, 1975), ch. 1.

5. C. B. Macpherson, *The Life and Times of Liberal Democracy* (Oxford: Oxford University Press, 1977), p. 108.

6. Joseph Schumpeter, *Capitalism, Socialism and Democracy*, 3rd ed. (New York: Harper and Row, 1950), Pt. 4; S. M. Lipset, "The Political Process in Trade Unions," in his *Political Man* (Garden City, NY: Doubleday, 1966), ch. 12; Robert A. Dahl, *A Preface to Democratic Theory* (Chicago: University of Chicago Press, 1956).

7. C. B. Macpherson, "Post-Liberal-Democracy," in his *Democratic Theory: Essays in Retrieval* (Oxford: Clarendon Press, 1973), ch. 9.

8. Robert A. Dahl, *Who Governs?* (New Haven: Yale University Press, 1961).

9. See Craig Calhoun, *The Question of Class Struggle: Social Foundations of Popular Radicalism During the Industrial Revolution* (Chicago: University of Chicago Press, 1982); Charles Tilly, *From Mobilization to Revolution* (Reading, MA: Addison-Wesley, 1978).

10. This is developed in Michael Taylor, *Community, Anarchy and Liberty* (Cambridge: Cambridge University Press, 1982).

11. Brian M. Barry, *Sociologists, Economists and Democracy* (London: Collier-Macmillan, 1970), p. 37.

12. Michels, *Political Parties*, p. 365. Also see B. H. Mayhew and R. L. Levinger, "On the Emergence of Oligarchy in Human Interaction," *The American Journal of Sociology*, Vol. 81, No. 5, 1976, pp. 1017–49.

13. Mancur Olson, *The Logic of Collective Action* (New York: Schocken Books, 1968).

14. Barry, *Sociologists, Economists and Democracy*, pp. 37–40.

15. Lester Milbrath and M. L. Goel, *Political Participation*, 2nd ed. (Chicago: Rand McNally, 1977), pp. 36, 38, 111, 112.

16. Dennis F. Thompson, *John Stuart Mill and Representative Government* (Princeton, NJ: Princeton University Press, 1976), p. 14.

17. Judith Shklar, *Men and Citizens: A Study of Rousseau's Social Theory* (Cambridge: Cambridge University Press, 1969), p. 166.

18. Robert A. Dahl, *After the Revolution?* (New Haven: Yale University Press, 1970), pp. 130–40.

19. Raymond Williams, *The Year 2000* (New York: Pantheon, 1983), pp. 160–65.

20. Thompson, *John Stuart Mill and Representative Government*, p. 28.

21. Karl Marx, *The Civil War in France* (London: Lawrence and Wishart,

1933), especially Pt. 3. For Marx's earlier statement on democracy, see his *Critique of Hegel's PHILOSOPHY OF RIGHT (Cambridge: Cambridge University Press, 1970).*

22. Richard Scase, "Relative Deprivation: A Comparison of English and Swedish Manual Workers," in D. Wedderburn, ed., *Poverty, Inequality, and Class Structure* (Cambridge: Cambridge University Press, 1974).

23. See Shklar, *Men and Citizens*, especially ch. 5; Thompson, *John Stuart Mill and Representative Government*, ch. 1.

24. Alan Cawson, "Functional Representation and Democratic Politics: Towards a Corporatist Democracy?" In Graeme Duncan, ed., *Democratic Theory and Practice* (Cambridge: Cambridge University Press, 1983), p. 179.

25. Herbert Marcuse, *One Dimensional Man* (London: Sphere Books, 1972).

26. Christopher Lasch, *The Culture of Narcissism: American Life in an Age of Diminishing Expectations* (New York: Warner Books, 1979).

27. A useful survey is Hugh A. Clegg, *The Changing System of Industrial Relations in Great Britain* (Oxford: Basil Blackwell, 1979).

28. Taylor, *Community, Anarchy and Liberty*, pp. 160–64. Also see Philip Abrams and Andrew McCulloch, *Communes, Sociology and Society* (Cambridge: Cambridge University Press, 1976).

Bibliographical Essay

The brief list of works that follows is designed to help the reader explore further the concept of participatory democracy.

Useful introductions to the way in which Greek political theory conceptualized democracy and how it was practised in the Greek city states can be found in Henry B. Mayo, *An Introduction to Democratic Theory* (New York: Oxford University Press, 1960) and Ernest Barker, *Greek Political Theory*, 5th ed. (London: Methuen, 1941).

Important though the Greek experience with direct democracy is, the modern concept of participatory democracy begins with the writings of Jean Jacques Rousseau, J. S. Mill, and G. D. H. Cole. Rousseau's *The Social Contract* [1762], translated by G. D. H. Cole (London: J.M. Dent and Son, 1950) lays the groundwork for subsequent work. He identified what constituted the main elements of participatory democracy: community, popular control, and the educative function of participation. John Stuart Mill followed his father, James Mill, and Jeremy Bentham in advancing the protective argument in favour of participation, but he steps out of their shadow by developing what he considered the more important justification for participation: human development. Consequently, like Rousseau, Mill viewed participation as self-sustaining and self-reinforcing. The most important locus of this thought is in *Considerations on Representative Government* [1861] (Indianapolis: Bobbs-Merrill, 1958), although another important statement of the benefits of participation, especially in reference to industrial democracy, is *Principles of Political Economy with Some of Their Applications to Social Philosophy* [1848] (London: Longman, Green, and Co., 1909), Bk. 4, ch. 8. G. D. H. Cole provided an important first effort to adapt Rousseau's vision to industrial society. Denying that one person could represent another in general, Cole conceptualized a society of functionally based producer and consumer associations, in which members' have the specialized knowledge necessary to supervise their representatives. His ideas arc best presented in *Self-Government in Industry* (London: G. Bell and Sons, 1919), *Social Theory* (New York: Frederick A. Stokes, 1920), and *Guild Socialism Restated* (London: Leonard Parsons, 1920).

Carole Pateman provides insightful summaries of these three major contributors in chapter 2 of her *Participation and Democratic Theory* (Cambridge: Cambridge University Press, 1970). Other useful and important secondary works are Judith N. Shklar, *Men and Citizens: A Study of Rousseau's Social Theory* (Cambridge: Cambridge University Press, 1969); Dennis F. Thompson, *John Stuart Mill and Representative Government* (Princeton, NJ: Princeton University Press, 1976); and A. W. Wright, *G. D. H. Cole and Socialist Democracy* (Oxford: Clarendon Press, 1979). More generally, a comprehensive survey of democratic theory is J. Roland Pennock, *Democratic Political Theory* (Princeton, NJ: Princeton University Press, 1979). And C. B. Macpherson traces the history of modern democratic theory in his important *The Life and Times of Liberal Democracy* (Oxford: Oxford University Press, 1977). Macpherson conceptualizes protective, developmental, equilibrium, and participatory democracy as four types of liberal democracy that accept the presuppositions of capitalist society in contrast to earlier theories of popular democracy, namely, those of the Levellers, Rousseau, and Jefferson, who had propounded a vision based on a classless or one-class society.

Other formulations of popular control emerged as a practical attempt to counter the alienation, exploitation, and repression of capitalist society. An interesting overview that covers visionaries, movements, and institutions of socialism and workers' control from the nineteenth century on is by Branko Horvat, "A New Social System in the Making: Historical Origins and Development of Self-Governing Socialism," in B. Horvat, M. Markovic, and R. Supek, eds., *Self-Governing Socialism: A Reader* (New York: International Acts and Sciences Press, 1975). The contributions of Robert Owen, Louis Blanc, Pierre Joseph Proudhon, Karl Marx, Friedrich Engels, and William Morris among a multitude of others should not be overlooked. But neither should the historical struggles of the working men and women who built the labour movements in Europe and America. Important statements of worker's control are by Karl Marx, *The Civil War in France* [1871] (London: Lawrence and Wishart, 1933) and Antonio Gramsci, "Selected Writing from L'ordine nuovo (1919–1920)" (in Horvat, et al., *Self-Governing Socialism*). Also, of interest are Dorothy Thompson, *The Chartists* (New York: Pantheon, 1983), a study of the Chartist movement in England during the 1840s, and Lawrence Goodwyn, *Democratic Promise: The Populist Movement in America* (New York: Oxford University Press, 1976), a study of the Populist movement among American farmers in the 1870s and 1880s.

More recently, the defence and revitalization of participatory ideals coincided with the upsurge of popular involvement and protest during the 1960s, giving rise to the New Left in America and Europe. The New Left is surveyed in Massimo Teodori, ed., *The New Left. A Documentary History* (Indianapolis: Bobbs-Merrill Co., 1969) and Paul Jacobs and Saul Landau, eds., *The New Radicals* (New York: Random House, 1966). Important statements of this movement include the *Port Huron Statement* by Students for a Democratic Society (in Jacobs and Landau, eds., *The New Radicals*); Daniel and Gabriel Cohn-Bendit, *Obsolete Communism: The Left-Wing Alternative* (Harmondsworth, England: Penguin, 1968) and Raymond Williams, ed., *The May Day Manifesto 1968* (Harmondsworth, England: Penguin, 1968).

Recent academic efforts to revitalize the cause of participatory democracy start with the critique of the reigning model of democracy, democratic elitism. The most significant works are Pateman, *Participation and Democratic Theory*, which defends the ideal and advocates its extension to the workplace, and Peter Bachrach, *The Theory of Democratic Elitism: A Critique* (Boston: Little, Brown, 1967), which espouses the developmental benefits of participation, while recognizing the inevitability of leadership in the modern context. Robert A. Dahl in *After the Revolution?* (New Haven: Yale University Press, 1970) offers an important and sympathetic discussion of the practical difficulties and limits of increased participation. Two interesting collections of articles that argue the case for increased participation are Terrence Cook and Patrick Morgan, eds., *Participatory Democracy* (San Francisco: Canfield Press, 1971) and C. George Benello and Dimitrios Roussopoulis, eds., *The Case for Participatory Democracy* (New York: Grossman, 1971).

The most recent scholarship defending participatory democracy argues the cause with greater sophistication. Jane J. Mansbridge in *Beyond Adversary Democracy* (New York: Basic Books, 1980; 2nd ed., Chicago: University of Chicago Press, 1983) combines theory with case studies of a New England town meeting and an urban crisis centre. The cases support her theoretical conclusion that democracy takes different forms as a result of different types of conflict: a unitary model when friendship fostered by common interests regulates decision-making and an adversary model in which interests conflict. Benjamin Barber in his *Strong Democracy: Participatory Politics for a New Age* (Berkeley and Los Angeles: University of California Press, 1984) criticizes democratic elitism and provides a theoretical justification as well as practical proposals for introducing wider participation in American politics. Barber argues that participation creates community among citizens and makes possible the liberty and freedoms for individuals that representative or ''thin'' democracy denies. A useful survey of much of the relevant literature can be found in Ronald M. Mason, *Participatory and Workplace Democracy: A Theoretical Development in Critique of Liberalism* (Carbondale: Southern Illinois University Press, 1982). Mason contends that workplace democracy fulfils the radical promise of participatory democracy by contradicting liberalism's separation of politics from economics. The reader should also consult the essays in J. Roland Pennock and John W. Chapman, eds., *Participation in Politics* NOMOS XVI, (New York: Lieber-Atherton, 1975), especially those by Donald Kiem and Peter Bachrach.

While the advantages of participatory democracy are clearly formulated and growing in acceptance, little effort has been made to analyse its practicality. As mentioned, Dahl's *After the Revolution?* challenges participatory ideals with organisational reality. Arnold Kaufman's two essays, "Human Nature and Participatory Democracy" and "Participatory Democracy: Ten Years Later," in William E. Connolly, ed., *The Bias of Pluralism* (New York: Atherton Press, 1969), caution enthusiasts about the difficulties and abuses of participatory forms, while sympathetically advocating participatory practice.

To explore the vulnerabilities of the participatory ideal, the reader should study Robert Michels, *Political Parties: A Sociological Study of the Oligarchical Tendencies of Modern Democracy* [1915], translated by Eden and Cedar Paul (New York: Free Press, 1962) and Moise Ostrogorski, *Democracy and the Organization of Political Parties* (London: Macmillan, 1902). The danger to liberty of participation is argued by J. Talmon in *The Origins of Totalitarian Democracy* (Boston: Beacon Press, 1952) and Alexis de Tocqueville in *Democracy in America* [1835–40], 2 vols., translated and edited by H. Reeve and P. Bradley (New York: Vintage, 1954).

The argument that elite competition and social pluralism constitute the essence of democracy and a defence against totalitarianism is found in the classic statements of democratic elitism: Joseph Schumpeter, *Capitalism, Socialism, and Democracy* (New York: Harper and Row, 1962); Robert A. Dahl, *Who Governs?* (New Haven: Yale University Press, 1961); and Seymour Martin Lipset, Martin Trow, and James S. Coleman, *Union Democracy* (New York: Free Press, 1956). Useful studies of the amount and prospect of participation are by Lester Milbrath and M. Goel, *Political Participation*, 2nd ed. (Chicago: Rand McNally, 1977), Sidney Verba and Norman Nie, *Participation in America* (New York: Harper and Row, 1972), and Anne Richardson, *Participation* (London: Routledge and Kegan Paul, 1983).

The motivation for widespread participation and community autonomy is an important element for any realistic theory of participatory democracy. Barrington Moore, Jr., in *Injustice: The Social Basis of Obedience and Revolt* (Armonk, NY: M. E. Sharpe, 1978) provides an important analysis of the moral bases of collective behavior. Charles Tilly in *From Mobilization to Revolution* (Reading, MA: Addison-Wesley, 1978) and Craig Calhoun in *A Question of Class Struggle* (Chicago: University of Chicago Press, 1982) provide evidence that community is fundamental to collective behaviour and protest. Hannah Arendt's *On Revolution* (New York: Viking Press, 1963) analyzes spontaneous and collective efforts to create a liberated social order. Michael Taylor defines community and shows how it relates to autonomy and liberty in his *Community, Anarchy and Liberty* (Cambridge: Cambridge University Press, 1982). Marshall S. Shatz, editor of *The Essential Works of Anarchism* (New York: Quadrangle Books, 1972), examines major themes of anarchism—community, self-management, antipathy to state and capitalism—through a selection of anarchists' writings. Mansbridge in *Beyond Adversary Democracy* discusses community decision-making in unitary democracy and argues that friendship presupposes its success. *Co-ops, Communes, and Collectives*, edited by John Case and Rosemary Taylor (New York: Pantheon, 1979), surveys alternative organisations of the 1960s and 1970s and *The Joyful Community* by Benjamin Zablocki (Baltimore: Penguin, 1971) examines the Bruderhof, a successful Christian commune.

That small size and close proximity are essential to unitary democracy is commonly asserted. Useful statements include Dahl, *After the Revolution?*, Mansbridge, *Beyond Adversary Democracy*, and R. A. Dahl and Edward R. Tufte, *Size and Democracy* (Stanford: Stanford University Press, 1973).

Leadership in democracy is best surveyed in Pennock's *Democratic Political Theory*. Thompson, in *John Stuart Mill and Representative Government*, provides insight into the problem of combining competent leadership and participation.

Finally, the extension of democracy into the economic sphere is essential for an eventual realization of the ideals of participatory democracy. Paul Blumberg's *Industrial Democracy: The Sociology of Participation* (New York: Schocken Books, 1973) provides a comprehensive survey of the evidence supporting the idea that participation reduces alienation. Paul Bernstein's *Workplace Democratization: Its Internal Dynamics* (New Brunswick, NJ: Transaction Books, 1980) uses a comparative survey to identify six essential elements for successful workplace democracy, while John F. Witte in *Democracy, Authority and Alienation in Work: Workers' Participation in an American Corporation* (Chicago: University of Chicago Press, 1980) questions the feasibility of incorporating industrial democracy in American industry. Jaroslav Vanek, editor of *Self-Management: Economic Liberation of Man* (Baltimore: Penguin, 1975), provides a useful collection of readings. And Martin Carnoy and Derek Shearer provide cogent arguments in favour of democratizing the political economy through a survey of American and European experiences in their *Economic Democracy: The Challenge of the 1980s* (Armonk, NY: M. E. Sharpe, 1980).

Index

About the Author

JOEL D. WOLFE is an Assistant Professor of Political Science at the University of Cincinnati. His articles have been published in *Comparative Politics*, *Polity*, and *The Review of Politics*.